#RVLife

#RVLife

Seeking Happiness Through A Nomadic Life

By

John Hebard

EDITED BY BRENDA NEJEDLO

ISBN: 978-1-7337668-0-7 (Paperback edition)
ISBN: 978-1-7337668-1-4 (eBook edition)
ISBN: 978-1-7337668-2-1 (Audio book)

Library of Congress Control Number: 2019902185

Cover photo by Opting Out of Normal
Cover design by ose_solutions
Edited by Brenda Nejedlo

Printed in United States of America

Published by Hebard's Travels, LLC
Hebardstravels@gmail.com
Visit www.hebardstravels.com

For my lovely wife Laura.

Thank you for always believing I could write this.

Live intentionally

Editor's Forward

———∽∼∽———

Whan I learned John was writing a book about their RV trials and adventures, I was excited to read the final outcome. We were together in Texas preparing for NomadFEST 2018, and I watched him work every day, headphones in, quietly typing, putting words to the page. When John asked if I would do a first-round edit on the book, I was honored and humbled to be asked. What I found was a candid tale of determination, many setbacks, and ultimately, happiness, freedom and acceptance with the lifestyle they choose to live. The writing is very much like meeting John in person. Free, open, sometimes blunt, and always enjoyable. No matter what life threw at them, John, Laura and Hebard's Luck triumphed in the end. Many stories will make you laugh, and others will make you think deeply about the perseverance and adaptability required to live your life on the road full-time. Their story is about not letting anything stand in their way, of letting the human spirit triumph over adversity, and in the end, finding the freedom they so longed for in their lives.

I look forward to the sequel.

Brenda Nejedlo
GeoAstroRV

Acknowledgments

I never could have written this without Laura's tireless work ethic and support. We may have fought over how much it pulled me away from working on Hebards Travels, yet you never once criticized me for taking on such a monumental project. You stood behind me through months of me sitting behind my computer with headphones on, 8-10 hours a day, seven days a week, ignoring the world around me. You picked up more house, social media, and ENTV work when you were already overloaded. Through all those long days and nights alone you even kept our YouTube channel growing. I want to take you on a very long vacation, you deserve it. I love you and promise the next book will be better.

I also want to thank Brenda Nejedlo for editing my first novel. As a new writer, I needed a highly educated, capable, unbiased third party to edit my first draft. You went so far above and beyond all my expectations it brought me to tears. Of course, I could have hired anyone to check spelling and grammar, but I highly doubt anyone else could have accomplished what you did. You fact checked the entire book, no small feat. You even analyzed the story to ensure it flowed well and actually made sense. Your thousands of suggestions may have been daunting and frustrating to work through, but I did the work happily. Your edits forced me out of my comfort zone. They made me analyze every single sentence. Your work showed that you cared about me and my book, that's not something to be taken lightly. Money can't buy that. My first draft was merely a shadow of the finished product. I owe most of that to you. I'm happy to call you a friend. Thank you, I know it wasn't easy.

Table of Contents

CHAPTER 1

How Did We End Up Here?

Hello. My name is John Hebard. My wife, Laura and I live and travel full-time in a 2016 Forest River Cedar Creek 36CKTS fifth wheel (RV/camper/trailer, whatever you want to call it).

Because you're going to see the term "full-time" throughout this book, I should explain it first. We often see discussions online about the meaning of "full-time." There are several definitions people subscribe to. What it means to us is this:

1. Living in an RV as a primary residence.

2. Not having a sticks-and-bricks house.

3. Moving the RV more than twice a year.

I'm going to tell you a story of how we found ourselves, two dogs, cat and a meager amount of our stuff, living in a small town during the summer of 2017.

And by small town, I mean if you blink, you'll miss it. But our living arrangements got smaller still. We were living in a bedroom at my grandma's house which is about the size of two large RVs parked next to each other. Sadly, my grandma passed away several years ago, and the house now belongs to my mom and uncle.

Built over 100 years ago, the house and the one next to it were part of a cheese factory. At some point, the two houses, which were originally one large building, were cut apart, moved back from the road, and turned into separate homes. That's where my grandpa found and bought the house in 1943.

So how did we find ourselves living out of an 8x12' bedroom in an old cheese factory? That's a good question, and I'm glad you asked it. Ultimately, we wound up there because we bought a new fifth wheel. What is a fifth wheel? It's a trailer you pull behind a truck, but it has a kingpin like a semi-trailer which connects to a hitch in my truck bed. Don't confuse it with a bumper pull travel trailer.

I apologize if I've been a little confusing so far. After all, why would buying a new RV end up with us living with my mom in a town of 400 people? I know it's a strange introduction, but this is a crazy story, and I stayed up a lot of nights writing just so I could tell you. It all started a long time ago in a galaxy far....oh wait, that's copyrighted. Our tale begins a few months before we bought our fifth wheel and turned our lives upside down.

CHAPTER

2

How our Story Began

---~~~---

Laura and I met during the fall of 2011. I was 29 and she was 24. Yes, I'm a cradle robber and proud of it. You'd understand if you saw her...so....uh ....anyway. When we met, she was fresh out of veterinary technician school. I'd been medically retired from the Army for a year and was managing a GNC store.

We were engaged after a year and married almost exactly two years after meeting. The wedding was within two weeks of our first date anniversary. We wanted them to coincide but just couldn't make it happen.

I wish I could say it was all rainbows and happily-ever-after's, but it wasn't. Like most kids getting married post Y2K, we didn't really know how to be married. There weren't many examples of good marriages left for us to learn from out there.

Both of us were forced to grow up through our parents divorcing. And like everyone else, we had our own lists of personal issues that made living together just oh so easy. (I hope you caught the sarcasm, if not please insert said sarcasm.) In reality there wasn't much about marriage that we found easy. I think what caught us off guard so badly was not knowing how hard marriage is. The easiest part was the wedding.

For most of our relationship Laura worked nights at an emergency animal hospital. I was a full-time student and was also working part-time. We couldn't ever get our schedules to line up. If we were really REALLY lucky, we'd get two half-days a week together, or 5-7 waking hours a week. They were half-days because of our opposite sleep schedules, normally I had to be asleep several hours before Laura. If I even stayed up to see how her day went, I'd get less than five hours of sleep.

Something else threw a big giant wrench into the mess, I was medically retired for PTSD after my third deployment. I'd been sober for several years, was on a few VA prescribed medications, seen several therapists, and thought I was doing alright. But you don't know what you don't know. And I didn't know how badly my PTSD was affecting me and our marriage. Very quickly Laura began walking on eggshells, always afraid of me becoming angry.

Let me explain something first. I never laid a hand on her or wanted to. I didn't throw or break things either. My dad was a screamer and thrower, so I vowed to never treat my wife how he treated me mom. Instead, I internalized my anger and I would shut down. I didn't want to be mean to Laura when I was angry, so I didn't want to talk and risk letting it happen. The alternative was almost as bad though. And I didn't know.

After a few years of being ground to a pulp, our relationship wasn't doing so hot. Our half-days off were reserved for the epic marriage battles that start over nothing and neither person will back down for no logical reason. You know the kind where you're ready to go buy a shovel and a bag of lye if they do that one annoying thing one more time? Luckily with all the free time we had together we totally worked out all our problems and lived happily ever aft......oh sorry, I was daydreaming and trailed off.

Sadly, when those fights are so regular you can set your clock by them, people start thinking maybe single life would be better. We had both danced around the idea of breaking up during different points in our relationship. I guess I was the quitter, because I was the first one to actually plan on leaving. Of course, she figured out what was going on before I could leave. We'd been together for four years after all. I'm surprised it took her more than a day to realize it, I chalk it up to us never seeing each other.

She begged for me to stay and I grudgingly agreed. It's not that she was or is a bad person, because she's not. I'd just had my fill of fighting.

I wish I could say that everything was fine after that, but it was only another notch in the old marriage belt. At least we both agreed to start working together and not against each other. What doesn't kill your marriage makes it stronger right? RIGHT!? Well, I guess the saying is true since we're still together, and no one's bought that shovel yet. We try not to think about those days anymore.

So back to the RV story, I suppose that's why you're reading this after all.

We'd been unhappy for a while before the whole almost-splitting-up-mess. Searching for ways to remedy the problems, Laura had begun watching YouTube videos about camping. She'd had great experiences camping with her grandpa when she was young and thought it could be a great way to bring us back together.

I was driving a 2006 Tacoma at the time and it could tow a few thousand pounds, so we were considering a little popup camper that we could take weekend vacations with. About a week after we decided to stay together, Laura was watching YouTube and found a channel named Chris & G Travels.

Chris & G lived in a small Class A motorhome and traveled full-time. They were always traveling to neat places and showing what living in an RV on the road looked like. They showed us that we could do it too. Watching them every day quickly became routine for us as we were instantly enthralled. They really got us thinking that maybe, just maybe, the RV lifestyle could pull our relationship out of its bottomless black pit.

We still had faith that we could make it work because we'd had some AMAZING times together. Two years before we almost split up, we'd been having many of the same relationship problems, so we took a vacation. Isn't that what normal people do when they're overworked?

We couldn't afford the vacation, but we REALLY needed it, so I drew from the IRA I'd saved while I was in Iraq. That vacation was one of the best decisions we've ever made. The week in Mexico was exactly what both of us, and our marriage, needed.

After the first day or two there, we started to finally unwind, I mean we began to find true relaxation. That's SO much more than just sitting in front of the TV for an hour before bed after a long day. Suddenly we were happy again. Happy to spend time with each other again. Before the vacation we didn't really have fun together, there wasn't time for fun around the weekly fights. We came home from Mexico more in love than ever. We were ready to tackle life together and never fight again.

Two years before I was planning on leaving, we returned from Mexico very much in love. What happened? Thinking back on it, I'm pretty sure I have a good idea.

We came home from Mexico, and went right back to work, school, errands, yard work, and never seeing each other. Our lives hadn't changed one bit. Everything that had been stressing us out and driving a wedge between us was still there waiting for us. We still didn't have any time for each other. We both slowly drifted back to our respective corners of the ring over the following months.

Society says that if you're having these types of marital problems to see a counselor. Done. We went to three different therapists over several months, but it didn't really help.

Society says that if you're depressed, stressed, anxious, can't sleep, can't stay awake, etc., to see a doctor and get some pills. Done, again. The VA had me on multiple medications for years, and they didn't really help.

Society says that with all the previous problems listed, you should buy and upgrade material stuff in your life. That can make you happy again, right? Done, again, and it didn't really help, again. Although it did accomplish building a mountain of super awesome debt though! YAY!!

Society says that with all the previous problems listed, you should take a vacation and get away to destress. Done, and it helped monumentally. Hmmmm. We'd accidentally stumbled upon what we needed to do. The only problem was how to capture those vacation feelings in daily life? Vacations are too expensive to take regularly. We weren't sitting on a million dollars, so how could we escape from the stress that was driving us apart, but still survive?

Until we were shown that full-time RV life was an option, we didn't have a clue how to pull it off. Chris & G showed us it was possible to live and work from the road. When they gave us the idea, we just had to figure out how to turn our lives upside down, sell everything we owned, quit our jobs, and move into an RV together. We didn't know if it would solve our problems, but we did know that what we had been trying wasn't working.

It also helped that Laura's grandfather had taken her on some cross-country RV trips when she was young. She had very fond memories of traveling in an RV. I doubt the decision to quit our lives would have been as easy without the trips with Grandpa.

There was just one small problem. How in the hell could we afford an RV of any kind large enough for two people, two big dogs

(150 lbs. worth), a cat and our stuff? Sure, we could buy an old beater that might lose a wall the first time we took it on the highway, but we're both conscientious and responsible people. If we were going to try this crazy plan, we needed something reliable and safe.

We quickly realized that neither of us knew anything about RV's. When you're thinking about buying a house on wheels you should probably learn a little about them first. Enter the research phase of our story.

CHAPTER

3

Hebard Luck

～～～

Thanks to Laura's years of working a crazy night shift schedule, she was basically an insomniac. Also, she is a HARD-CORE researcher, and has been all her life. She told me stories of presenting a researched plan to her dad for a very expensive new phone she wanted in high school. She did such a good job that he bought it for her.

When we began kicking around the idea of full-time RVing, she started spending most of every night reading. We learned A LOT about the RV industry very quickly, or so we thought.

Did you know there are about 20 different categories for RV's? You've got Class A's, the big flat faced buses; Class C's, a motorhome with some kind of bunk or storage over the cab; Class B's are the large vans meant to live or travel in; finally, there's fifth wheels and travel trailers, which I already explained.

Laura's research was even more confusing because some of them are rated for full time living, others are classified as luxury, there's toy haulers with a garage bay for motorcycles and stuff, pop ups, truck campers, the list goes on. To throw another wrench into the pile of RV's, you have crossovers between A's and C's, and between C's and B's. Totally exhausting, I know.

Laura was a trooper though. She figured all of this out during many lonely nights as I lay sleeping next to her.

As people new to the world of RVing, our heads were spinning after the first few days of research. We couldn't even figure out what class we wanted. If you find yourself in the same position, there's a really easy way to narrow everything down. Look at what you can afford. We quickly realized the highest quality RV we could possibly buy would be a fifth wheel.

But wait, there's more!

Unfortunately, my little Toyota Tacoma wasn't going to pull a fifth wheel. For our plan to work, we had to buy a large heavy-duty truck. Oh great, research time again. Finding the truck was my job since Laura had her hands full attempting to narrow down the lists upon lists of different fifth wheels. I already knew a little about trucks anyway. Well, let me backup, I THOUGHT I knew about trucks. After a few hours of research, I quickly realized that I didn't really know much at all.

I had no idea what GVWR (gross vehicle weight), GCWR (gross combined weight), or GAWR (gross axle weight rating) meant. I had been working on cars for over a year and felt like I'd never even seen a vehicle before.

It turns out that when you're towing heavy stuff, it's important to know all those numbers. Otherwise, you could damage your truck, or find yourself using an underpowered vehicle to tow with. That may not seem like a big deal but try pulling your 18,000-pound trailer up a mountain in the summer with an underpowered truck. It may protest by breaking down halfway up the pass.

We knew we wanted a fifth wheel. We knew we wanted one over 35 feet long so that we'd have enough space for us and our pets. We knew we wanted one rated for full-time living, and we knew that we needed one rated for four-season weather. All those things equal weight and money, and LOTS of both.

After a few weeks of late night (or early morning?) research Laura had narrowed down the list of companies and models, and nothing she was looking at was under 11,000 pounds dry weight. Dry weight is before you cram all your stuff in the RV. So, we were really looking at a fifth wheel with a weight of 15,000-19,000 pounds after we packed in whatever we chose to bring with us and put some fresh water in the tank.

I've seen a lot of people try to pull large fifth wheels with ¾ ton trucks, most are grossly overloaded. An easy test to see if the trailer weighs too much is how much your truck bed lowers when it's hooked up. If it drops more than 2-3 inches, that's probably too much weight.

Some people will add airbags to level out the truck, but that doesn't make the frame stronger. Just something to consider

We've read A LOT of forums and Facebook posts where RVers argue over trucks and what they can tow. Truck arguments turn nasty very quickly! Everyone has an opinion, and I found that many of them were being quite unsafe by towing with a truck that was far too small for the load. Sadly, they couldn't see around their egos.

I knew whatever we bought would be REALLY heavy, so I scratched the ¾ tons from my list. Even though every other guy on Facebook swears he can pull his 19,000-pound luxury full-time fifth wheel with a 15-year-old F-250, I decided not to risk it. I made it home alive from combat three times. I try not to tempt fate anymore.

I understand people not wanting to buy a one-ton truck, the ride while it's unloaded is kind of terrible. But I'd rather deal with that and be able to tow easier. Something else to think about. So, I decided on a 1-ton truck. With the first choice out of the way I just had to decide on what manufacturer I wanted, and whether should I pick single or dual rear wheels?

I forgot to mention that I was cramming all this research in during lunch breaks at work and dinner breaks during homework. Fun times for sure.

Right about the time I was trying to figure out how to get my coffee intravenously, a friend at work told me about frame twist tests. My reaction was, "The what what's?"

A frame twist test is when you take two ramps and stagger them so that one front wheel begins going up a ramp before the other. This accomplishes raising a truck off the ground at an odd angle. General Motors trucks did well, as their frames twisted very little and the back wheel was off the ground. Sadly, Ford trucks didn't fare nearly as well. Their back wheels were still both on the ground. In some cases, the frame had twisted so badly the tailgate couldn't be opened.

I'd already scratched Dodge from my list. After working on cars for a year I'd decided to never own a Chrysler product, they were the cheapest built of the big three from what I'd seen. Although, I didn't have much experience with their one-tons. We didn't get many diesels in the shop. Later I learned that Ram isn't actually under Dodge, it's a separate division of Chrysler. I've since met many full-timers towing with Rams and haven't heard any complaints.

With the brand finally chosen, I started researching single rear wheel (SRW) and dual rear wheel (DRW) trucks. Here's the BIG difference between them, DRW's are built ONLY for towing heavy stuff. Because of that, you get cool upgrades like an exhaust brake (not all the SRW's had that, depending on the year); a better rear axle gear ratio which raises tow capacity; no need for anti-sway control; an extra tire on each side in case of a rear blowout; and many of them have long beds which makes tight turns easier with a fifth wheel.

There is a downside to buying a long bed dually, however. They're primarily made as work trucks. You have to spend a lot of money to upgrade into a nice interior like the ½ tons have, and they're few used nice dually's on the market because of this. If I'd wanted a basic work truck interior, I had plenty to choose form. But since I knew it would basically be an extension of our living space, I wanted a nicer interior.

With the decision made, I secured a loan pre-approval from the bank and started looking for our perfect truck. I set my search parameters to be a Chevy or GMC, 2011 or newer, since that's when they upgraded the towing capacity. $30,000 or less, no work truck interior, long bed, DRW, less than 35,000 miles, and within 1000 miles of Kansas City.

> *I'm glad you kept reading because I have a funny story about this one time when I was an idiot…*

I found three in my first online search, and two had been wrecked. The other may as well have been wrecked, it was trashed. I changed my search parameters and raised the price to $35,000 and the mileage to 40,000, but that didn't help much. Finally, I took the price up to $40,000 and mileage to 50,000. Then I finally found a few that were in decent shape. Sadly, I think the closest one was about 500 miles away.

Immediately I started calling the dealerships and told them I was already pre-approved for a loan, and that I could be there within a day if they'd just hold the truck for me. They all said they had to ask their boss and get back to me. They were all sold out from under me before they called back. I knew I couldn't take the price higher since we'd still have to get a loan on the RV, so I kept looking hoping that another truck we could afford would post online.

After a few depressing weeks the "Hebard Luck" struck, as Laura would say it. Hebard Luck is a running joke between us. It's somewhat similar to Murphy's Law, "Whatever can go wrong, will." But Hebard Luck is more like "Whatever can go wrong, will. The first few attempts to fix it ourselves will fail miserably. But, defying all reason, it turns out amazing in the end." It actually happens quite often. But sadly, not with gambling.

It struck in a BIG way!

Around 6:30 p.m. on one of our half days together, I ran my 1,365th search (I'd lost count by then) and a 2014 Chevy popped up that met my revised ridiculous list, and it was only thirty minutes away! I called the dealer and they confirmed they still had it on the lot. I asked if anyone would still be there to let us look at it if we arrived thirty minutes before they closed. They said yes, and we jumped in Laura's SUV and hit the road five minutes later. We had to let the dogs out first of course.

Not only was it still there when we arrived, but it was in better condition than we could have hoped for! All seven tires were new, and a good brand. It already had a spray in bed liner, running boards, an aftermarket deck with GPS/Bluetooth/WIFI/etc., long bed, 55,000 miles (a bit higher than I wanted, but still low for a diesel), all maintenance was up to date, and it was in phenomenal shape overall.

We test drove it and took it home that night. It was an interesting test drive. I don't think I'd driven anything that wide since HUMVEE's in the army ten years prior. The sales team stayed an hour late to close the deal. After we added an extended warranty, we were into the truck for about $45,000.

Laura had always been nervous with me driving, but that fear disappeared when she was in that large truck. Of course, I had to take her around the block before we drove home, she was too excited to wait. It was fun watching her loosen up.

We were literally giddy with excitement driving home that night. The hours and weeks of research, planning, and conversations were well and all, but they weren't tangible like the truck. Buying the truck solidified our dream. We were on the hook for a $45,000 loan, we couldn't back out anymore.

After we got back home, we began discussing a name for the new truck. In the middle of talking we noticed the temporary tag they'd given us was AHNJ and some random numbers. Immediately I thought of Andre, Andre the Giant. The name AHNJ (pronounced awnjay) stuck. It's a big truck and ANHJ seemed perfect.

How serendipitous was that Hebard Luck though? We found exactly what we wanted, at a price we could afford, and on a rare half-day together and Laura could come with me. I really didn't want to buy a truck without Laura seeing it first. And it solved the problem of buying a vehicle by myself and getting to it without trading in my Tacoma. The Tacoma needed some work before I could have sold it, otherwise I wouldn't have got much for it.

CHAPTER

4

Be Vewy Vewy Quiet, We're Hunting RVs

ow that we'd found our truck, it was time to go RV hunting. Laura had done a fantastic job researching fifth wheels and was putting the finishing touches on a master list right around the time we brought AHNJ home. After narrowing down the manufacturers and models, she cross referenced rigs rated for full-time living and those with four-season packages.

A four-season package usually means it has real rolled insulation instead of pressed foam walls, thermal windows, tank heaters, and ducted heating in the storage bays that protects the pipes and tanks in freezing temperatures. However, these features can vary by manufacturer.

A quick note on "full-time" rated units. VERY few manufacturers will state their RVs are rated for full-time use. Finding this information was one of the hardest aspects of Laura's research. She spent weeks reading and watching blogs, forums, reviews and YouTube videos. It was based off a general consensus among owners.

Full-time rated units are usually built with higher quality materials, such as real wood cabinets instead of pressboard or particle board, higher quality furniture/appliances/electronics, and the overall build quality is usually higher.

There was just one little problem, EVERY fifth wheel on the list was at the high end of the price range. Even looking at units just a few years old, we were still having a hard time finding anything in decent condition under $40,000.

For some silly reason I thought we could buy a used RV, that was still in good shape, from our master list, for under $40,000. Oh, one more caveat. The company still had to be in business. That was going to be tough, as many went under around the 2008 crash.

Are you laughing yet? If not, I'll start, and you can join in.

Laura's master list included companies such as Redwood, DRV Suites, Cedar Creek, Montana, Bighorn, Big Country, Grand Design, Luxe, Arctic Fox or Landmark. We didn't care nearly as much about the floorplan as we did about buying something built well. If you do a quick search, you'll see that these are all VERY expensive units, even used ones.

Later we learned that New Horizons and Spacecraft should have been on the list. Although we couldn't have afforded them even if we did find one for sale. Those companies will spend weeks or months building a fifth wheel, instead of hours. Quality comes with a price tag.

We were dead set on no dinette booth as Laura had bad memories of sleeping in a converted dinette in her grandpa's RV, no corner shower and the TV couldn't be at a 45-degree angle from the couch or chairs. Other than those few things, we were open to almost any features.

Our must-haves list included slide toppers, a medium to large size fridge, a master bedroom large enough for us and the dogs, ceilings and doorways tall enough that I wouldn't have to duck since I'm 6'2", a couch or recliners directly facing the TV and enough cargo capacity to carry everything we'd need to live on the road. Should be a piece of cake, right?

Maybe I should do RV comedy? I could take this show on the road.

With our shiny new master list in hand, we decided to take a trip to our closest RV dealer, Olathe Ford RV Center, and have our first look inside these RVs we'd been researching. After all, why shouldn't we? We'd just spent a month researching RVs and we knew that we knew everything about them! Cue the well-deserved laughter and circus music.

Our first dealer experience started off on the wrong foot before we could even walk through the door.

A woman was walking inside at the same time and held the door open for Laura and me. She chatted us up for a minute and it turned out she worked there on the sales team. Huge surprise, I know. She asked if we had an appointment, and we said no. We should have seen the cartoon dollar signs in her eyes, I guess we just weren't paying attention. Later we learned she had jumped their turn system and stole us from another salesman.

We sat down with her, showed her our master list, explained our must-haves and have-nots lists and told her our budget. It was going well until we mentioned budget. She didn't listen to anything else we said except the $40,000 price.

She took us straight out to look at new, very tiny, very flimsy, Chaparral light fifth wheels that (wait for it!) just happened to be priced, new at $40,000. I don't think I've ever touched something that felt cheaper in my life. I'm pretty sure if China got into the RV business, they'd make higher quality units than those. The cabinets sounded as if they would shatter when closed without the utmost of care. The cabinet hinges would have been more appropriate on a jewelry box. And I smashed my head on the short slide standing up from the couch.

After showing us a third Chaparral, we finally put our foot down with the saleswoman and told her we wanted to see any used RVs they had that fit our list. She begrudgingly agreed and took us to the back row, where the used RVs were located.

The first used one we walked through was a 2013 Bighorn with terrible water damage around a slide. Another was a 2013 Cedar Creek with a destroyed interior and missing furniture. Another one had clearly been owned by a chain smoker. Yet another had its underbelly falling down and the insulation was exposed to the elements. Who knows how many mice were living in there?

The dealer actually had the audacity to ask top dollar for their used junk. We did a quick search online and saw that we could find the same units elsewhere for at least $10,000 less. They also appeared to be in much better shape, and we told her so.

Surprisingly, she didn't even try to negotiate with us or show that she cared we could save money not buying from her. She immediately switched tactics and tried to convince us to trade our vehicles in so we could afford a more expensive, newer, RV which we weren't even interested in. We left the dealership.

We did go back and try a second time, hoping for a better experience. The second salesman listened slightly better, but the experience still made us feel like they weren't listening to our needs.

After our fantastic experience buying the truck, we were very unhappy with how they treated us. We were also quite concerned about the damage and abuse we'd seen on those used RVs. Would all used fifth wheels we looked at be in such poor condition? Why would a dealer be selling damaged RVs at all? What other product is sold this way? We'd never seen anything like it before and it was extremely worrisome.

After striking out twice with a dealership we changed tactics and went to an RV show instead. At the end of February Overland Park,

Kansas has a small RV and Outdoors show. Lucky us, it was only 15 minutes away.

Knowing it was coming up, we were both able to move work schedules around beforehand. The morning of the show we crawled out of bed at the crack of 8 a.m., barely conscious. I distinctly remember walking around the convention center with the largest coffee I could buy at Quick Trip that morning, I almost fell asleep in one RV. Our terrible schedule was starting to take a toll.

The RV show was a radically different experience vs. the dealership. There were no high-pressure sales tactics and we were able to browse at our leisure. Sadly, most of the RV's there were smaller bumper-pull travel trailers. Out of the few fifth wheels they did have, only one fell into our price range. Still, it was fun to finally walk through RV's and get a feel for them without someone hounding us every step of the way.

That show was the first opportunity we had to just sit in an RV and talk about all our future plans and dreams, which we spent an hour doing. Also, it was our first chance to get hands on an RV. We played with the cabinets and appliances, sat on the furniture, laid on the bed, and imagined the day we could live in one and travel.

Unfortunately, the one fifth wheel in our price range didn't fit our list of haves and have-nots. We left feeling slightly panicked. We didn't have much time left before our landlord wanted us to move out, and the RV show season was over for the area.

After the first dealership experience, we were hoping to buy from a show and never have to step foot in a dealer again. That plan just wasn't in the cards though. We had to change tactics again. For the new plan we thought maybe buying through a nationwide chain would be a good idea. The logic being that if we needed repairs on the road there would be shops available to us in most states. It made sense to us.

Shortly after the RV show, some friends came to visit from out of town. We excitedly told them about our radical idea, our last-ditch effort to save what was left of our lives. They seemed mildly interested, so naturally, we took them RV shopping with us.

That time we went to Camping World in Grain Valley, Missouri. We thought, "It's a nationwide dealership. They have to be more reputable than the first dealer, right?" We were confident we wouldn't have any problems with them.

> *Don't try this at home kids. We were professional newbies making stupid mistakes that should only be learned from, laughed at, and never repeated.*

When we walked through the door, we were quickly introduced to a salesman. We told him the same things we had told the person at Olathe Ford RV. He was very nice, listened to everything we had to say, but ultimately didn't listen to what we wanted either. Instead of showing us used models, of which they hardly had any, he instead took us straight to the new, more expensive models.

Being ignored was starting to feel too familiar. The salesman played the typical high-pressure sales ploy of starting with a model which was inferior and not what we wanted. Then he followed up with one that was very nice and beautiful, but much more than we could afford. Finally, he showed us the in-between we could afford. By that time, however, we had become annoyed at salesman not listening to our needs, so we called it quits and went back to his office.

That salesman taught us a several very interesting lessons about RV loans and RVing in general.

1. Interest from loan payments may be a tax deduction because it's considered a second home.

2. You may be able to deduct some expenses if you have an LLC and use it for your traveling business. Just be sure to keep your receipts.

3. Veterans can get incredible benefits like free or discount camping on government land, better RV sales discounts, and free RV club memberships.

4. If you finance an RV, you are not applying for a home or vehicle loan. It's something completely separate and doesn't look like either. If you secure a loan above $50,000, you can get up to a 20-year rate. This will lower your payments but raise the interest. Again, the interest is usually deductible as a second home.

5. Used RVs will have a much shorter loan term with higher payments.

> *Obviously, I'm not a lawyer or tax accountant, I'm simply relaying what we were told. If you have questions you need to ask a professional. It's a good idea to run any contract by an attorney before you sign it anyway. Just think of the bill as if you're paying for insurance.*

The salesman made it sound as if we wouldn't be able to secure a loan unless we chose a new RV over $50,000. But we were sure we'd never qualify for such a large loan. We left feeling overwhelmed, ignored and dejected.

We returned to our rental house more confused than ever. Not to be dissuaded, however, we dove right back into more research. We wanted to know why used RVs were in such poor shape and why dealers had so few used RVs available from our list.

Information and answers to our questions were surprisingly hard to find. So naturally, we figured what we'd seen was a fluke and dismissed it. It must have just been the dealerships.

> *A lot more on RV quality later, stick around. If you haven't watched our Lemon RV series on our YouTube channel Hebards Travels you're in for an interesting story. If you have, you're going to learn a lot more.*

A few days after going to Camping World, I called them again for one more try, as there weren't many RV dealers around the Kansas City area. I got the same salesman and, again, had a conversation with him about what we wanted, compared to what he had shown us.

"Hopefully he'll actually listen this time," I thought.

I told him we only wanted to look at used RVs because of our budget, which we'd now raised to $50,000. We'd learned that we had to be a bit more realistic with pricing. Halfway through my pitch, he cut me off and said he had a pair of Cedar Creek's that fit all the criteria on our list. They were new, but a model year old. As such, they were heavily discounted. The list price was about $88,000 and were being sold for around $55,000. We wondered why they hadn't been mentioned a few days before.

Laura and I couldn't drive out there that night, so we were there when they opened the next morning to look at them. The RVs had been sitting on the lot since April 2015. We asked to have them both opened up and connected to temporary power so we could walk through both and really get a feel for the layouts.

They were both Cedar Creek 36CKTS 2016 models, so only one was opened/turned on since they were nearly identical. The color scheme was lighter in one, and it had theater seating, while the other came with a pair of recliners and darker colors.

They met all our criteria and then some. We spent several hours looking through it, opening cabinets, trying out the couch, chairs, dining table seating, bedding and more. We decided it was the right fit for us. It was 41 feet and had plenty of room for our four-legged kiddos.

We loved what we saw and gave them a down payment to hold it while they began to work on financing. We're frugal, so we of course chose the one with recliners and darker colors that was $500 less.

When we spoke with the loan officer, we requested a Splendide washer/dryer stackable set and a fifth wheel hitch to be included in the loan. We were told their financing department would do some work and call if they could find us a lender.

We often see questions regarding living in an RV full-time. You don't have to look any further than the common posts on Facebook RVing groups to find out this is a polarizing subject. The common belief is that if you tell someone you're a full-timer, a few things will happen. You won't receive a loan for an RV, you will void your warranty, and you won't be allowed to insure your pricey investment.

Obviously, we aren't lawyers and nothing I write here should be taken as legal advice. These are things we either saw firsthand or heard from others who experienced it firsthand. If you're really worried about these things, then it's best to spend the money and speak with an attorney associated with these four subjects.

1. Loans: When we purchased our rig, we'd already been warned several times by people in person and on Facebook, that if you tell the dealership you're going to use it full-time, they won't give you a loan. In reality, it's the bank that possibly won't give you a loan. While speaking to the salesman handling our paperwork, we mentioned that we planned on full-timing in it. He responded by saying that he didn't hear that was our plan and to please not mention it to anyone there again. We were both shocked when he said that, and it scared us a little. We were finally buying a home, but we couldn't tell certain people it was our home.

2. Insurance: Our personal bank, USAA, doesn't offer RV insurance themselves, but they partner with Progressive. When I called Progressive, I was very nervous, and I kept beating around the bush. Finally, I think out of frustration, the loan officer told me they insure RVs for full-time use. I was

very specific when I asked him if that meant we could use it 365 days a year. He responded by saying they offered policies for full-timers or vacationers. It ended up being a comprehensive plan with a wonderful mix between automotive and homeowners' coverage. Not only is the RV itself insured just like a vehicle would be, but all our belongings inside are insured as if they were in a home. They gave me the choice of increasing the policy at my discretion depending on how expensive our property was. There's quite a bit of misinformation online about whether or not this is legitimate. I'm telling you it is, at least with Progressive. In the policy it says 365 days a year. There is no stipulation on amount of time we have to be out of the rig each year. I can't comment on other insurance companies as I didn't speak with any.

3. Manufacturer Warranties: Our contract did say we weren't allowed to stay in it full-time, but it didn't define what full-time meant. We couldn't find any stipulation regarding an amount of time we are or are not allowed to be in our RV. We wondered how they could even prove if someone was using it full-time? It seemed to me the burden of proof would be on them, but to be fair, we never asked a lawyer. With the amount of new RVs sitting in the shop waiting for repairs during the first year, it's highly unlikely anyone could live in a new RV every day during the warranty period, however long their manufacture warranty is for.

4. Extended Warranties: Every extended warranty is a little different. The best part is that if you purchase an extended warranty and it turns out they don't cover what you need them to, you can return it for the prorated portion. Essentially, they'll buy you out of the contract. It's not as easy as it sounds, but it is possible. This is handy considering most of us purchase warranties out of fear. Most people I've spoken with about extended warranties complain about how many of the problems they encountered weren't covered under their plan. Many have told us they're just a waste of time and money. We haven't tried to use ours yet, so we don't know firsthand. This isn't to say extended warranties are bad, some people have had great success using them. However, our standpoint is, if you can learn to be handy by asking questions and watching videos on YouTube, you can learn to repair just about anything on an RV. It may be cheaper to just buy a lot of tools and take some classes. Some warranties will limit your time allowed in the rig and exclude full-timers. We've never heard firsthand that someone's warranty was voided because they were found to be living full-time in their RV, even if it's listed in the paperwork.

CHAPTER

5

We Buy Our First Home!

S everal very tense days passed after placing the down payment. Our phones were never turned off and we leapt at every call. Finally, after almost a week, Camping World called on March 29 and said they'd found a lender who would cover the RV, washer/dryer and hitch.

WE WERE FINALLY GETTING OUR RV!!!!

He said it would be a few days before their techs could install the washer/dryer. In the meantime, we could drop off the truck to get the hitch installed, then we could take the RV home the day it was ready. The next moment Laura and I had together we dropped the truck off and sat back waiting to hear when everything would be ready. We told them what our schedule was so they could try and have it ready on a day we would have off together.

On one of our next days off they called to tell us everything was ready. We jumped in the SUV and left immediately. When we arrived, the salesman shook our hands and congratulated us. He then sent us out to our new RV for an inspection.

If you've never bought a new RV, then you've never experienced a dealer RV inspection. Consider yourself lucky. Our inspection was given by someone I'll refer to as "The Walkthrough Kid." We wondered if he was even old enough to vote. The "walkthrough" basically consisted of him just parroting a series of buzz words he'd been told, but it quickly became clear the only thing he really understood was how to turn on the TVs and lights.

I asked The Kid multiple technical questions, none of which he could answer. He gave us an "owner's manual" that consisted of a few pages with lines where we could write in the information. You'd think it would come completed from the manufacturer, wouldn't you? Well, it turns out they don't, not for Cedar Creeks at least. It wasn't even a model specific owner's manual. As far as we could tell, it was the same one that was issued for all Cedar Creeks.

At some point later, I realized we were at the mercy of a kid that may have still been getting rides to work from his mom. During the walkthrough, I noticed a large area with dried fluid and wipe marks on the floor of the front cap storage area. I pointed it out to The Kid, and he said if there was a leak, he was sure the techs would have fixed it already (that problem becomes VERY relevant later). Sadly, we believed him and didn't push harder. As new RV owners, we were very overwhelmed with the entire experience, and we clearly weren't on our A game.

> *We recently learned that National Indoor RV Center (NIRVC) conducts proper inspections. They also allow buyers to stay a few days on their property in their new RV to test it and look for problems. Whenever we buy again it will likely be through them, or another dealer with the same policies.*

We should have filmed the walkthrough. Not just for evidence, but for reference afterwards. We should have also demanded a knowledgeable and competent person show us how to use our first RV. Don't let a dealer bully you into an inadequate walkthrough because their techs are "busy." Camping World sure wasn't too busy for us before we bought it.

After the walkthrough, we went to see the loan officer. We'd obviously been approved, but barely. After the washer/dryer and hitch, we'd maxed out what the bank would loan us. The "Hebard Luck" had struck again. We burned all our credit for those two loans, but we finally had our house and a truck to pull it. Only three months after being introduced to the idea of full-time RVing we were fast tracking to hit the road.

We landed a fifth wheel with everything we wanted, we couldn't have been happier. While we were in the office going over final paperwork, the techs gave it a once-over to ensure it was ready to go that day. They found that one of the air conditioners didn't work, so they just yanked one off another unit and put it on ours. Odd, but at least it didn't take days or weeks to get fixed. They still didn't find the leak in the storage area though.

We had to wait a few hours for the AC swap, so we did some shopping in their store. How convenient for them. We were given a Good Sam membership for buying an RV through Camping World, which provides a discount at their store. Even with the discount we still spent about $750 on extras that day.

We needed water and sewer hoses, power cord adapters, wheel chocks, bug screens, tire covers, a lube plate, a surge protector, and more. We thought we purchased everything we needed, but our Amazon budget was fairly high over the next few months.

If we'd planned ahead and bought it all on Amazon, we would have saved hundreds of dollars over the Camping World store. But before that day, we didn't know if we'd even get an RV.

Shortly after we finished shopping, the techs also finished replacing our air conditioning. We loaded our stuff into the truck and backed it up to our new trailer to hook up.

Until that time, I'd never towed anything behind a vehicle. I've spoken with many new RV owners that had never towed or driven anything that large before. Most states don't require a CDL or any extra training for driving or pulling RVs. Kansas and Missouri are no different. No one even asked if I knew how to tow it. I'd watched whatever YouTube videos I could find about hooking up and towing, but sadly there weren't many.

I didn't know what I was doing so I asked someone for help. Lucky us, they sent The Walkthrough Kid back out to help us. After about 10 minutes of messing around, we were finally hooked up and ready to go. Fantastic, almost time to see if I could get it to the RV park without crashing and burning.

Before we continue with the story, if you've never hooked up a fifth wheel before, here's the process we've learned since that first day.

1. Most importantly, if you don't have a fifth wheel tailgate, lower the tailgate on your truck.

2. Have a partner with a two-way radio behind you to help guide you in. It becomes easier with practice, but I needed help badly in the beginning.

3. Have your partner raise or lower the king pin to line it up with the hitch. You'll want the king pin as low as possible. If it's too high it can still go into the hitch, but the jaws won't be able to close, or the hitch handle won't push in.

4. Back up onto the kingpin until you hear the loud "THUNK!" That's the best way I can describe the sound. But don't back up hard enough to move the trailer. It can take a little practice.

5. The second most important step is to set the parking brake, then shift the vehicle to park. If you don't set the parking brake first, the truck can roll a half inch, preventing the jaws from being able to close around the pin. Don't let your foot off the brake until you set the parking brake, don't let it roll any amount.

6. If the kingpin is in far enough, and at the right height, you can then push the handle in and close the jaws. That's how our Reese 20k hitch works anyway.

7. Lock the handle, attach the emergency brake cable and plug in the trailer wiring.

8. Remove the wheel chocks from the RV.

9. With the RV jacks still down, perform a "tug test" by driving forward an inch. If the kingpin isn't secured in the hitch correctly it's best to let the trailer fall on the jacks and not on your truck. At least that's our opinion.

10. Close tailgate.

11. Raise all jacks on the RV.

12. Using the radios, conduct a trailer lights test with your partner.

13. Check for trees or other obstacles before you begin driving. Not surprisingly, many campgrounds have trees with damage 10-13' high. If there are obstacles present have your partner outside watching them with a radio until you're clear.

Back at the Camping World parking lot, the only thing that stood between us and the RV park we were headed to for the night, were two back-to-back 90-degree right hand turns. With my extensive limited knowledge of towing, I figured I'd need to swing wide to make the turns. Easy enough, or so I thought.

I wasn't very used to driving the dually, so even when I thought I pulled up as far as possible, I actually had several feet left. And I wasn't even using the left lane. I made a hard right towards the exit but stayed on the right side of the road. In hindsight, I should have used the left lane. The things I know now.

Thinking that I pulled out as far as possible without driving off the road, I cranked the wheel and prayed the camper wheels wouldn't go in the ditch and roll our new fifth wheel. I would have been biting my nails if they weren't pulling on the wheel hard enough to fry the power steering pump.

I took the corner at a snail's pace, trying to look through my mirrors, but I couldn't see the right-side trailer tires at that angle. Laura was behind me in her SUV watching and later told me what happened.

To her horror, she watched the right wheels go off the road, heading straight for the ditch. Fortunately, Camping World had put some blacktop in the street-side corners. Unfortunately, the blacktop was smashed down probably from others doing the exact same thing. Laura said the trailer tipped to a near 45-degree angle before the tires went back on the road.

To this day I still don't know how close I was to rolling the rig, but I know I was a lot closer than I'd like, and all within the first five minutes of pulling it. I think Laura still has nightmares about it. I wouldn't be surprised one bit if there was an angel pushing on the side to keep it from rolling.

After clearing the corner with nothing but dumb (or Hebard) luck holding up the camper, we were finally on the road with our new house. Well, not really. We'd forgotten to do a lights check, and so had The Walkthrough Kid. We stopped less than a mile from dealership, and it turned out the trailer brake lights weren't working.

Good thing we stopped! (It was Laura's good idea, she has a lot of them).

Oh great, our first problem and we weren't even a mile away. At least we got that out of the way quickly! I called Camping World and they told me to check the truck fuses, wish I'd thought of that.

The trailer brake light fuse was burned out, so I pulled one from a system we didn't need, and we got back on the road (we carry spares now). We had scheduled a night at the only RV park in the western Kansas City suburbs and we drove straight there for a shakedown night.

Since both of us were absolutely terrified, we only went 55 mph the whole way, it took us over an hour. The whole "almost rolling the brand-new RV in the first five minutes" thing didn't help one bit. If you ever drive up behind an RV going very slowly, please give them space. They may be towing for the first time.

CHAPTER

6

The First Night in Our New Home

—◦◦◦—

The first night in our new fifth wheel was spent at Walnut Grove RV park in Merriam, Kansas. We reserved one night to test it out. That was a mistake, it should have been at least an entire weekend. The things we know now.

I hope you're taking notes. I know this is all funny and interesting, but for the love of God please don't make the same mistakes we have.

I was in the right lane as we approached the RV park, once again, I barely made the turn. In my defense, it wasn't a good corner for

RVs. Although, I still didn't realize that I needed to be using the left lane to swing wide for tight right turns.

Luckily, we had one of the very few pull-through spots in the park. By that point I was genuinely surprised I hadn't hit anything. I felt like I was towing an aircraft carrier behind me. It honestly felt like the RV was a lane and a half wide.

We were both thanking God for small miracles as we made it into the pull-through without taking out a power pedestal. Our joy quickly dissipated when we realized the Walkthrough Kid hadn't explained how to unhook the RV. We must have tried ten times before a very nice neighbor offered to assist us. He was driving a Jayco Super C but had owned a fifth wheel before.

A little bit about the neighbor before I continue. We've been lucky enough to run into this gentleman three more times at the same park. The last time was over a year later. He's one of those amazingly friendly, knowledgeable, willing to help with anything RVers, that you always hear about. He left his hot dinner to come help us because he saw us struggling. He asked for nothing in return and actually refused to let us repay him in anyway.

He showed us there was a lot more to unhooking than just putting the front jacks down. It wasn't until several months later that we learned how he actually unhooked us. In case you're wondering how to do it, here's what we've learned since that first time. We were using a Lippert 6-point auto level system.

1. Evaluate how level the site is. We've had several unlevel sites where the front jacks couldn't extend far enough to level the camper. If you may need leveling blocks under the front

jacks, now is the time to put them down. Otherwise you'll have to hook the truck back up to lift the jacks up. Also, look at the side-to-side angle of the RV. You may need to drive one side of the trailer onto leveling blocks before you unhook.

2. Place wheel chocks around the tires to prevent rolling. Make sure they're on both sides just in case. I commonly see people place them on the uphill side, I don't know why. DO NOT use X chocks at this point if you have auto level.

3. If you don't have a fifth wheel tailgate, lower the truck tailgate.

4. Extend the front jacks until the fifth wheel hitch is level with the ground (ours pivots in four directions) and you've removed the trailer weight from the truck. The hydraulic jacks are quite strong and can lift the truck to some degree if I'm not paying attention. Don't lift your truck with the trailer.

5. Reverse the truck an inch, until there is no play in the hitch. This step is very important.

6. Set parking brake BEFORE shifting to park. This step is also vital. If you don't do this, the truck will move just enough when you place the vehicle in park that the hitch handle won't be able to pull out. Months of frustration ensued until we learned this incredibly simple, yet necessary, step. It removes the tension from the jays. Trust me, there's no amount of pulling that will unbind the jaws when they have 1,000 lbs. of pressure on them.

7. Now you can pull the hitch handle out to unlock the jaws, unplug the trailer wiring and remove the emergency brake cable.

8. SLOWLY pull forward until the kingpin clears the hitch. If you didn't lift the camper high enough, there can still be a lot of weight on the kingpin. If you pull forward too quickly, the trailer will "drop" off the hitch. I almost smashed our propane grill once doing that.

9. Close the tailgate once you are clear of the camper.

10. Secure the trailer wiring and emergency brake cable. I normally put it all up inside the pin box.

11. Place leveling blocks under the other jack legs as needed. I have to line up each one as I lower each jack leg. It takes a few minutes, and a lot of running around, but prevents the jack pads from slipping off the leveling blocks later. We've added RV Snap Pads which also help them from slipping.

12. Level the trailer. We have Lippert's 6-point Level Up system. Use several levels, or a leveling app, and check to see if the RV is actually level though. The system may need to be recalibrated. Ours was horribly unlevel from the factory (more on that later). You should be level front-to-back, and side-to-side after the auto-level procedure.

13. Once level, you can place X chocks between the wheels. I crushed one by placing it between the tires before I auto leveled the camper. I learned the wheels will move while leveling the RV. That was an expensive lesson.

With the jacks all down, we put the slides out and had a wonderful first night in our camper......Oops, I'm off daydreaming in fantasy land again, sorry. That's how we wish our first night had gone. What happened instead was such a HUGE mess, that it made us seriously reconsider buying an RV at all.

Back in the real world, when I pushed the slide button, nothing happened. I was using the outside button and I could hear something clicking, but that was it. I opened the front storage bay and found that hydraulic fluid was leaking from somewhere and had made quite a mess. Not surprisingly, the puddle was right where I'd seen the cleaning marks during the walkthrough.

On top of the slides not working, the jacks wouldn't operate either. We were stuck. Laura immediately went to Facebook looking for answers. Several people told us to check the mini breakers, however we had no clue what they were or where they were located, and no one could tell us where to find ours.

I checked all the 120v fuses and breakers but didn't find the problem. Then I checked the 12v fuses in the front storage bay, but they were also fine. Since I was unable to locate the 12v mini breakers, we decided to call for help.

> *Too bad I didn't know the mini breakers were merely inches below the 12v fuses. We've since directly helped dozens of other Cedar Creek owners with this exact problem. Now, after two years in the RV, I know they "pop" due to low voltage and other random reasons. I guess the batteries weren't charged. I eventually replaced ours with self-resetting breakers and threw out the cheap ones.*

Because we were given a Good Sam membership when we purchased the RV, we called them for a mobile mechanic. We were informed that we couldn't use Good Sam for roadside assistance, or to request a mobile RV tech, until we'd had the membership for at least 24 hours. I guess they figure nothing can go wrong on the first day.

Even though we were starting out on a bad note, we decided to make the best of the situation. The RV park was only 10 minutes from our house, so I ran back there to get the dogs and a few other items since we had nothing in the RV yet. We ordered pizza and spent the night watching Netflix from the laptop through an HDMI cable plugged into the bedroom TV.

The next day, around 4 p.m., exactly at the 24-hour mark, I called Good Sam back and requested they dispatch a mobile RV tech. They found one in the area, gave him our information and told us he'd be there in about two hours. Great!

We sat back and relaxed, sure that our problems would soon be fixed. I apologized to the RV park and told them we'd be out of their hair soon. I still reserved a second night, just in case.

We also called Camping World. I told them about the wipe marks when we bought it as evidence of a preexisting leak. I explained that someone had clearly tried to clean up something. They said they could get us in the shop in a few days. So, our plan was to get it road ready with the mobile tech, take it to storage until Camping World could get it in, then go back to Camping World to find out why the slides and jacks weren't working.

The two-hour mark came and went. An hour later, at 7 p.m., we received an automated call from Good Sam asking if the service had been completed. I selected "no" and was instantly transferred to a person, that was a nice feature. The new representative told us our membership was active the moment it was given to us, and they didn't know why we'd been told otherwise. Maybe everyone that works at Good Sam should know that?

They reached out to the mobile tech and were told he only needed another 15 minutes. Great. We sat back and relaxed again.

At 7:45pm, we received another automated call from Good Sam asking if the service had been completed. Since the tech still wasn't there, I chose the "no" option again and I was again transferred to a person who once again reached out to the tech who once again said he only needed another 15 minutes. We were annoyed by this time. But we said ok and went back to waiting. Besides, what else could we do?

At 8:30pm we called the mobile tech directly to ask what the holdup was. He informed us that he'd just finished the previous job, some sort of engine rebuild on the side of the road. That sounded a bit outlandish, but whatever. At least he answered the phone.

He went on to say that he'd told Good Sam the previous job would take much longer and that they'd given us an incorrect ETA. We were so sick of the whole mess by then that we didn't care anymore. We just wanted him to actually show up and fix our brand-new RV.

The tech said he was leaving his shop right then and would be at our location in just a few minutes. Great, again. We were very unhappy by that point, but we had it directly from the horse's mouth that he was on his way. We sat back to wait, again.

Because we couldn't use our kitchen with the slides in, and I didn't want to leave with the tech "about" to show up, we ordered pizza for dinner again. We'd already put off dinner for several hours waiting for the tech to show up.

At 9:17pm we called Good Sam again, who called the tech again, who claimed he was 10 minutes away that time. By then we knew he was lying, unless he just happened to stop en route to help a woman giving birth on the sidewalk. We discovered his "shop" (house) was only 15 minutes away, according to Google Maps.

Good Sam said they would call back in 10 minutes. If the tech hadn't arrived then they would cancel, schedule service with another company, and file a new ETA. Very unfortunately for us, that never happened.

At 9:45pm the mobile tech FINALLY arrived! Only four hours late.

> *I so wish that I could end this story here, I really do. Sadly, I can't yet.*

He arrived in a white box truck with no company markings on it. I went outside to speak with him. I didn't know anything about working on RVs and saw that as a great opportunity to possibly learn a little from him.

That attitude helped me A LOT working in the shop. A few conversations with guys that had been working on cars for years could teach me in minutes what may take years to learn otherwise.

When he opened the rolling back door, I saw several tool chests, a generator, welder, large air compressor, an enormous floor jack and random piles of mechanics stuff. Clearly, he was prepared for almost anything.

I explained the problem to him, and he got right to work looking for the cause. Maybe I was talking too much, I've been known to do that from time to time, or he just didn't want me out there with him? I'm not sure why, but he was really short with me and acted annoyed that I was even outside.

In just a few minutes he located the source of the hydraulic fluid leak. It was a loose solenoid next to the fluid reservoir. Just as he was explaining the leak, our pizza showed up, and I went inside to finally eat dinner with Laura.

At 10:15pm I went back outside to speak with the tech again. While we were eating, he determined that we had in fact popped a mini breaker. It sure would have been nice if the Walkthrough Kid had given us a heads up about the 12v mini breakers, what they're for, and their location. We didn't even know they were a thing, let alone where to find them.

The tech quickly fixed the leak, reset the mini breakers, moved the slides in and out a few times, gave us a pile of red shop towels to clean up the hydraulic fluid, then said goodbye.

Wait….what? No bill, no invoice, no paperwork of any kind? I wondered what in the heck was happening.

I stopped the tech right before he got in his truck and asked him about a bill or paperwork. He informed me that because Good Sam dispatched him, he would bill them directly and that he didn't even have an invoice to give us. I thought that sounded pretty strange, but being so new to the RV world, I took him at his word.

I watched him drive away while holding the handful of red rags he'd given me. I went to clean up the leaked fluid before it dried and found there was A LOT of fluid everywhere. It must have leaked even more while he was fixing it.

I started mopping up the sticky fluid and found that we had another problem. Because some idiot thought installing the refrigerator's power inverter directly underneath the hydraulic fluid reservoir was a good idea, there was now fluid all over it as well.

I thought it was strange the tech didn't clean up at all, but I was happy for the rags he'd left me. I wiped up what I could, but hydraulic fluid isn't easy to clean up. Everything it had leaked on was still slightly damp and sticky. So, laid the rest of the dry rags out on the damp areas hoping to soak some more up and went inside to call it a night.

Later, we came up with a hypothesis about why the mobile tech lied about how long it would take him to arrive. If he'd told Good Sam that he wouldn't be available for 3-4 hours they would have scheduled someone else. So, our thoughts are that he lied to secure his next job. If true, it's a slimy tactic that only benefits him.

7

New RV Owner Growing Pains

———∿∿∿———

With our brand-new RV finally fixed (HA! Man were we naïve) we sat in our new plush leather recliners for the first time and watched some TV. We'd never had nice furniture before and couldn't believe how comfortable it was.

With the slides out there was so much room, it actually felt like a home. The dogs could run around and play, and we weren't bumping into each other every other second. After spending the first two days with the slides in, it was night and day different.

With everything "fixed," all doubts about buying it disappeared. We were over the moon with our new house. As far as we were concerned, we were homeowners. But it was far better than a traditional house. We could park our house on a beach or in the mountains, at our whim. We could migrate with the seasons and say goodbye to the harsh Midwest summers and winters. We spent the evening contemplating where the new adventure would take us.

We decided to leave the next day. I'm sure there were some good laughs had from anyone watching us trying to hook up for the second time ever. We still hadn't figured out most of the list I described earlier. After a while, we got lucky enough to accidentally figure it out.

We checked out of the RV park and profusely thanked them for allowing us to stay longer at the last second. We got back in the truck and prepared to pull our new home for the second time. No pressure at all after almost dumping it in a ditch the last time. I was more than a little nervous.

Lucky for us, the storage lot was only ten minutes away. Unlucky for us, the on-ramp for the highway was a steep hill with a short merging lane, maybe $1/4^{th}$ of a mile total. I hadn't pushed the truck hard while towing yet and had no idea how AHNJ would handle it. But we were about to find out.

I made the tight right turn slowly and punched the gas. Well, diesel in this case, but you get the point. The 6.6L Duramax roared to life like a pissed off dragon! We virtually flew up the hill. We were doing almost 40 mph after the hill, and 50 mph by the time I had to merge. Granted, the truck and trailer were both empty, but we hit the highway genuinely impressed with our new truck.

Since that time, we've added about 4500lbs between them, but I've also added an Edge CS2 tuner and a Stealth module to the truck. AHNJ is permanently in beast mode now and handles the extra weight as if it's still empty. The Stealth module gives me several additional MPG's, while also increasing power and throttle response. I can't recommend it enough.

We drove the few minutes to the storage lot and found, to our dismay, that we had to back the trailer into our spot. That wouldn't have been such an issue except the spots were all slanted parking, slanted the WRONG WAY!

There was a class A parked next to our site, which made the situation exponentially worse. After what must have been an hour, and an Austin Powers 30-point turn, we finally had it parked. Then came another half hour of trying to figure out how to unhook the truck, which we accidentally figured out again. Luckily before dark.

Before we left, we decided to level the camper. Because why wouldn't we level it in storage? Laura stayed on the passenger side to watch for any problems while I pushed the auto level button and stood back to watch the magic happen.

Oh, we watched some magic all right. The magic of how our trailer didn't tip over from the uncalibrated auto level. As I look back on it, I think it was about an inch from actually tipping over. That's because the parking lot had a severe slant which put the driver's side higher, and the auto level wanted to lift the driver's side as high as possible while also dropping the passenger side to the ground.

Laura started screaming about the same time I saw the driver's side tires lifting off the ground. I sprinted back to the control panel, which was almost at eye level by this time, and smashed the off button almost hard enough to break it off.

With our hearts racing we asked each other what in the hell had just happened? I manually leveled the trailer just as it was getting dark and called it good.

Before we left, I checked the battery disconnect and ensured it was in the on position, because "on" means that the disconnect is on and working. Right? Well, why bother checking to make sure the lights don't work when you can just assume and go home?

Since going home seemed like a great idea, that's exactly what we did. We went back to our daily life and work for a few days until it was time to take the RV back to Camping World. On the morning of our appointment we drove down to the storage lot, ready to hook up and haul it across the city to find out what was wrong with our new house.

Everything was going just fine until I tried to move the jacks. When I turned on the auto level control panel, it said low voltage and the jacks wouldn't work. While we were standing there wondering what we would do, Laura noticed a problem with the power inverter for the fridge. It was mounted just to the right side of the control panel, and she saw that the inverter's LCD screen was full of hydraulic fluid.

That was the last straw and we both almost lost it.

Our brand-new batteries were dead, and the hydraulic leak had gotten inside the inverter. Neither of us could figure out what had killed them for the longest time. We searched online and learned the battery disconnect was mislabeled. It should have been labeled "Batteries On or Off," not "Battery Disconnect On or Off." I had left the batteries on and the fridge killed them.

We called Camping World to tell them we would miss our appointment and informed them about the new inverter problem. They said being late was fine and to just bring it in whenever we could. Strangely, they didn't seem concerned in the slightest about all the issues we were having. That should have been a clue.

We quickly realized that we had to charge the batteries to move our camper. First, I tried my jump pack on the camper batteries, it couldn't provide enough power to operate the jacks. Next, I plugged in the trailer wiring to the truck and tried again, but it still showed a low power warning. I then left it plugged in and let the truck idle for about 15 minutes. I figured that would be enough time and tried the jacks again. They barely moved before the low power warning came on again.

I didn't want to spend five hours with the trailer wiring charging the batteries, so I changed tactics. I have a set of trucker's jumper cables that were long enough to reach, and I hooked them up. I tried every combination of hooking them up, but either nothing happened, or the cables heated up immediately. The batteries received a small charge while the cables were heating up, but I was worried that would damage something. I decided to scratch the jumper cable idea.

Our next idea was to drive thirty minutes to Cabela's and buy a Yamaha EF2000isV2 2000w generator that we'd been considering. We didn't have the $1000 for it, but I did have a Cabela's credit card.

We knew that we'd need a generator anyway, so we went ahead and bought it.

We did consider the larger 3000w, but it just cost too much. Besides, we knew that in the future, if we wanted more power, we could buy a second 2000w model and the parallel kit to make 4000w. This seemed like the better option at the time.

We also bought 50-30 amp and 30-15-amp dog bone adapters, a 2.5-gallon gas can and a Yamaha cover for the generator. Unfortunately, we got home too late to get back into the storage lot that night. Instead, I went to the store and bought a quart of generator oil and made sure the generator was running for the next day.

The next morning, with our shiny new generator in hand, I was at the storage lot the minute the gate would let me in. Being so early, I had to leave Laura in bed since she had to work that night. I fired up the generator to let it warm up for a minute before I put a load on it for the first time. I pulled out the power cord, screwed it into the trailer, then attached our fancy new $350 50-amp surge protector (because I'm paranoid), the two dog bone adaptors and plugged the RV into the generator.

When I plugged the 15-amp dog bone in, the surge protector began its two-minute power test. As I sat patiently waiting, the surge protector gave me a fault code. It wouldn't connect. "Oh crap, what is it now?" I know I said something to that effect. Maybe a bit more colorfully though.

I called Yamaha and they told me to call a Cabela's Yamaha repair facility. I didn't know that was a thing. Anyway, I found one and spoke with them. They determined the generator was working just fine. The surge protector was the problem.

> *Several months later I learned why it wouldn't connect. I won't make you read five more chapters to see why though. If our surge protector detects the power supply is irregular, too high, too low, etc. it won't connect. In this case it was too low. It doesn't like anything less than 30 amps.*

I removed the surge protector and BAM! The generator revved right up, and the trailer had power. I'd read up on deep cycle AGM batteries (what our RV had) and I knew that running them below 50% can seriously damage them. My plan for that day was to sit there with the generator until I had them charged to at least 50%.

While I was waiting, I had the bright idea to film our first YouTube video. It was going to be a review of our new generator. I tried to show how loud it was inside and outside and talked about it for a few minutes. Sadly, that footage was never used. At that time, we didn't know anything about video editing, uploading videos or creating a YouTube channel.

Every hour I would unplug the power cord and check the dummy lights inside. After 3-4 hours, the second light finally lit up. I thought I'd killed everything, so the batteries could have all the power, but I have no idea if the electric water heater was on sucking power. Just another newbie mistake in a long line of mistakes. If you're only plugged into a 15-amp connection (essentially what that generator was) the water heater will use most of the power.

When the batteries were charged at last, I packed up and went home to work on the house. It was too late to drive across the city, and we didn't have much longer until we had to move.

CHAPTER 8

A Whole New Set of Problems, and Laura Has A Brilliant Idea

⹿⹿⹿

The day after I charged the batteries, we hooked up the trailer to take it back to Camping World. The drive was, thankfully, uneventful. We dropped it off and they said they'd call us when they found something.

We went home confident they would diagnose the problem and fix it quickly. We had just bought it and the leak was clearly present beforehand. Why wouldn't they cover everything, we thought?

The next day the service manager called. He informed me that the hydraulic fluid reservoir had been overfilled, which had caused it to overflow. He could tell it had been overfilled because the cap has a sponge that allows air in and out of the reservoir to prevent it from creating a vacuum. Because the inverter is mounted beneath the reservoir, the extra fluid had drained directly onto it.

He then proceeded to ACCUSE ME of overfilling it. He told me that because the damage was caused by owner negligence, the warranty wouldn't cover it. He actually stated, "I know you did it." I was appalled at their terrible customer service. Couldn't a hard bump also slosh it up into the sponge? How could he possibly "know" that I had overfilled it?

Midway through his rant I'd had enough, and decided to pull out my, "I'm a sergeant and you're an idiot private screwing up" voice. It had been years since I'd used it, but it didn't need much dusting off. I then proceeded to chew his ass completely off his body and hand it back to him, just like a good sergeant does.

The look on Laura's face was priceless! She'd never heard me talk to anyone like that. Here's the PG version. Obviously, I wasn't being this nice to him.

I told him that I'd never put anything in the fluid reservoir, and that I'd worked in a shop for over a year and I knew better than to start adding fluids to systems I didn't understand. I informed him it was either his techs or the mobile tech that did it. Also, not only did I not do it, but what in the world was he thinking calling a customer, accusing them of lying (or anything for that matter) and yelling at them?

Boy, did he change his tune in a heartbeat! Suddenly, the conversation sounded much more like, "It must have been the mobile tech, sir." Unfortunately, the service manager insisted he couldn't (or wouldn't, pick one) replace our inverter, because it wasn't a warrantable issue.

We called Good Sam and told them about the situation. They couldn't (or wouldn't) do anything to help us, even though they were the ones that sent the mobile tech to us, they still wouldn't accept any responsibility.

We were, we felt, understandably very unhappy with how the service manager had treated us, so Laura started firing off emails explaining the situation to the Camping World we'd bought from. We were met with a brick wall. The girl that answers their emails ignored our three requests to speak with someone in management. In addition, all my voicemails were ignored. Apparently, their managers never answer their phones or return calls/emails.

Since they chose to ignore us, we were forced to escalate the situation. Laura had a wonderful idea to write a long Google review for that Camping World explaining everything that had happened. About 30 minutes after posting it someone from their corporate rapid response team called us. It was great they reached out to us, but we had to wonder why a business would need a "team" like that anyway?

They couldn't believe what happened, they would help us any way possible, so on and so forth. On our behalf, they called the service manager, the store manager and Good Sam.

We received some calls back. We thought, "Good, we're finally getting somewhere." The service manager had dropped his accusatory tone and finally offered half off the labor to install a new inverter, but they still wanted $1000 for just the part.

Cue us panicking again. We'd just spent $1000 we didn't have on a generator, and we couldn't do it again.

Good Sam also called and said, again, there was nothing they could do to help. It was basically our word against the tech's. By that point, we were extremely frustrated and angry. No one would do the right thing. Everyone said they couldn't help, or it wasn't their fault. Finally, we decided to call the mobile tech to see if he'd take responsibility. Before we did however, Laura had an idea that changed everything.

I clearly remember it, we were sitting in bed, and I was in the middle of dialing the mobile tech when Laura stopped me. She said that we should record the conversation. That hadn't crossed my mind, but it seemed like a great idea.

First, we did a quick Google search and found that Kansas is a one-party consent state which means, legally, only one person needs to know a call is being recorded. She opened a voice recorder app on her phone, I finished dialing and put the call on speaker when it was answered.

We struck Hebard Luck pay dirt. The tech that worked on our trailer answered. I asked a few open-ended questions and he confirmed that he remembered us. I told him the solenoid had leaked some more and that I needed to add more fluid. I wasn't happy about lying, but it was a necessary evil. I then asked him what type of fluid he'd added, and how much. He clearly remembered and immediately answered my question. I thanked him and hung up.

We were overjoyed! I think we even high fived each other. We FINALLY had real evidence that it wasn't us, and that we weren't just crazy liars.

A short while later we called the tech back, recording the conversation again, and informed him about what happened with the inverter. I politely told him that because he'd clearly caused the damage that he would need to cover the repairs.

Well, I'm sure you can imagine how he took that. Oh man was he ANGRY! He instantly began yelled at me, saying that at the bottom of every invoice is a legal blurb about how he's not responsible for anything, ever, in any way.

To which I replied, "You didn't give us an invoice or a receipt."

To which he screamed back, "GOOD LUCK PROVING I WAS EVEN THERE!" right before he hung up.

We called Good Sam to inform them of the new evidence we'd acquired. We sent copies of the two voice recordings to them and they played them while still on the call. They laughed, a lot, when they played them. The customer service rep we were working with said he'd never had such an easy case. Apparently, no one had ever produced such strong evidence.

The recordings proved everything we'd been saying. Good Sam said they'd cover all the repairs. They also informed us that because the tech had lied to them, they would remove him from their network. Which meant no more calls from one of the largest roadside assistance companies in existence.

Maybe the tech should have just owned his mistake and fixed it? I still believe he knew exactly what he'd done. Why else would he have given me a pile of new rags and no receipt right before he sped off?

The people at Camping World never apologized for blaming us. They did, however, get it fixed and the repairs only took a few days, which I now know is basically a miracle when it comes to RV service time.

When we picked up the RV, the paperwork listed the problem as caused by the customer. We refused to sign it until they changed the wording. Surprise surprise, the same girl that had been answering our emails/calls and refusing to put us in contact with higher management, was the one handling our paperwork.

She was clearly angry about us not signing it. She was actually downright rude to us, huffing, puffing, sighing, and slamming papers down, etc. She was acting like a 14-year-old that can't go to a party with her friends. We just stood there and stared her down until the temper tantrum petered out. Eventually, she rewrote the paperwork, we signed it and happily left, hoping to never go back.

That time, when I pulled out of the parking lot, I swung a bit wider and easily cleared the ditch. I just needed a nearly disastrous situation to learn from. We drove back to the storage lot, which required another 20-point turn to park, and began the next leg of our epic adventure.

Why Did We Have Such A Difficult Time Hitching Up?

The directions I wrote out for hitching up and unhitching both state that using your parking brake is imperative. Well, when your parking brake doesn't work, that's a problem. Have you ever thought to test your parking brake when considering a used vehicle? I was even working in a shop and didn't think to test AHNJ's parking brake when we bought it. That lapse in judgement caused us no small amount of difficulty.

Shortly after we took the RV back from Camping World, I went to a friend's house with a steep driveway. Before shifting to park I set the parking brake for the first time. I thought it was odd how far the pedal pushed down, but then I took my foot off the brake and AHNJ rolled hard until the transmission caught it. Immediately I knew something was wrong.

On my next free day, I drove back to the dealer hoping to get it fixed. I spoke with the service manager first. He was very sorry but said he couldn't just cover the cost of fixing it. The pads were totally shot and had to be replaced. On a GM heavy duty axle, it's a $1,000 job and about 8 hours of labor to replace both sides, they have to tear apart the axle. He felt bad for me but said he could only cover half the bill. He then suggested that I go speak with the used department as they were a separate entity and could possibly help me more.

The used department Manager was also very sorry, but I was a week outside of their 30-day used vehicle warranty. I plead my case reminding him they sold it as having been inspected and in good working order. It seemed that we had all forgotten to check the parking brake. I guess that made sense to him because he agreed to cover $500 of the repair bill.

There's that Hebard Luck in action once again. After the service manager covered half of the remaining half, I only had to pay a $250 "remember to check the parking brake in the future" idiot tax. I won't make that mistake again.

Once I learned how important the parking brake is with our fifth wheel hitch our early struggles suddenly made sense. I had been setting the parking brake because our neighbor that helped us had told me to. But the truck was still rolling that inch until the transmission caught it so the hitch jaws wouldn't open. I would have been pulling my hair out, but it was already gone.

CHAPTER

Moving Out and Moving In

O nce we finally had the RV fixed and back, our lives were put into high gear. Laura was still working full-time, and I was still a full-time student with a part-time job. On top of all that, we had to start selling and packing all our belongings. Our landlord had given us until the end of June to move out so they could sell the house. That gave us only two months to sell, pack, and move. Our plan of attack was this:

1. Sort everything we owned into three categories.

    - Going to storage
    - Going to the RV
    - Selling

2. Move the storage pile into storage, obviously.

3. Move the RV pile onto the RV. MUCH easier said than done.

4. Once the house was clear of everything we wanted to keep, hold an estate sale for everything left.

5. Clean the house.

6. Move into the RV.

7. Drive off into the sunset.

Piece of cake. Right?

We had accomplished a small amount of sorting and some Craigslist selling in the previous months, but nothing more than your typical spring cleaning.

In case you're looking to downsize and start selling stuff online, I have to warn you about the scammers. If you haven't experienced them yet, they're very sophisticated. The common scam I ran into was the "person overseas" pitch.

The first time someone contacted me with this scam, it sounded way too good to be true, so I Googled the exact verbiage they wrote to me. I wasn't the only person searching for it. It seemed that many people had fallen for the scam. I found several articles describing step-by-step how the scam worked. I was already in the third of fourth step, it was right before agreeing to their outlandish deal.

Here's how it works, just in case you ever run into it.

1. They would usually claim to be a service member on deployment overseas. They would contact me saying that whatever I was selling was exactly what they wanted, they

didn't need to inspect it prior to purchase, they were fine with the price (who EVER says that!?) and to please take down the ad immediately as they would like to quickly buy it. The grammar and spelling in the email or text would be terrible, that was always an easy way to tell it was a scam.

2. If you respond to their initial message, they will offer to send you the money through PayPal, plus extra because they would have to hire a shipping company to pick it up since they're out of the country.

3. The extra would be for you to directly pay the shipping company when they picked up the item. I couldn't figure out why they couldn't just pay the shipping company themselves. Then I read about the scam and it all made sense.

4. The final step of the scam involved them claiming their PayPal account had been hacked, and PayPal would immediately withdraw the money from your account, and the scammer would get all their money back and whatever they bought, for free.

So, I decided to have some fun with them.

I was trying to sell Laura's elliptical machine and scammers were contacting me every few hours since the price was over $1,000. A $1,000 price tag is like bait, I learned. I wrote one of them back with a message that went something like this.

> *"Yes, it's still for sale. However, mice have eaten out all the wiring, the display no longer works, and it's so rusted it doesn't move anymore. Also, please send a second*

> *shipping company in case the first can't make it past the*
> *landmines, razor wire and snipers' nest."*

I still can't figure out why they stopped contacting me. Oh well, back to downsizing.

I want to give you an idea of just how much stuff we used to own. We had bought six sets of industrial shelving between Home Depot and Costco to organize all the totes and whatever else we had in the house. We set them up in the basement and garage. One brand was weaker, and the shelves actually bowed from all the weight we'd packed on them. There were also several stacks of stuff that didn't fit on the shelves scattered around the basement floor. But isn't that normal?

I also had an enormous 8' wide, 5' tall, and 3' deep workbench with four shelves packed full of reloading, hunting and shooting gear in the basement. Laura had bought me a 2X4 Basics kit to build it with two years before, and I built a massive reloading/shooting workstation. 2x4 Basics is a kit with plastic end pieces that have slots and screw holes designed for you to plug in a 2x4 and build something easily.

Sadly, I was always so busy that it was rarely used it for anything but storage.

In the dining room we had a kitchen cabinet designed for a sink. It was Laura's craft/sewing space (pre-built cabinetry is far cheaper than pre-built craft tables). It was also packed full of her supplies, and this was in addition to everything else we had in the bedroom, bathroom, kitchen, and closets. When we moved into that house, it was the first place we'd ever lived in together with a basement and garage, and somehow, we'd figured out how to fill every space.

One explanation for the large amount of stuff was that my dad had passed away several years before, and I was his sole beneficiary. Even after an estate sale and multiple garage sales, I still had a lot of his things. To summarize, we had way, WAY too much stuff (I still feel like we do).

We knew it wouldn't be easy to accomplish everything, but luckily, we had two months. In addition, I would have a break between spring and summer semesters to really knock out the to-do list. We were already quite used to sleepless nights from the research phase, so we figured why start sleeping now?

Once the RV problems were solved, we rolled right into sorting and packing. We poured all our free time into it. There were many nights spent in the basement and garage digging through black and yellow totes from Costco.

The house we were renting had an extra room, so we designated it the "keep" room. Everything that was going to the RV or being kept in storage was moved in there. Two separate piles, of course.

We were also buying many items online for our upcoming RV life. We had Amazon packages arriving almost daily. After a few weeks, the "going to the RV and storage" piles had grown very large. I was selling as much stuff online as possible prior to the estate sale. I knew it would bring in more money, but it was also to ensure everything would be gone by the time we had to move out.

Once the piles were too big to walk around, we rented a large storage shed at the same location the RV was being stored. We waited as long as possible on the shed to save money. It was much easier moving out with AHNJ vs moving in with my little Tacoma. I spent many nights moving stuff out alone because Laura couldn't get time off work to help. She felt bad, but there was nothing she could do about it.

Right about the time we were making enough progress to sleep more than five hours a night, my landlord called me with some horrible news.

Until that point, we had been on very good terms with our landlord. Laura had gone to vet tech school and had worked with his wife for several years. My second date with Laura was a double date with them. We'd been friends for years, that's why we were renting their house. He'd been offered a promotion they couldn't pass up, but it required them to move six hours away within two weeks. They didn't know what to do with their house, and we were sick of apartment living, so we worked out a deal.

We rented their house for the cost of the mortgage and insurance. It was several hundred dollars less per month for us, and it allowed them to move immediately to take the job. We were all quite happy with the arrangement. Also, our dogs finally got their own yard to play in.

So, you can imagine our surprise when he informed us that we had to be out of the house a month earlier than we'd previously agreed upon. We were already drowning in work trying to move, and when he called me it only left about three weeks to finish moving out. We lost half of the time we'd thought we had left.

If you've ever moved, you know there's always more stuff than you think there is, and it will always take longer to move than you planned on. I knew that from previous moves, and it made me panic a bit since I already felt short on time. Thank God we're not procrastinators.

The landlord also expected us to clean the carpets with the shampooer they'd left at the house, and his wife wanted us to repaint the interior walls. To be fair, I'd agreed to clean the carpets, but only when I thought we had the additional month.

Right about the time our landlord called, my spring semester ended. Sure, I was happy about finals ending, but I didn't have any more time to sleep since I was still working at the shop. I had one week to get everything left that we were keeping out of the house and prepare for the estate sale. That's when I had to kick it into high gear.

We were shorthanded at the shop and they couldn't give me any additional time off. However, they were nice enough to rearrange my schedule so I could have a few days off to run the sale. That helped, but it meant I was working every day leading up to and after the sale.

Unfortunately, Laura's boss wasn't as cooperative. She was given no shift changes or time off. Because of that, we had to have the RV set up to live in before the estate sale even began. Laura was still working nights and couldn't sleep until 2 p.m. with people showing up at 7 a.m. for the sale. We also needed someplace for the animals to stay during the sale. We were coming down to the wire a lot faster than we were ready for.

Laura was working around her crazy schedule to help any way she could. I was going to the storage lot every night that week and staying an hour after close every time. Laura had a few days off in the middle of the week and we killed it (or ourselves?) those days. Thankfully we finished moving the storage and RV piles to their respective locations.

It was a very surreal feeling once everything we were keeping was gone. Suddenly, the building we'd lived in for two years no longer felt like home. We were mentally ready to move into our new home and to move on with our lives.

A few days before the estate sale was set to begin, I moved the RV from storage back to the park we spent our first night in, except that time we had scheduled more than one night. Being new to RVing we didn't yet understand that most RV parks are usually near capacity. When I called them, a few weeks before we needed a site, and said I needed to reserve a monthly site they almost laughed at me.

All their monthly, or "long term," sites were full. The sites still open were for weekly or daily rates, where they can make more money, but there's less guarantee of money over a monthly site. Because I was still going to school, and we were both still working, we couldn't stay at a park on the other side of the city and commute an extra 30 minutes. We couldn't afford the fuel or time. And Laura had this thing about driving across the city at 3 a.m. with all the drunks on the road. Moving was already going to add more to her commute.

I pleaded to their humanity and explained our situation. They made an exception and gave us the monthly rate in a weekly site. The only stipulation was that we needed to move into a monthly site when one opened. That was more than fine with us.

I didn't get a pull through that time, I had to back it in. I don't remember how many attempts it took, but my nerves were fried when I finally got it in there. The next hour was spent attempting to figure out the auto level system. The auto level still wanted to raise the driver's side as far as possible. It didn't help that the site itself was quite unlevel, and I didn't understand the simplicity of leveling blocks yet. I spent the whole hour online trying to find answers. Finally, out of frustration, I called Lippert. I wish I'd started there.

My experience with them was great. After a short-automated menu, I was speaking with a person. Not just any person though, but a native English-speaking American who understood me, and quickly answered my questions. It's always refreshing when a company doesn't farm their customer service out to a foreign call center. I don't think the call lasted more than 10 minutes. Most of that was ensuring that I did in fact recalibrate the system correctly.

The calibration process was quite simple. First, I had to manually level the RV front to back and side to side. Once I confirmed it was level with a level (how ironic) I could reset it. With the pad turned off, I pressed the up arrow ten times and then the down arrow ten times. It displayed a message saying something about zero-point calibration being reset and I pressed enter to confirm it. I've had to reset that a few times since then, it's good to know your systems.

With the RV parked, and level, we finalized the move-in process. We had moved most of the items in already, but not the day-to-day things. We didn't have clothing, personal hygiene, bedding, dishes, food, etc. in there yet. That was another day of packing and moving. Because we were using it, or it was refrigerated, it hadn't been packed yet. I always underestimate how much is in the fridge.

As soon as the RV was set up for us to live in, I was back in the house working on final preparations for the sale. I took apart my reloading bench and got it ready to move for when it sold. I bought a pile of yard signs so we could advertise at street corners around the house and hopefully pull in people driving by. Laura helped me fill them in. She has much better handwriting than I do.

Two days before the estate sale we moved into the RV. It should have been a monumental occasion in our lives with a small party and celebration. However, we were so tired that I honestly don't remember a thing about it. I know it happened, because we weren't still at the house when the sale started. But we may as well have been teleported there by aliens for all I can remember.

With us and all the things we were keeping moved out of the house I was finally able to start making some headway preparing for the sale. Every night I after work I would let the dogs out and go back to the house to work a few hours until Laura got off work later.

It was a surreal experience working in there alone that night. I don't believe I'd ever spent a day in there alone before. Sure, I'd spent many many nights there without Laura, but I'd still had the dogs and cats with me. It had still felt like a home back then. There was such an empty and forlorn feeling walking through there knowing it was one of the last times I'd see it.

I think the strangest part was that most of our stuff was still there. Maybe it's because I'd already mentally separated myself from those belongings? Maybe it was because somewhere deep below my mental emotional dam lived tattered memories of cleaning out my dad's house after he passed? Who knows?

Those memories get frisky every now and then and try to screw with me until I beat them back down into my emotional basement. I need a good emotion's beating stick I can hang on a peg next to that door. Wow….just like the axe handle my dad hung on a peg outside the front door to knock the mud out of his boots before coming inside. It was also used for my spankings when I made bad decisions. They only happened a handful of times throughout my childhood though. I think I was a pretty good kid, or maybe I was just afraid of the axe handle hanging next to the door.

> *This is one reason I love writing. It brings things forward from the depths of my memories, emotions and imagination I don't even know are there. I didn't know what I was going to write in those last two paragraphs until my fingers flew over the keys and I saw them appear.*

I'd been to estate sales before and had an idea of how they were run. Typically, there's many folding tables around the house with a myriad of items on them. Usually there would be some sort of order to them, clothing in this room and electronics over there. I wanted to do the same thing.

I borrowed several folding tables from neighbors and began hauling totes out of the basement and tried to organize everything so people could easily see what we had to sell. No one wants to dig through boxes at a sale.

Unfortunately, since I'd been moving and working so much the few weeks prior, I was really getting worn down.

A year before then I'd hurt my back. It happened while working in a warehouse where I hand loaded pallets of groceries. Even though I'd been through physical therapy twice, it was never the same. It still really bothers me. The day before the estate sale was set to kick off, my back finally gave out on me.

10

The Estate Sale
and Final Move Out

The morning of the sale, I went by Quick Trip for their largest coffee, a bunch of ready to eat food since I wouldn't be able to leave all day, and a bunch of change. I wanted to start the sale with a stack of small bills to make change with. I didn't want to turn away a sale because I couldn't break a large bill.

I was at the house by 5 am to work on final preparations. I ate a handful of Aleve and got to work. I was able to haul a few lightweight things out of the basement, but the Aleve just wasn't enough. Instead, I concentrated on unloading and organizing what I'd already brought up. I did what I could until 8:00 am, then I threw the signs in the truck and drove around the block putting them up at all the nearby intersections.

A few days before, I'd posted the sale on every online forum I could find and listed an early morning start time since we didn't have time to run it a second weekend. Before I could even put up the last signs nearest the house, I had people showing up. I literally ran back alongside people driving to the house, and the sale kicked off. I didn't even have half the stuff laid out, and nothing was priced, but I was out of time.

Between engaging potential customers, I was still trying to bring items up from the basement. I didn't have a choice since the vast majority of our things that had been down there, were still down there. To make matters worse, there wasn't nearly enough room to empty the totes and display it all in the basement.

I was in serious trouble. It was the only weekend I could have the estate sale, and I didn't have anyone that could help me. Around 10:00 am, a 30ish year old man wearing a suit walked in and started browsing. I don't remember his name, so I'll call him Gabriel. I was trying to haul a large tote up the basement stairs and was clearly struggling while the two of us talked.

I didn't have time left to worry about my back. I learned a little something about doing what it takes to get the job done in the infantry. Pain is temporary, failure is forever.

Out of the blue, Gabriel asked about my back injury. To be clear, he didn't ask if something was wrong, or if my back hurt. He asked how long it had been hurt, how I'd hurt it and what kind of physical therapy I'd been through.

We spoke about it for a few minutes and I told him what had happened. Gabriel then said he was in school to become a chiropractor, and that he wanted to help me. No, he didn't offer to adjust my back. He wanted to move our stuff for me.

I was floored. I couldn't believe a total stranger would just volunteer to help me like that. I asked him what he wanted for payment, since I really did need his help. He didn't want anything, and even refused to allow me to repay him. Then Gabriel took his suit coat off, laid it over the stair banister, rolled up his sleeves, and dove right in.

People were starting to pour into the house by that time and Gabriel was killing it. In just a few hours he'd brought most of the items from the basement up to the first and second floor without one word of complaint. There was a fair amount of sweat though, and he accepted my offering of water.

Not only was he lugging things upstairs, but he was unpacking and arranging it all as well. I tried to stop him, but Gabriel never missed a beat saying I needed the help. He told me I didn't have time to deal with unpacking/arranging everything while still talking to potential customers. I felt bad, but he was right of course. So, I let him keep working.

Eventually I told him if he saw something he wanted to just let me know, and he actually agreed! I'd finally found a way to repay him. He picked out my best pair of cold weather camo gloves, worth about $50, which I'd bought for goose hunting. He was also interested in my compound bow but refused to just take it. However, he did agree on a $100 discount from what I was asking.

After several hours of work, and totally saving my butt, Gabriel was ready to leave. But not before I thanked him profusely. He came back the second day to pick up the bow and pay me. He even offered to help again if I needed it, which I didn't.

I named the mystery man Gabriel because I needed a guardian angel that day, and then he walked through the door. For all I know he may have actually been an angel. "Gabriel," if you ever read this, I can never thank you enough. You know who you are.

With Gabriel's help, the estate sale was going well, items were moving very quickly. Since I didn't have time to price anything, it was a straight barter system. I told everyone as they walked in that nothing was priced, to just grab what they were interested in, put it in a corner or carry it around, and come get me when they were done.

Whenever someone was ready to check out, as it were, I'd offer a very reasonable price, and hardly anyone haggled with me. I needed everything gone, and a few bucks was better than nothing from giving or throwing it away. I did have a few predatory people show up and basically try to rob me. I was already asking .10-.15 on the dollar, but that wasn't good enough for them.

I had to chase one man off several times. He did everything to rob me but pull a gun. I'd be in mid conversation with someone who wanted to buy something, and he'd try to interrupt us with a super low-ball offer on some other item.

I got lucky during the second day when a family that had just immigrated from South America walked in. They had come with nothing and needed to fully furnish their apartment. They bought the couch, table and chairs, the mattress, and multiple other smaller items.

I didn't have any luck selling my hunting gear though. It was May, and no one was interested in duck and goose decoys six months before the season opened. After years of piecing items together and finding sales, I had finally collected the essentials for duck and goose hunting. I'd invested so much time and money that it hurt the worst letting it all go for almost nothing.

On Sunday, the last day of the sale, I ran into some problems. The neighbor across the cul-de-sac came over to complain about all the people and traffic. To be fair, I'd warned all my neighbors' months in advance that this was going to happen, and the moment I knew the exact dates of the sale, I told them. It wasn't even noon and she came over to demand I take down the signs and end the sale, like she was in charge or something.

Somehow, I stifled the explosive laughter that would have probably given her hearing damage. I told her that all the online ads had it running through 5 pm that day. Taking down the signs wouldn't matter, and I sure wasn't going to turn away anyone that showed up, just because she didn't like it. I had no intention of stopping while people were still coming in. I still had so much left to sell I was getting worried. I actually wanted to keep the sale going for another day, but I knew I couldn't.

Over the weekend I'd collected phone numbers from people that were interested in the more expensive items, but couldn't buy them that day, for whatever reason. That afternoon I went down the list and called each one. Even if they couldn't afford a decent price, something was better than nothing. I made it very clear that I was willing to negotiate. A few did come back, and I helped them load the larger items.

When I finally closed down the sale, we still a lot of stuff left.

I hadn't sold our TV or washer/dryer set. We'd bought them new on credit a few months before we got the idea to go full-time. No one wanted them. Well, no wanted to pay a fair price for them. I started off just trying to get what we owed. I thought 30% off was a fantastic deal, until I couldn't find a buyer.

When I realized I couldn't even get what we owed I kept dropping the price. When the estate sale ended, they were all still in the house. Since we only had a week left to get rid of them, I started to worry. I reposted them online and called everyone I knew in the surrounding 100 miles to see if they were interested.

Thankfully, Laura found buyers for all of them. Her dad bought the TV, and absolutely loves it. Then, one of Laura's coworkers bought the washer and dryer set. We didn't get what we needed for the loan amount, but thankfully we didn't give them away either.

One of my friends that lived two hours south of us, drove up the day after the sale and loaded up his truck with leftover items. I was thrilled to give it to someone I knew could use it all After he took what he wanted there wasn't a lot left over, but anything was still too much. The RV was at capacity, and we didn't want to store things that we didn't want to keep. With my final days off work, I cleaned the house and listed everything we still had left online, in the slim hope that someone might take it off our hands.

As the weekend approached, I realized we weren't going to make it. My back was still extremely painful, and I was having difficulty accomplishing simple tasks like walking and showering. We were running out of time and there was nothing we could do about it. I'd already pushed myself far past my limit, but it just wasn't enough.

There was still a pile of things left in the garage and living room, and there were several large items that I couldn't bring myself to give or throw away. However, most of it was leftover junk, so some went to storage and I was able to sell it online during the following weeks.

The final Friday came, and the landlord arrived. We still weren't done, of course, because the revised agreement had given us until Sunday. The landlord and his wife were visibly upset about the house not being spotless when they arrived. I was barely able to walk but they couldn't have cared less. Oh, I forgot one thing, they had planned to take all the pictures to list the house during that weekend. I still have no idea what their rush was.

They weren't happy that the carpets were still dirty. They weren't cleaned because at the last minute, they changed their minds and said to have them professionally cleaned. I didn't have everything out of the house, so I had been unable to schedule the cleaning. I was hoping to squeeze that in on Sunday.

They wanted everything gone, cleaned and done immediately. It wasn't enough for them to cut a month off our agreement, they had to take my last two days away as well. The next morning, I went back to the house very early on my way to work and hauled everything left out to the curb. I posted a free ad on Craigslist and continued on to work. Shortly after I left the house, my phone started ringing off the hook with people wanting to take it all. I told them if it's not there, someone else already took it.

A little later my landlord called me to say he'd hauled everything back inside the garage. The same neighbor that had complained about the estate sale called him whining about the free stuff pile. I was then told that I wasn't allowed to have anyone else come to the house, and that I still had to get rid of it all. Great, I love having my hands tied. That just reinforced why we wanted to RV full-time. Now we can leave if we have bad neighbors.

After I got off work, I went back over and started loading my truck. I took what I could to Goodwill and what they didn't accept went in the trash. With the house finally empty, my landlord said they would deal with the rest of the cleaning. That was fine with us since they didn't clean the house before we moved in. They could finally do something to help. I was done.

Until then, we had been good friends with the landlord and his wife. We were always on good terms, but their actions irreparably damaged the friendship. We were both sad to lose the friendship, but it hurt Laura much worse. She really tried hard to salvage it, but we haven't really spoken with them since.

We weren't even mad about the whole moving out mess, because we were finally moving into the RV. It was the beginning of June and my summer classes were starting. We were both still working, but we tried to relax as much as we could after the previous crazy months.

11

Final Preparations
to Hit the Road

O ver the summer months we bought books about RVing, continued watching YouTube, and kept reading RVing blogs trying to learn as much as possible before we hit the road. Since Laura spent most of her time at home alone, or with me unconscious, she used it watching YouTube. Her time was almost evenly split between videos about RVing and videos of Florida, since that's where we were going first.

Those were a rough few months. It was a brutal Kansas summer and we regularly say days over 100 degrees, a few even went over

110. We were very worried about the dogs while we were gone. Even with both air conditioners running 24/7 inside temperatures were regularly reaching mid 80's during the afternoon. Many people don't realize this, but an RV will heat up like a car left in the sun if the air conditioning turns off. If the park lost power, temperatures inside the RV could reach lethal levels for our pets within an hour.

Our answer was a device called Piper. Laura found it and it worked great. Piper is a home monitor that worked with an app on our phones. We couldn't just see the dogs, we could talk to them, and it also showed us the temperature. If it lost connection, there was a sudden loud noise, rapid temperature change, etc. it would send us a warning on our phones. Then we could call the park to see if they had lost power.

It wasn't a perfect plan, but Laura could be home in about 15 minutes, plenty of time to get the pets out if we lost power. Luckily, we never had to race back home, and we eventually stopped using it. But the peace of mind was well worth it. Otherwise we didn't want to leave the RV and risk losing our four-legged kids.

We began the summer with a hard goal in mind, I would finish school in mid-October, we wanted to leave within a week of my classes ending. We just couldn't escape the ticking clock.

Laura, being the research goddess she is, found an RV park with availability in paradise. Technically it was on Pensacola Beach, but that was close enough to paradise for us. Pensacola Beach is a barrier island about ¼ mile wide off the coast of Pensacola, Florida. The RV park even has its own chunk of waterfront. We made a four-month reservation, set to begin before the end of October.

Laura's birthday is October 30th, and she was turning 30. It was her golden birthday which was a big deal to her. She really wanted to spend it on the beach. It was a race against time to finish school, get on the road, and make it to Pensacola by the 30th. I was dedicated to making it happen though.

As summer was winding down my last semester began. It was grueling.

I had to take the most difficult class of my degree, complete a 16-week internship's worth of hours in 8 weeks, keep working part-time, find time to spend with Laura, continue to plan and prep for leaving and somehow sleep more than an hour a day. I don't think I made the sleep goal. I was a walking zombie for two months. On the first day of class, I went to Costco and bought a case of energy drinks. I should have bought three, or five.

My internship was with a private security company. They gave me two midnight to 8 am shifts, and one 10 pm to 2 am shift per week. I thought my sleep schedule was bad before. Unfortunately, the internship was downright boring. Due to my history in the army, and since I was finishing a criminal justice degree, the security company just put me on the schedule with my own shifts and posts. Afterwards I realized how big of a mistake that was.

I didn't learn anything during those two months. I rarely saw another security guard. Other than two days of shadowing a senior officer to learn the duties of his post, there was virtually no training. I couldn't have been happier when it was over.

During those two months, Laura was still working the graveyard shift, averaging about 60 hours a week. Even though she'd given her boss eight months of warning that she'd be leaving, they still weren't trying to hire her replacement. Shortly before we'd planned to leave, Laura realized they hadn't interviewed anyone to replace her. It became clear her employer didn't believe she would actually go through with it.

As it turned out, Laura was telling the truth. Six weeks before we were set to leave, she turned in her two-week notice, and they panicked. Not only were they already shorthanded, but they didn't even have another vet tech that could fill her shoes.

Of course, there were a few other techs who were about as knowledgeable as Laura, but the hospital needed more than two good techs on staff. Laura leaving left them in a severe experience deficit. She felt bad, but she had warned them over and over for almost a year. We felt sorry for her coworkers.

After Laura quit, she had more time to finish final preparations. We took the opportunity to finish cleaning out the storage shed. When we first reserved it, we rented a size that was far larger than we needed, on purpose. We knew we'd be moving things in and out often and it gave us space to work without having to sling everything out in the hallway every time we opened it. But we didn't need or want all that extra space while on the road, since it's quite expensive.

We moved from a 10x12' to a 5x7' shed. It took several days to accomplish this swap. First, we went through everything in the RV to see if we really wanted to take it with us. We'd been living in it for a few months and anything we hadn't used in that time was on the chopping block. We took a lot to storage.

Next, we went through everything in storage to see if we wanted to take any of it back to the RV. After we moved everything we wanted to the RV, we consolidated everything still in storage into containers that would stack easily as the smaller shed would be packed to the ceiling. When that was finished, we got to play life-sized Tetris, fitting everything into the smaller shed. After half a day we were finally able to close the door. Our success meant we were another step closer to leaving.

I also had to get the truck set up before we could leave. Not only would it be an extension of our living space, but storage as well.

Before we could leave, I needed to deal with our bikes. We knew we wanted to take them with us, we just didn't know how or where we'd put them. Our fifth wheel doesn't have a hitch receiver on the back, so a bumper mount bike rack wouldn't work. The only other viable option I could see was mounting them on the roof of the truck. After a lot of research, I found that Thule makes no-drill roof racks. Unfortunately, they're very expensive.

I spent several days online attempting to find all the parts used and was able to save us a few hundred dollars between eBay and Craigslist. I only had to pay full price for one piece. Putting the roof mounted bike rack system together came right down to the line.

I also decided that I wanted to take all my tools with us, which was no small feat. I had an enormous two-level toolbox packed full of stuff at the shop. To take it all meant I needed a very large truck toolbox, but not a tall one that could damage the front cap during tight turns.

One morning, after an all-night guard shift, I stopped by a place named Chux Trux. I told the guys there what I wanted and why, they measured the truck, and dug through catalogs in search of a box that would work. They found a 15 cubic foot box from DeeZee that fit my requirements. I figured it would hold all my tools, luckily it did. At the last minute I asked them if I could also fit an auxiliary fuel tank in the bed. After some more measurements they determined DeeZee's 40-gallon tank would fit as well. I would even have half a foot between the tool box and hitch left.

They offered a very nice veterans discount, which was good, because I hadn't really planned on the fuel tank. Sure, I'd brought it up with Laura a few times, but she kept saying no. From my truck research a few months earlier I'd seen many RVers rave about how much they loved having an extra tank and how much time and money it saved them. I made a unilateral decision and ordered it without telling her. Of course, she found the receipt later and I had to explain that. She was justifiably angry.

The day I took the truck in to get the tank and box installed I had a conversation with a salesman about tuners. Everything I'd read said they would void manufacturer warranties, so I wasn't considering one. He told me (incorrectly) that one model he carried couldn't be traced. He gave me the veteran discount on it as well, so I also installed an Edge CS2 diesel tuner. It really did help the truck run better while towing, there was a noticeable difference.

I wish I'd known about the Stealth modules back then because they actually can't be traced. Well, as long as you unplug it before you take your truck in for service.

Laura wasn't happy about the tuner either. Although, I think it had more to do with me spending large amounts of money without telling her. I can't imagine why that would be a problem.

While I was working on the truck Laura was figuring out how to make everything fit into the RV. The cabinet dimensions in RVs really don't make sense. Our pantry cabinet has spaces tall enough for one or two more shelves. Laura measured every single inside storage space, then she went online and found containers that would fit them. I couldn't believe how difficult something that should be simple turned out.

Figuring out complex problems is something she excels at and that task was no different. She did such a fantastic job that we hardly waste an inch now. The downside is we're able to store so much that the rig is always near its maximum weight. Oh well, nothing is falling out of cabinets after travel days.

Right as we were planning to hit the road, we encountered our first problem with the RV since the power inverter. The entry-side pass-through storage slam latch door wasn't latching. There was a large gap at the bottom and the latch wouldn't catch. Even if the handle was locked, we could open it. We didn't have time to take it to a shop, so we came up with a temporary solution. Two small sheets of plywood, two sets of lock hasps and two padlocks secured it quite nicely.

The plywood kept items from shifting, opening the door and falling out on the highway. The locks would keep people out if they realized we couldn't lock it. It worked well enough that we were confident to travel with it.

After all of Laura's RV research she knew we needed an RV GPS, Google doesn't care about low bridges. We decided on the Rand McNally tablet RV GPS. It helped that it included lifetime map updates, and Laura found it for a great deal. She's really good at that stuff too.

I finished my course work and internship, quit my job, packed my tools into my new tool box, sold my old tool box and joined Laura ready to leave. With the RV packed and organized, storage consolidated, the truck set up, and my degree finished, we were finally ready to hit the road.

There was one last hurdle that we hadn't overcome though, making money on the road. We had a loose idea of starting a blog and YouTube channel, but not much past that. We had a decent windfall saved up with our 401k's and ROTH IRA's though. So, we weren't too worried about money. Also, we hadn't been able to sell Laura's little SUV before leaving, so we planned on her driving behind me until we could sell it.

Happy Birthday and Goodbye

We were planning on leaving right before Laura's birthday, and she was adamant that she wanted to spend it on the beach. I was worried because I didn't know if I could pull it off. We'd never traveled with the RV before and getting it to Florida seemed like a fairly impossible task with my entire two hours of towing experience.

So, I devised a backup plan, a surprise birthday party. A month or so before her birthday, I began to contact everyone she knew that lived near us. I told them I was planning a surprise party for Laura and got a list of people who thought they could come. The whole surprise day was planned around a concert that would be in town right before we left.

I planned the special day to begin with time at a spa to get her hair, makeup and nails done. From there I would take her to an early dinner at her favorite restaurant, where her friends and family would be waiting to surprise her. After dinner we'd drive downtown to see Lindsey Stirling in concert. It would be our first concert together, so I knew she'd never see it coming.

The day of the party, everything went off without a hitch. I surprised her over and over. But the main act was yet to come. Even while standing in line for the concert, she had no idea what was happening. Luckily, there weren't any signs outside giving it away. Even when we took our seats, Laura still didn't know what was going to happen. I think I may have been having more fun than she was with all my plans working out.

After the opening act the crowd was really getting fired up, I could feel the anticipation in the air. Of course, Laura sitting next to me couldn't have been more confused. Suddenly, an electric violin fired up and a silhouette of someone playing it appeared behind a screen on stage. Then it switched to another screen, then another, over and over, for a few minutes until a small break in the song. Then the lights lit up the aisle to our left, and Lindsey came RUNNING down the aisle and jumped up onto the stage, all while playing her violin. And without missing a single note.

I picked Lindsey Stirling because Laura played the violin for over 10 years. If you haven't heard Lindsey's music, go look it up.

Aside from the incredible music (which she writes), there's another element to her performance. She dances while playing the violin. I knew Laura hadn't heard of her, and I was really looking forward to the opening song. Lindsey didn't disappoint.

The look of shock on Laura's face was priceless. After a two-hour concert her surprise party came to an end. She'd had a chance to say goodbye to some friends and to see Kansas City again before we left. I hope I can top it someday, but that will take some serious work.

12

Why Don't We
Just Leave Tomorrow?

W̲e planned our departure day to be one week after my semester ended. There was no real significance to the day we chose, other than that's when our monthly rent at the RV park was up. Two days before we had planned to leave Laura looked at me and said:

"Why are we still here? Why don't we just leave tomorrow?"

That simple, yet profound statement, shattered my reality. It was one of our first baby steps in a very long journey of nomadism and freedom. A journey where we can go wherever we want, whenever we want, and whyever we want. (I know it's not a real word and I don't care.)

I sat there stunned for a few minutes, trying to process that we could leave simply because we wanted to. We didn't have to tell or ask anyone. Laura had already planned our route to the Pensacola Beach RV Resort. All we had to do was fuel up, pack up a few things outside, hook up and leave.

My response, after a few minutes, was, "Why not?"

Even now, after two years of being on the road full-time, we still love the ability to change plans at a moment's notice when we want to. We can leave early, stay late, or decide to go somewhere completely different than we had planned. It's a fantastic freedom that "normal" life doesn't afford.

Laura immediately called her parents so they could come over and say goodbye. They weren't free that night but could be there in the morning before we left. After she hung up, we moved things around inside so the slides could come in, told the RV park we were leaving early so they could book our spot, fueled up the truck, and finally put the bikes on the new roof racks before we went to bed.

I won't lie. I don't think either of us got much sleep that night. It had been nine months since we were first introduced to the idea of full-time RVing and we were FINALLY LEAVING!!!!!

The next morning, we woke up early. Well, early for us. Anything before 10am felt like the crack of midnight after working nights for so long. We got right to work. Laura finished up a few things inside while I dumped the tanks and put the hoses away.

Laura's dad arrived as we were finishing up. Unfortunately, he came alone and told us her mom couldn't make it due to work. Laura talked to him for a bit while I tried to get the truck hooked up.

Two hours after checkout time, we were finally ready to leave. Laura said a tearful goodbye to her dad, we loaded the dogs into her backseat, and we hit the road. The first leg of our trip had us driving from Mission, Kansas to a rest stop just before St. Louis, Missouri, about a four-hour travel day.

With Laura driving behind me, we used a pair of two-way radios to communicate. We were so excited to leave that we talked all day about anything and everything and killed the batteries before we even reached St. Louis.

I hate to admit it, but I had no idea what I was doing. Sure, I'd been driving the dually for several months, so I was getting used to a wide profile, but towing 40 feet behind me was a little scary. It didn't help that I couldn't go the speed limit. The Westlake trailer tires were only rated for 60 mph so that's how fast I drove.

That was my first experience on the highway longer than an hour with everyone else flying past 20-30 mph faster than me. A lot of them merged in front of me much earlier than they should have. Laura kept thinking they were going to hit me as they were merging. She would call me on the radio to warn me every few minutes. Eventually I had to tell her to stop warning me about things as the warnings were distracting me from watching traffic.

I soon learned that any quick movement resulted in the trailer swinging out of the lane. And by "any," I mean a ½" movement of the wheel translated into the back of the trailer moving a foot. So, every time I took a drink of water, reached for anything, or changed the music, Laura would tell me I was swerving. As frustrating as that was, it was something I had to learn.

I was so happy to finally pull into the rest stop that evening. Learning how to tow on the fly was a bit nerve wracking. Laura had her own problems that first day. Bullet, our yellow lab, wasn't used to being in a vehicle. He would get so excited that he would cry and whine the ENTIRE TRIP!

I think he get so crazy and excited because when he was a puppy, he only got in the truck to go swimming. I'd drive him to a lake and off leash dog park, he loved it more than anything. A LOT of people have commented on our videos when he's crying telling us he needs to be drugged, walked, muzzled, fed, etc. Thankfully, after two years of traveling, he's much calmer now while driving.

Four hours of his glass shattering whining can grate the nerves a bit. On the other hand, Kimber, our fluffy mutt, will sit in the front seat watching everything and not make a peep the entire day. Unless she sees a squirrel or some other small fluffy thing that she thinks she could chase. Then she'll let rip a blood curdling ahhhwoowoo with all the fluffy cuteness she can muster. Trust me, she can muster a lot of fluffy cuteness. She rarely barks like a normal dog, instead she squeaks or ahhhwoowoo's.

Our first night on the road was spent on the phone with Laura's mom. Already, we were changing plans to detour south to Houston. Laura's grandpa was very sick, and her mom was headed down to help take care of him. Laura hadn't seen him in almost 20 years. We planned the entire route there and went to bed excited.

Being that we planned our first stop outside of St. Louis, I had called a friend I deployed to Iraq with, who lived near there. I was happy that we could finally see each other after so many years. Unfortunately, all our plans were violently changed against our will the next morning.

13

The RV Honeymoon Is Over

———— ∿∿ ————

Our first time overnighting went fine. It wasn't our first night with the slides in, so we already had an idea of what to expect. The most difficult thing about boondocking, lotdocking or overnighting with our trailer, was the lack of power.

I understand I just used a lot of words many people won't understand. So, here's how we define them. Definitions will vary between people.

Overnighting: Parking your RV somewhere and sleeping there for a night before moving on. Typically, we won't detach the truck, put the jacks down or slides out, and won't set up any of our outdoor items. This is usually done in rest areas, truck stops, or pull offs.

Lotdocking: This is essentially the same as overnighting, except that it's only done in parking lots. You'll often hear people say they Waldocked, meaning they spent the night in a Walmart parking lot.

Moochdocking: Parking in someone's driveway and usually using a 15-amp connection and water. This is usually done with friends or family.

Boondocking: Staying somewhere with no hookups that's not an RV park, parking lot, rest stop, or driveway. This will usually be Bureau of Land Management land (BLM), U.S. Forest Service land, State/County/City parks. Length of stay will vary depending on their rules, but you can often stay up to 14 days.

Back to our first overnight.

Yes, the lights, water pump, and all other 12v systems were powered from the batteries. However, none of the household 120v outlets were powered. The RV came with a 1,000-watt inverter, and it only powered the outlet behind the fridge. During those early days, before we installed solar, we had to charge everything in the vehicles while driving. Otherwise, I'd have to leave things in the truck to charge. I used the truck instead of the SUV because it has two batteries.

Although we rarely use rest stops anymore, we chose to stay at one our first night. The whole night we had truckers pulling in and out, leaving their engines idling the whole time. After a restless night, I got up the next morning ready to eat and hit the road for Houston.

Everything changed when I opened the fridge, and the light didn't come on.

I didn't panic immediately, somehow. The first thing I did was check breakers and fuses. No breakers were tripped, but....all our 12v fuses were burned out. Naturally, I grabbed the pack of extra fuses I'd bought for the trip and went to replace them. I was patting myself on the back for planning ahead right up until the time I tried to put the new fuses in. I'd bought small automotive fuses and they didn't fit. Crap.

We weren't near a town, so I looked up the nearest gas station, jumped in Laura's SUV, and sped off to find the right fuses. The third station I went to had the correct large size. I grabbed two packs and raced back. After replacing all the burned-out fuses, I was confident that when I opened the fridge door, it would be working. That was, until the light didn't turn on again.

Double crap.

I went back to the drawing board and thought maybe it was a power issue. I pulled out our Yamaha 2k generator, fired it up, plugged it into the shore power line, and opened the fridge again. To my extreme disappointment the light didn't turn on again.

Triple crap, if that's a thing.

We didn't learn until almost a year later that Cedar Creek used a 30-amp transfer switch for our fridge, but not the rest of the RV. What does that mean? Well, without at least a 3k external power connection our fridge wouldn't turn on if the inverter and batteries couldn't run it. BUT, the lights, slides, outlets, etc. would work just fine. So naturally we thought the fridge was broken.

By that time, I was finally starting to panic a bit. We had over $500 of food in the fridge. We'd loaded up on our favorite Kansas City barbeque, vacuum sealed and frozen it before we'd left.

Unable to get the fridge running, my last option was to buy a lot of dry ice and hope for the best. While I ran back to town, again, Laura started looking for RV parks with availability that day since we needed to plug in. The third store I went to had dry ice and I bought 15lbs of it.

By the time I returned Laura had already lined up a park a few hours away that had an RV repair facility next door, which was perfect. What wasn't perfect though, was that we had to scrap our new plans and cancel on our friends and family.

With the dry ice in the fridge and freezer, we plugged the new address into the RV GPS and took off for our new destination. I set the GPS for fastest route since time was a factor. I learned another hard lesson that day. Shortly after we left, the GPS told me to exit the highway.

Here's a little tip. If it's your second day towing, you may want to set your GPS to the "prefer highways" setting. That may add some miles and hours to your trip, but hopefully it won't take you on a roller coaster road. Ours took me down a twisty bumpy farming road so narrow that I was riding the lines on both sides of the lane. Laura was fairing slightly better since she was in a smaller vehicle. Although, Bullet didn't appreciate the road. The roller coaster feeling was making him nauseous. To make matters worse, the road was very busy with constant oncoming traffic, and nowhere to turn around. I had zero margin of error.

BUT WAIT, THERE'S MORE! Bad luck seems to usually come in threes. And it was time for the third act of the day.

Right as I was coming to terms with my second day of towing school, I turned a corner and found a random hill tall enough to have multiple switchbacks, right in the middle of Missouri farm country. The road was just as narrow going up the hill and there were still no shoulders. Just to spice things up, I'm guessing, there was an extremely steep drop off on our passenger side with no guardrails.

I wish I was making this up.

I don't know if I asked out loud how our day could have been any worse, although, if I had, it may have explained what was happening. I quickly reminded myself that I'd survived invading two countries, IEDs, snipers, mortars, RPG's, being run over by a semi, and lastly, surgery by the VA, clearly the most dangerous on the list.

I followed up my little mental pep talk by audibly saying something along the lines of, "I can do this." Was I lying to myself? To this day I still don't know, but I'm here writing about it, so it could have gone much worse.

I grabbed the radio and told Laura what was in front of me, and that I wouldn't be on the radio until I was up the hill. My only thought the entire way up was to keep the driver's side trailer tires on the centerline. Just like you don't look down from a high place, I didn't look in the passenger side mirror. I knew I was in the other lane a little too much, but at least I didn't roll our house off a cliff on our second day.

A few hours later, we reached the RV park. To our extreme surprise, the fridge fired right up when we plugged into shore power. Luckily the dry ice had done the trick, and we didn't lose our food.

The whole fridge experience was odd enough that we decided we still wanted someone to look at it. The service center next to the RV park was closed that day, so I set my morning alarm for 15 minutes before they opened.

We spent the night online, attempting to figure out what was wrong with our house. We couldn't find anything that explained what was happening. The fridge unexplainably turning back on was really confusing. Before we went to bed, I pulled the fridge out of its cubby to save the tech time the next day.

The next morning, I called the service center when they opened and requested a mobile tech before he could get tied up with another job. He arrived shortly after I hung up. We told him what had happened, and he went to work testing the outlet behind the fridge, checking fuses and the batteries. We got some bad news when he tested the batteries though. They were all dead and swollen. At that time, we didn't ask how or why that happened, although we really should have.

Our camper came with four 6v lead-acid deep-cycle batteries. The shop didn't have any of those in stock, but they did have a few 12v RV/Marine deep cycle batteries. We wanted to get back on the road, so we bought two of them at the "emergency" markup. The tech installed them and took our four dead batteries.

We stayed at the park an extra day, just to watch the fridge in case it decided to stop working again. With the problem fixed, or so we thought, we got back on the road the next day headed to Florida. Our breakdown had eaten the extra days we were going to use to see Laura's grandpa. We couldn't delay any longer, because if we were late for our reservation in Florida, they could cancel it and give our spot to someone else. They were very clear about that.

We spent the next three days traveling and ran into a few more problems.

1. The third RV park we'd ever stayed at had serious power issues. I spent an hour trying to figure out what an E7 error is on a Dometic thermostat, and why only one AC would turn on. I learned that it was a low power error. That made me think to check the display on our surge protector since it could analyze the power source. The display showed that only one line was powered.

The spot they put us in only had one of the two 50-amp legs working. With only one working, only half of our breaker panel was receiving power. Our site was in full sun, and it was hot enough that day that we needed both ACs running. I'm sure if we'd stayed longer, we would have noticed the other systems didn't have power either.

We should have listened to the reviews online. Several people said they had similar power problems. Luckily, I was able to get us a refund, but they only agreed after I threatened to leave a negative review online. We left and found a shady spot to park in and ran the fantastic fan all night.

That was our first experience with an RV park that refuses to upgrade or fix obvious problems. Luckily, we rarely run into parks like that.

2. We learned to never drive in the right lane though cities. In Birmingham, Alabama, I was almost forced to exit into downtown with no warning due to a blind corner and no signs warning of the exit. Thankfully, I was able to stop in the space between the highway and exit lane, without Laura rear ending me, and no one rear ending her (small miracles). She was able to pull out and block traffic for me while I got back on the highway and up to speed. Now I stay out of the right lane if there's three or more to choose from.

3. The inverter randomly shut off several times. I learned how to reset it, but it kept turning the fridge off. This issue bothered us very much. Clearly the new batteries hadn't fixed the problem.

4. Be sure to research toll roads ahead of time. We had two bridges to choose from that crossed over to Pensacola Beach. Had we known, we would have picked the other bridge. There was a $50 difference between the two tolls. That was an expensive lesson

14

Life Finally Gets Better, Kind of

W e pulled into Pensacola a day early just as we'd planned. By then I was finally beginning to feel comfortable towing our new home. Of course, looking back now that seems laughable.

We Waldocked that night, as checking in a day early would have been an extra $50. I was really trying to control unnecessary spending because I was extremely nervous about money. Sure, we had savings, but no source of income yet.

We were thrilled to have made it to the RV park in time so that we didn't lose our reservation. That was a big deal for me. We made it in time for Laura to have her beach birthday.

If you've never been to Pensacola Beach, put the book down and go put it on your bucket list right now. It's part of the Gulf Islands National Seashore and has miles and miles of white sand beach all open to the public, it's even open in front of the hotels. If one spot is too crowded, you can simply walk, or drive a bit, and find a different area. It was a perfect location to start our new lives.

We arrived at the RV park right when their off-season was beginning. That meant monthly rent was less than $700, almost half the summer rate. We thought $700 a month was a steal, especially considering the perks. The RV park had its own section of waterfront that faced mainland. And if we got tired of that water we could simply turn around and walk a ¼ mile to the other side of the island to enjoy its white sand and mild surf. We've never stayed in another park that offered such direct access to the water, Laura was in heaven. We'd roll a cooler over, carry our chairs, and sit watching the surf for hours.

Our anniversary was about a week after we arrived. Laura wanted chicken wings and fried pickles on the beach, so I went to the only restaurant on the island that was open on a Sunday, and serving that kind of food, Hooters. We packed up our beach stuff and anniversary dinner then drove a few miles down the island until we found a deserted beach. We took our super extra fancy anniversary meal and beach chairs to the edge of the surf and sat out there for hours until dark.

After we'd been out there for a bit, watching the surf, when we suddenly had a mutual epiphany (it's a real thing, I was there when it happened). I distinctly remember this, we looked to each other at the same time because we both had the same realization at the same time.

We….were….finally….FREE!!!! We actually both said something to that effect at the same time. I wouldn't have believed it was possible until it happened to us.

That thought hit me like a ton of bricks. We were free from the terrible schedules that only gave us two afternoons a week together. Free from getting just enough time off to buy groceries, mow the lawn, and fight about never having time together. But most of all, we were free from a suburbia life sentence of chasing the "American Dream."

We sat on the beach and talked for hours about what this new-found freedom meant for us.

We had been so programmed to achieve the American dream that all we could previously focus on was buying a house in a nice area, each having our own vehicle, taking a vacation we couldn't afford every year, owning an enormous TV, living in a nice area with low crime, buying furniture and knick knacks to fill all the extra space in the too-large-for-us house, buying (making monthly payments on) the latest cell phones, constantly upgrading everything to the latest and greatest, and taking up expensive hobbies to fill what few spare seconds we may have accidentally scrounged up. The list could literally go on forever. What in the world were we thinking?

Here's the problem with that list. NOT ONE THING on there actually matters. Not. One. Damned. Thing. Go ahead and read it again if you don't believe me.

Nothing listed there helped us have a better marriage (something we desperately wanted), gave us more time together, reduced debt, made us happier, or freed us from ANYTHING. In fact, they all did the exact opposite.

When we finally unplugged from the Matrix and stepped back, we realized that if we had accomplished everything on the list, we would have lived the rest of our lives locked in a cage under a mountain, guarded by a dragon named Debt. There's a joke about Hobbits in there somewhere.

Anyway, that debt would have meant we would have had to work even more and have even less time together. I think that's literally the definition of a vicious cycle, don't quote me though.

I thank God we broke away when we did. If we'd stayed in that previous life long enough to "buy" a house (AKA, get a giant loan we'd pay on the rest of our natural born lives), I doubt we'd have ever been able to break free. It's almost as if the system's survival requires people to stay stuck in it forever. But maybe I'm just being paranoid.

We spent our first few weeks in Florida sitting on the beach, riding our bikes all over the island trying to get back in shape, watching football at a local bar, and taking random drives for entire days. We finally spent time together and tried to remember who we were before all the pain.

Even though we were free of all the things I listed, our past life had taken a serious toll on us and our relationship. I even looked for a marriage seminar in Florida before we left. We never went to one, but I wish we had. Getting away was a big step for us, but there was so much more we needed to work on. As I write this almost two years later, we're STILL working on stuff.

It wasn't, and hasn't been, an easy road. The bad memories don't ever go away. The hurtful things that were said aren't unsaid just because we had a few nice days together on the beach. But, neither of us have given up on the other, and we're still trying.

However, after those few weeks of fun I did some math and started to seriously worry. Living the way we were was quickly burning through my retirement. I calculated that if we didn't change something soon, we'd have to stop traveling and go back to regular jobs within six months. I realized we had to start bringing in more money, and fast. Our credit cards were either maxed out or about to be. Getting on the road hadn't been cheap.

I Find A Job

We knew that we needed more revenue to survive. The only problem was that I needed a job I could do while traveling across the whole country, and one I could work when I wanted to, not when they demanded. For once, I wanted to place my marriage above work.

I may as well have been looking for a job breeding unicorns' in space.

After a few weeks of research, and talking to other RVers, I was still coming up short on a job that would fit the new lifestyle. Maybe I had discovered why so few young people are full-timing?

One day in the RV park I met a new neighbor. She full-timed in an older class A and used her toad (tow behind vehicle) to drive for Uber. She told me that she'd done this in several states for over a year and it was how she funded her travels.

I was instantly intrigued. It sounded like the exact job I was seeking. We hadn't been able to sell Laura's little SUV before we hit the road, and it was perfect for Uber. We had several conversations about me using it for Uber, but Laura didn't like it. It was her first nice vehicle and she was rightfully afraid that it would be destroyed by drunks and careless passengers.

After assuring her, several times, that I would clean or fix anything caused by Ubering, she agreed to it. Although I think the fights were more about me going off to work and us not spending time together. You know, the exact thing we were trying to escape from (I can't imagine why she was angry). I talked her into it, but she still wasn't happy. However, we didn't know of a better option at the time, it was the best compromise I could come up with.

Within a week I was in the system and driving for Uber. It provided some money for us. There's a lot that goes into making a profit with that job. I had a week or two of trial and error, but I quickly learned that I had to work until 3 am Thursday through Sunday if I wanted to make any real money.

I also learned I wasn't the only one with this genius idea. The Pensacola area was saturated with other Uber drivers. Thankfully, after I learned the area and its patterns, I was able to earn enough to keep our heads above water. The sad part was that I had to work late, which is what we were trying to leave behind. Laura wanted me home by midnight, right when work was starting to pick up. We hadn't been on the road for a month and we were already fighting about work again.

Ahhh the good old days.

We eventually hashed out a compromise that let me keep working. I don't remember the specifics, but the bills were getting paid and we were still getting time together. At least the important things were covered.

More Repairs

Shortly after arriving in Florida, one of our slide topper arms came loose. Now, "came loose" doesn't really do that situation justice, let me explain. We were in the living room watching TV when that spring-loaded topper arm came loose and unwound. It sounded like Muhammad Ali was using our slide as a speed bag. It scared the hell out of us!

I was able to wind it up and put it back in place, but it still wasn't secure. I found out later that you shouldn't ever wind them back up yourself since losing control could be very dangerous and possibly result in a mangled hand. That tip came from one of our viewers Kevin Barone. He's been instrumental in helping us keep this thing on the road. Probably because he's worked on RV's for several years. I wish I'd known that information before my attempt at rolling it up though. My hand hurt for a week.

We emailed Cedar Creek to request authorization for a mobile tech to come fix it and they agreed. Since we were living in it, we couldn't just drop it off somewhere. We already had a list of several things that needed to be fixed, including the slide topper arm. Also, the fridge was still having problems even after the new batteries were installed, we wanted to get that resolved as well. So, we contacted a local RV repair company that offered mobile service.

The techs were able to fix several things on our list. They explained what had happened with the slide topper arm, there wasn't a rivet or screw to hold it in place. I guess the rivet guy was at lunch that day. Once the wind pushed the slide topper over far enough, the arm slipped out and unwound. The mobile tech used some screws to secure the arms that weren't riveted. Some were secured from the factory, and some weren't. So weird.

The techs also found a problem that explained why the batteries had died (Later we learned it was only part of the problem). Our converter was overcharging the batteries by pushing too many amps. We finally had an answer for why the first set had swollen and wouldn't hold a charge. Lucky for us, the techs had an extra converter in the van and were able to replace it right away. Sadly, they couldn't fix the pass-through storage door not latching. The plywood wall lived on.

These repairs kicked off our first problems with Cedar Creek. We wrote their customer service department and explained that we also needed to be reimbursed for the mobile tech and batteries from our second day on the road. After a little back and forth, they agreed to pay for the current and previous repairs, but not the batteries.

I emailed scans of all the bills and was told they would send out reimbursement checks. Great, problem solved. We sat back and waited for the money to come. Unfortunately, the checks didn't arrive before we left Florida. It wasn't explained to us that checks could take several months to arrive. We emailed them again as we were leaving and told them to cancel the first checks and to reissue new ones to a different mailing address.

The Hit and Run

We were on the receiving end of said hit and run. But the title's catchy ain't it?

Anyway, we were inside the rig doing....I don't remember, when our neighbor suddenly began pounding on our door like there was a fire. I ran to the door and he told me someone had just hit our truck. I grabbed my phone and sandals and ran outside.

I immediately began taking pictures of the damage. Then my neighbor told me the person who'd hit us was leaving, I hadn't realized they were still there. He pointed at 40' Class A driving towards the park's exit. I took off after it in the best sprint I could muster wearing sandals, hoping to get a picture of their license plate. The driver must have seen me coming because he punched the gas. I've never seen a rig that size take corners so fast. It was leaning so far that I thought it would tip over.

Sadly, I couldn't run fast enough to catch him in those stupid sandals. I walked back to the RV park sucking wind and cursing myself for getting so out of shape. I went to the office hoping they would give me the guys information. I told them what site he'd been in and expected they would help me.

I was wrong. They would only hand over the information to my insurance company. Fine, whatever. While I'd been waiting the 15 minutes for them to figure that out, I'd already reported the wreck on the USAA app. It was a Sunday, so I couldn't call anyone.

I left the office quite unhappy. While walking back to the RV, I decided to wake up early the next morning, make some calls, and get that mess figured out. Right about then, I was walking past the two-story house that's oddly built in the RV park, in the middle of a row of RVs. We'd wondered why it was there, and I found out that day.

A man about 60ish on the second story balcony called me over and asked me to come up and speak with him. It turned out he was the owner of the park, an attorney (one of the best in Pensacola we learned), and he had witnessed what happened. That wasn't even the good news, he was willing to be a witness if I needed one, and he had the office give me the man's information that hit and ran.

The Hebard Luck had struck again!

I wonder if he helped me because he was worried about liability? It did happen on his property, after all. Either way, his help was instrumental. My insurance would have covered a hit and run, but only after I paid the deductible. The park's owner saved us $500, weeks or months of hassle, and the Class A owner got a ding on his insurance, as he should have.

I went home and surveyed the damage to the truck. The rear bumper, tailgate, and right taillight assembly were all bent or damaged. My neighbor was still out there and told me the driver's wife had even been behind guiding her husband while he backed up, but she was only watching one side. After he hit AHNJ, she yelled at him, he got out, surveyed the damage, audibly said, "It doesn't look that bad," then got back in to leave.

That's when my neighbor came and pounded on our door. He was waiting to say anything hoping the driver would do the right thing.

We were incredibly lucky he didn't hit the truck any harder. We were parked in a long narrow spot that could barely fit both vehicles and the RV. We had to park the SUV's hood under the kingpin and then pull the truck up to its bumper to make them all fit. If he'd hit us much harder, it could have damaged all three.

I finished taking pictures, then went inside to call the driver. I put it on speaker so Laura could listen as well. He answered almost immediately, and I told him who I was and why I was calling. He was SOOOO angry I'd found his number, I had a hard time not laughing.

I told him that we needed his insurance information. He replied by trying to pay us off. He said that he would just give us some money for the repairs if we didn't report it. Well the joke was on him thanks to the USAA app. I told him it was too late for a bribe.

Oh man, I thought he was angry before. It still brings a smile to my face knowing that we didn't let him get away with it. We wondered how many others he'd paid off?

After some angry blustering he finally coughed up the information, I think because he realized he couldn't weasel his way out of it. We were curious about this guy, so Laura looked him up online. He lived in Pensacola, was 70 years old, and was selling a 1.5-million-dollar house at that time. He was rich, and he still ran. Some people's kids.

The insurance companies did their job and we got the truck fixed at no cost to us. We were even given a free rental while AHNJ was in the shop. I love that perk. Thanks for taking care of us USAA!

The body shop had it for almost a week. It needed a new tail light assembly, new rear bumper, and a new tailgate. The tailgate had to be painted, LineXed, and have emblems placed. It was over $3500 in repairs. I'm really glad we didn't consider the cash offer as I highly doubt he would have given us enough.

We Meet A Pyro

We've all had an inconsiderate or rude neighbor while camping/RVing. If you haven't, it's just a matter of time. Even though we'd only been on the road for two months this guy is still the worst we've encountered yet.

The night before I was going to pick up the truck from the body shop, we were watching TV and heard fireworks in the distance. I got up and looked out the rear driver's side window, because if we could see them, we'd go out and watch.

When I looked outside, I couldn't believe my eyes. Because instead of fireworks, I saw a fire not two feet from our home. It wasn't just a little campfire in a fire pit though. Sticks of wood were haphazardly jammed in the aluminum tube, poking out in all different directions and one had even fallen out and lit the grass on fire while there were 40+mph winds that night.

I ran outside fast enough that I may as well have teleported. I unhooked our black tank flush hose from the RV and began spraying down the grass before the fire got to our camper. While I was playing firefighter, I looked to my right and saw that our neighbor had placed a large padded moving blanket over a folding table, against the side of his RV, then stacked his pile of dry firewood on the blanketed table just three feet from the open flames. Oh, and the blanket hung down to the grass.

I guess if he was wanting to burn down the RV park, he had a good plan. There was maybe 15' between RVs. It wouldn't have taken much for a whole row to burn down. And he would have got away with it too if not for us meddling kids!

Seeing the potential for a terrible situation, I sprayed down EVERYTHING. I started with the fire and grass, but I also sprayed down both RVs, his whole pile of wood and that stupid moving blanket. Once I could safely put my hand in the fire pit, I quit soaking it. I'm glad we weren't boondocking because I would have run our tank dry using our little spray hose.

The neighbor, which I'd met earlier that day when he pulled into his spot, was using tall narrow metal tubes for fire pits, and he had two of them. I saw them earlier in the day and thought they were impractical fire pits. Nevertheless, he'd packed one full of wood, lit it, and took off for the evening.

I was seriously concerned about the mental state of someone who would choose to make a series of such horrible decisions. Especially with no apparent regard for even his own RV. I called the RV park's emergency number to report what had happened. The groundskeeper, who lived on the property, came over and I showed him how our neighbor had tried to light both our rigs, and possibly the rest of the park, on fire.

The groundskeeper agreed it was ridiculous and told us he would speak with our neighbor in the morning, and that he wouldn't be allowed to have another fire. I felt satisfied with the outcome, but after the groundskeeper left, I still sat in the rental truck and waited for our neighbor to return. I wanted to make sure he wasn't going to light another fire again while we were asleep.

Thirty minutes later or so he and his wife returned, they appeared to both be around 70. I told him what had happened with his fire, and what I'd done to keep our rigs safe. I tried to approach the situation as, "maybe there were some coals you didn't know about that started the fire back up after you left." Instead of just accusing him outright of being an idiot.

He never denied that he'd lit the fire and left for the evening. In fact, he said that to him, camping meant having a campfire. I agreed and just asked that he please not leave while it's lit, to which he agreed. Satisfied we were on the same page, and hoping he wasn't crazy, I said goodnight and went inside.

The next day I left early to return the rental truck and get AHNJ back from the body shop. Everything with that went fine, they'd fixed him up well and he looked better than before. Then on the way back home, Laura called me.

The pyromaniac had escalated.

Now, I don't mean that he simply built a second fire, or even a larger one. No. He'd pulled out all his pyro toys and was having fun. Did you know there are flamethrowers you can attach to a propane tank? Neither did we before that day. Mr. Pyro had three, one for each of his extra 20lb propane tanks. By extra, I mean extra over the ones in his RV.

Laura had been asleep (still trying to kick the night shift schedule) when she was awakened by what she thought was a jet engine outside. It wasn't a jet. Mr. Pyro had filled both of his tall "fire pits" with wood and then stuck a flame thrower into each to light them. Laura actually witnessed him light the second one. That's when she called me.

I told her to call the office and remind them he wasn't supposed to have another fire, and to watch him in case she needed to call the fire department.

She ran outside and jumped in her SUV to watch him, and in case he lit our rig on fire. She called the office from there and they said they'd send someone out. While watching him, Laura witnessed him using the flamethrowers again. He also opened a brand-new Costco-sized bottle of charcoal lighter fluid, sprayed the entire bottle into one fire, threw the bottle in after it, then immediately went back inside his rig.

Why would anyone do that?

Laura called me and the office again. I was still 30 minutes away, and still couldn't do anything. Again, the office said they'd send someone out, they finally did that time.

The situation spiraled out of control at that point, and this is why I call him a pyro. After the office staff came out to tell him he couldn't have a fire, he realized it was because Laura had reported him. She was sitting in her SUV watching him, after all.

He had food cooking in a smoker, along with the two fire pits burning on a sunny 85-degree day. In a rage, he pulled the hot food out, by hand, and proceeded to throw it at our rig and Laura. He was pacing, randomly yelling and screaming in the air, all while throwing the food.

The temper tantrum was strong with that one.

Laura called me again, frantic that time. She was afraid he'd use one of his three flamethrowers on the RV. He was clearly unbalanced and retaliatory. I told her to film him, hung up and called the police. I was still 15 minutes away and very worried.

I told the dispatcher what had happened, and they sent some officers out. When I arrived home, two Sheriff's deputies had beat me there. Mr. Pyro was enraged. He was screaming at them, Laura and the office staff that had come down from their tower to finally do their jobs.

The deputies explained to me that they'd given our neighbor a warning. And even though we were under a fire ban he hadn't broken any laws so there was nothing else they could do. Wondering what to do next, I thanked them for their time. After the deputies left, the office staff scurried back to safety, clearly unwilling to do anything.

We were left wondering what in the hell had just happened. This guy was clearly a mental case, almost burned down his own RV along with ours, and no one could or would do anything about it.

Since we were under a fire ban, I went inside and called every local and state government agency that could have possibly done anything to stop that guy. No one could or would do anything.

Shortly after I ran out of people to call, I looked outside to find, wait for it......ANOTHER FIRE!!! That's right, he was back at it.

By now I'll bet you're wondering why we didn't just leave, and that's a great question. We weren't doing anything wrong, so we felt the pyro should be the one to move. Also, we'd paid for an entire month at the RV park. The office was very clear there would be no refunds if we left and it was early in the month. We couldn't afford to throw away $700.

I called the office again for the….I lost track of how many times. Someone came out, again. We thought they would finally do something. Sigh...we couldn't have been more wrong. Instead of stopping him, they helped him move, and set up, his incendiary device collection to the empty site on his other side. Shortly after the move we had to call the office, again, when we could see the flames over his fifth wheel. I wonder if he got so bad because no one had ever confronted him before?

Well, the office ACTUALLY did something then. And by something, I mean they moved him across the park to an upgraded waterfront site and let him stay several more days.

We Make Some New Friends

During our time at Pensacola Beach RV Park, we met a lot of wonderful people. Two years later, we still talk to several of them.

A few days before Christmas Laura asked me to make cookies. Normally I make a half batch, but that time I messed up with one ingredient and had to make a full batch of chocolate chip cookies from scratch. Oh shucks.

To deal with the extras, Laura had the great idea of putting them in zip lock baggies and dropping them off at our new friends' campers. Even better, we decided to knock-and-run and to film it all!

Sadly, our old GoPro 4 didn't film well at night, so the footage wasn't usable. On a positive note, we had a blast giving away cookies! The next day we were hanging out and everyone was talking about the mystery cookies they received the night before. They were trying to figure out where they came from while we struggled to keep up our poker faces.

We had to drop the act though when someone said he wouldn't eat them because he didn't know where they came from or what was in them. At that point we had to tell them it was us. They were all still really happy, and it was a delicious prank.

Before we left the park, two of the couples decided to put on a shrimp boil for us. Laura had never eaten shrimp. In fact, she'd hardly eaten any seafood. Growing up in Kansas, good quality seafood was tough to come by, so her parents just didn't buy it.

Our friends knew of a local shop that sold every kind of seafood you could want. Everything native to FL was caught that day, but they also had a nice selection of Pacific fish on ice. They put on a feast we'll never forget. Laura tried the jumbo shrimp and snow crab legs and liked them. Although, you won't see her ordering seafood these days.

That shrimp boil wasn't cheap, and they refused to let us help pay for it. We were so moved by their generosity. That was our introduction to the RVer spirit of kindness and giving. We've been trying to pay it forward ever since.

RVers are some of the nicest and most generous people you'll ever meet. If you have your hood up in an RV park, expect several people to stop by and ask if you need help. Rarely will anyone accept payment for their help though. Instead, they usually ask that you pay it forward and help someone else.

A Day at the VA

The story that follows is a perfect example of why 20 some veterans a day are committing suicide.

Before we left Kansas City, I'd seen my shrink at the VA, and he put several refills of my medications in the system. He told me that I could pick them up at any VA pharmacy in the country whenever I needed to.

I knew that I'd need refills before we left Pensacola, so I took a day and drove an hour or so to the Pensacola VA hospital before I ran out. My Doctor in Kansas City had made the refill process sound extremely quick and simple. After I showed my VA ID, I was supposed to be handed my medications. Back in reality, this is the VA I was dealing with, they're not really known for quick or simple.

Feeling fully confident, I walked up to a pharmacy window, showed them my ID, told them I had refills in the system, and requested my prescribed medications. I was then told they couldn't give them to me.

Sigh.....I should have known better.

"Ok, why?" I asked them. Well, a major policy change had been sent out the week prior. My doctor in Kansas City couldn't have foreseen this disaster so I don't blame him. I would love to know what bureaucratic idiot was listening to the Good Idea Fairy though.

A new policy had been sent out VA wide stating vets couldn't have controlled meds filled outside their state of residence.

I can only think of one reason that may explain this mess. The VA has been trying to force vets into only receiving meds by mail for years now. I think this was an effort to further that agenda. I say that because everyone at the hospital just kept telling me I could only receive them by mail.

Fine, I guess I'll have them mailed to the RV park and pray they don't take the usual two months. Oh wait, they can only be sent to my registered home address. And what if I don't currently have a stationary home address? Oh, in that case I'm SOL (Sh!t out of luck).

Knowing how terribly I would, or wouldn't, sleep without Ambien I persisted. I found some sort of supervisor and explained my situation, hoping they might actually give a crap about the vets they're supposed to be serving.

There was no Hebard Luck or lucky break had that day. That doesn't happen with the VA, I think they have jammers installed or something. Instead I got treated like a junky drug seeker. The scary part was that reaction was immediate, and by almost every person on staff I spoke with. Maybe someone sent out a memo? One lady even audibly scoffed at me when I tried to plead my case.

The scoffer just pointed to a piece of paper pinned to the wall next to her as if it should explain her terrible attitude. It was one of 10-15 other papers pinned to the wall, the wall behind her desk where

I couldn't read any of them. I had to ask her what she meant and that's when the attitude every vet that's ever braved the VA knows all too well came out.

The "I'm in charge because I'm behind this desk and you'll do what I say if you ever want anything to happen. And you better not dare talk back or I'll lose your paperwork for the next 2-5 years" attitude.

Vets have three basic choices when presented with this attitude.

1. Loudly correct their attitude with a barrage of well-placed insults. It's highly unlikely this choice will produce positive results, although it'll feel great.

2. Report them. It's possible this choice may result in corrective action against them at some point in the distant future, hopefully before the nuclear holocaust. But it doesn't help you get anything done that day.

3. Take it with a smile. Man, that sure feels reminiscent of the military. Being forced to do something by someone who couldn't fight their way out of a wet paper bag. But show me a better option, I won't hold my breath.

I did what millions of other vets before me have done, I ate that plate-full of attitude with a smile and asked for seconds. I was in long enough that I can squash my emotions, throw on a fake smile and say or do whatever it takes to get through some bullsh!t. My acting skills were still up to par and she backed down, but only a little. She said she'd find someone that could help and dismissed me. I sat back down to wait.

After an hour or two of waiting they called my name. I'd been given an appointment with a doctor for a new evaluation. To be given any controlled medications their only option was to have me see a new doctor and have new prescriptions written. Fine, it's not like I had anything else to do for the entire day. But first a nurse needed to record my vitals, then I waited another hour or so.

The next time they called my name I was finally able to speak with the doctor. I gave him the rundown and he seemed apathetic at best. The meeting maybe lasted 10 minutes. He was extremely hurried and clearly didn't want to be speaking with me. He wrote down a few things and told me I'd need to undergo a urinalysis to check for illegal drugs.

What, why? Oh, that's right, they all thought I was a drug seeking junkie. Thanks for the vote of confidence everyone!

What choice did I have if I wanted to sleep? I jumped through their hoops, put up with their attitudes, wasted about eight hours of my life and endured the humiliation of their know-it-all complexes. After I'd been spit out of the wringer, they ever so graciously gave me three weeks' worth of meds. Not even a full month's worth.

I left and never had another refill of either drug. I'm happy to say their plan worked and I'll never inconvenience them again. I eventually weaned myself off the medications and no longer need them. It was easier than dealing with the VA's crap again. Gotta love that free healthcare.

Millions of veterans endure this broken system every day. They deal with horrible attitudes, waiting months or even years for services a civilian hospital can accomplish in days or weeks, they're told they should be grateful for the free healthcare and ignore the bad attitudes and service, they're placed on secret waiting lists to hide how far behind the VA is, they're treated by doctors that had their medical license revoked in another state, most of the doctors they see are from another country working at the VA for a green card and barely speak English, and if vets protest too loudly they'll be arrested and thrown out of the hospital. The VA has their own police department, just in case we don't like being treated like crap.

Then when someone at their wits' end commits suicide in a VA hospital parking lot the media and politicians all act so shocked and can't understand it. While vets read the same story and wonder how many years of hell they endured before they finally gave up.

I know that many people working for the VA care about their jobs, and I truly appreciate them. The problem starts at the bureaucratic top and trickles down wrapped in red tape. People who care have their hands tied and will actually get in trouble if they try too hard to help, and people who don't care are protected by unions and policy. Even the reporting process is a joke.

I've spoken with one (1) guy who was able to get a horrible doctor fired after proving his medical records had been falsified to protect the doctor, that's it. They're so protected they can treat us however they want with little fear of true repercussion.

Many people don't know this, but vets can't sue the VA for malpractice, well not like you can with a civilian hospital. So, that ace in the hole most people have to protect themselves with is non-existent in the VA, and they know it. Shockingly, people are still surprised when they hear a veteran committed suicide at a VA facility. If everyone had to use the VA, there would be riots in the streets.

I'd like to see someone fix that mess and allow the people that care to care and fire the people that don't. I'd also like to win the Powerball.

15

Starting Our YouTube Channel

———— ～～～ ————

We hit the road with plans of starting a YouTube channel that would hopefully fund our new lifestyle. After a month on the road, we figured it was a good time to start working on it. We knew it would be a while before YouTube would pay us anything, so the earlier we began the better.

After Laura pestered me for a few days I finally got off my butt and we made our first video. I was procrastinating because I was camera shy. Now, if you haven't seen our first video, don't worry. We made it private because it was impressively terrible. It consisted of me sitting on the couch talking, like a statue, for almost 20 minutes.

There was no pretty scenery, no shots of us doing anything fun, no graphics, and no reason to watch past the first two minutes.

Laura put the video together using the free GoPro editing software. Not only had we never used the program, neither of us had even made a video before then. It took Laura several days to edit it, there's a reason that software was free. Even though we didn't have an old computer, the GoPro program would crash the laptop every hour or so.

After we uploaded that first video, we shared it everywhere. Twitter, every business, personal, and Facebook page or group we could think of, and we even directly sent links to friends and family.

No one watched it.

We were so confused, and a bit hurt. Not only were we merely receiving single digit daily views, but no one wanted to subscribe to our channel either. We were begging everyone we knew to please subscribe, and for good reason. YouTube won't allow you to claim your channel name until you reach 100 subscribers. We were afraid someone else would take it first, then charge us to get it back.

Sadly, that's something people actually do. After Laura bought the www.hebardstravels.com URL for our website, a company contacted us wanting to sell us every possible combination of URLs that were a letter off. They'd bought 30-40 URL's close to ours. If we ever want another domain that's anywhere close to ours, we'll have to pay for it. These companies exist by grabbing up every possible URL people may want and charging big money to release them.

We dipped our toes into the filming water during our two months in Pensacola Beach and made several videos. Each one was progressively better, and we left them all up for public viewing. After about six weeks our 100th subscriber signed up and we officially became Hebard's Travels on YouTube.

Looking back now I understand why people wouldn't watch or subscribe, we weren't any good. I was HORRIBLE on camera, Laura didn't want to be on camera, I didn't know how to film, and Laura didn't know how to edit video.

To top it off, we were putting far too much time and effort into filming. We'd spend a week randomly driving around, filming everything that looked interesting and burn tanks of diesel doing it. All with no real idea or plot for the video.

When Laura would start editing, there'd be hours of footage to sift through. It would take her all week to put something together, and it still wouldn't be good. That was largely my fault though. Because I didn't have a storyline beforehand, my plan was to film everything and make a video out of it later.

Laura didn't appreciate that plan, and I don't blame her.

After many hours spent trying to make videos, we had a chat. She told me my plan had to end because it was driving her crazy. It did, somewhat. There was a lot of trial and error figuring out how to make videos. Two years later we're still learning and adjusting.

To make matters worse, we had cheap filming equipment, and we didn't even know how to use it. Our main camera was a GoPro Hero 4 Black. If you've never used one before, they're great action cameras but not so good for vlogging. We constantly ran into audio problems. Any wind over 5mph would destroy the audio. I can't tell you how many times I had to re-record clips because you couldn't understand what I was saying. Several times we had to delete clips or entire videos because we couldn't recreate the shot.

Our other camera was a Nikon D3300 DSLR. Though it was an entry level camera, it was still complicated enough that neither of us could use it off auto mode. We didn't have an external mic for it, and its audio was worse than the GoPro's. However, it gave us the ability to film from a distance. It also took better pictures than our phones. It had to be on a tripod to film with though, so it was mostly used for photography.

Right before we moved into the RV, Laura bought me a DJI Phantom 4 drone for my birthday. It was about $2,000 worth of birthday! OK, maybe not all our equipment was cheap. But until we arrived in Pensacola, I'd never flown it. Luckily, our wonderful neighbor Cody, who'd warned us about the hit-and-run, had a Phantom 3 and taught me the basics of flying a DJI drone. After a few trial runs I was flying all over the island filming everything from 100-year-old gun battlements to ghost ships washed up in a storm.

To summarize the challenges we faced, we had to learn how to film in general, learn how to create a storyline that people would want to watch, learn how to use our equipment, learn how to fly a drone, learn how to be on camera, learn how to edit video and figure out how to get people to watch the finished videos.

If you have any aspirations of starting a YouTube channel, start practicing yesterday. You don't want to be in the same position we were, trying to learn everything when you already need to know it.

My Basic Filmmaking Recommendations

1. Don't get hung up on the latest and greatest equipment. Otherwise you can easily spend $5-10,000 up front.

   - Used gear is a good way to get the latest model without spending as much.

   - Older models are another good option to save money. If you're opposed to buying used, you can usually buy a slightly older model online that's still new. Sometimes the newest model isn't even that much better.

   - If you need a specific piece of gear for a short time, renting may be your best option.

2. Any camera is good enough.

   - We know people that only use their cell phone for all their pictures and videos.

   - Clear steady shots are more important than a fancy camera. A gimbal is a great investment. Our current gimbal is a Smove Mobile that was about $160.

   - 4K is pretty, but usually unnecessary. It will drain batteries and fill memory cards faster. You need a more powerful (expensive) computer to edit, and a blazing fast signal to upload. Also, by using 4k, you'll often lose features such as image stabilization, higher frame rates, HDR, or auto low light. Currently I only use 4k on drones and time-lapses.

3. Audio, audio, audio.

- The best shot in the world can be ruined by bad audio.

- If you want to talk to your audience, they must be able to hear you.

- There are tons of affordable options from small plug in mics for cell phones, to professional quality hot shoe mics for DSLR's. If you're really on a budget, you can even put a "dead cat" sticky windscreen over the mic on your camera to block wind. That's also a great option for point-and-shoot cameras that don't have an external mic input. I use one on my GoPro case over the mic hole and it drastically improves my audio.

4. You get what you pay for with software.

- Good editing software is expensive for a reason.

- There are a few free programs that are adequate, but don't expect too much from them. In my opinion, the best free editing software is iMovie. Laura can film, edit and upload an entire video with her iPhone using iMovie.

- We've paid for Adobe Premiere Elements 15 and Final Cut Pro. We liked them both, but Final Cut has worked better for us.

5. You need a decently fast computer

    - We started on a laptop. It was far from fast enough and had to be upgraded.

    - You will most likely need to upgrade your current computer or buy/build a new one.

    - To render video, you should have at least a solid-state hard drive (SSD), 16GB of RAM, and an i7 processor. Anything less will make life difficult. I.E. longer render times requiring more of your time. These are the basics as I see them, obviously if you can afford more it will make life easier.

6. HAVE FUN!!

    - Don't listen to the trolls and naysayers, just block them. There's a great feature on YouTube called, "Hide user from channel." It will allow people to watch your videos and even comment on them, although you'll never see their comments, and they won't know that you don't see them. It's the perfect anti-troll tool.

    - No matter what you produce, someone won't like it. Ignore those people. Unless multiple people are saying the same thing, then it may be something worth looking into changing. If much of your audience is complaining about audio (a common one we used to hear) then you should probably buy a mic.

- Don't get depressed if your first videos are bad, everyone's first videos are bad. You have to produce the bad ones to learn, it's just part of the process. Get the bad ones out of the way early.

I hope these tips help you. We spent a lot of time and money to learn all this the hard way.

Can You Earn A Living on YouTube?

Yes….but don't expect to anytime soon. However, you'll still want to monetize your channel the instant you can. You never know when you'll post the next viral video!

Typically, it takes years to gain a following large enough to earn even a few hundred dollars a month. Once you get that large following, it may open doors with sponsors, so stick with it! Sponsors and advertisers may, or may not, pay you directly. Sometimes they might give you a discount or send you products instead of money. But if it's things you were going to buy anyway, I see it no differently than being given a check.

Once you have a modest following, don't be afraid to reach out to potential sponsors. You may be surprised how willing they are to advertise through you. For instance, if your videos are all about hiking, a boot company may jump at the idea of advertising to an audience who might be interested in their product. On the other hand, sometimes they just won't see the value.

Because YouTube takes so long to begin paying content creators, you need a secondary source of income. Since I'm a disabled vet, that's our other source. Whatever you choose, ensure it's generating enough income to survive on before you invest all your time in YouTube. It's not 2010 when anyone posting videos could build a giant channel in a year, it's become much more difficult these days.

One of the common ways people on YouTube pay the bills is to start a Patreon channel once they get a larger following. That's usually because they're sick of working their butts off for such a small return. We average .4 cents per view, or about $400 for 100,000 views. Not really enough to pay the bills without 10,000 views on every video.

Achieving 10,000 views per video is EXTREMELY difficult. Of our 300+ videos (at the time I wrote this) only 31 have over 10,000 views. Of those, only a handful broke the 10,000 mark in less than month. Most of them slowly achieved their view count over many months. My point is this, it takes a very long time to earn money from YouTube. Sadly, we didn't realize this until we had invested a significant portion of our money and lives into building a channel to earn a living.

Please don't be mean to channels that also utilize Patreon, as they're likely just trying to keep their heads above water. Don't be afraid to become someone's Patron either. It's a fantastic platform that gives people who want to support content creators the ability to do just that. It could be parents, friends or die-hard fans. Either way, if content creators don't give people a way to support them, then they likely won't. When was the last time you went searching for a way to give someone money?

16

You Need an Emergency Fund

⸺∼⸺

We'd been in Florida for over a month and Laura was really wanting to go diving. She's been a certified diver since high school, and it had been years since her last dive. Laura loves it so much that she even kept all her dive gear and brought it on the RV.

Hoping to surprise her, I called several dive companies and found that we'd just missed SCUBA season. Once I learned that, I broke the bad news to her. I could see she was sad, so I did some research and found a beach on the island where we could at least snorkel. I knew it wouldn't be the same, but it was the best I could do. We even went and bought a diver down flag, so no boats would run over us.

We checked the weather and picked the warmest day in the forecast to go out. We made a big day out of it and packed a lunch, snacks, drinks, beach chairs, snorkels and fins.

The day came and the weather forecast was correct, mid 80's and sunny. We packed all our stuff in the truck like we were running from a volcano and took off for the beach. We couldn't believe what we found when we arrived. The beach was pristine white sand, devoid of other human life, as far as the eye could see in either direction. The only noise was the surf, wind and gulls.

It was so wonderfully desolate I felt as if we should have gathered driftwood to make a giant "HELP" sign. Even if we had been stranded on a deserted island, I think we'd have waited a few days to gather that driftwood. As long as we had the dogs with us of course.

After we set up the chairs, we hunted shells in the surf line. Laura pointed out a few she liked so I went and flailed around in the surf gathering the best ones I could find for her. After a while no one else had showed up so we finally felt safe leaving our things unwatched. We grabbed our snorkels and fins and hit the water.

That was my first attempt at putting on fins in the surf. If you've never tried, it's a real hoot. Every time you think you've finally got your fin on the next wave hits you. It knocks you off balance while trying to steal both your fins, mask and dignity.

After a few minutes of floundering around like a pool inflatable with a hole in it, I finally got both fins on and we took off. We didn't go out past the break because we were worried about boats, but we did go up and down the shore for an hour. We found a lot of conch shells and saw some beautifully colored fish.

I'd spent very little time in the ocean, in fact, I'd spent very little time swimming anywhere. I wasn't a good swimmer and I knew it. For me to go deeper than where I could stand was a real challenge for me. I really struggled overcoming my fear. Laura had been a competitive swimmer for over 16 years, and she loves water more than air. I decided it was time to try and work through my fear. I needed to get over it anyway, there's just too much fun stuff to do and see in the water!

After an hour we decided to head back. The waves were kicking up too much sand and it was getting hard to see underwater. It also didn't help that Laura had a shark come within a few feet of her, through that sandy water.

I was exhausted from swimming for so long. Laura, of course, was fine. I swear she's actually a fish, she can just randomly go swim a mile or two if she wants to.

We decided to take a break and eat. A few bites into my food, it suddenly felt as if someone had jammed a red-hot poker in my mouth. I instantly spit my food out in the sand.

I couldn't figure out what had happened, so I grabbed my water to rinse my mouth out. Apparently, while we were swimming, someone had swapped my water out for acid. At least that's what it felt like. I promptly spit that out as well.

By that time, Laura realized something was very wrong. She asked me, but I still wasn't sure. I stuck a finger in mouth and started feeling around. Then I found it. I'd broken a molar, and half of it was missing.

I figure that due to my fear of water I was clenching my teeth and broke it. I knew I had a few cracked teeth, but I'd never had one break in half and fall out before.

As I've said, I was medically retired from the Army. After three years in combat I thought that I may have "some" PTSD. I was depressed, gambling, street racing, couldn't sleep and was drinking myself to death. So, maybe more than "some."

One random day I decided to end my career and walked into the mental health department. Some Army shrinks diagnosed me with PTSD, anxiety, depression and a few other things. They determined it was all severe enough that I shouldn't go back overseas for a fourth time, or even stay in to finish my third enlistment.

One of the worst things about my PTSD is sleeping. I don't really have a sleep pattern to speak of. Some nights I'm up for hours, other nights I'm asleep the instant my head hits the pillow. But all those nights, I dream.

I only know I'm dreaming though, because Laura tells me I am. I may remember a dream once a month, often it's less. However, I dream almost every night, and I guess they're often bad. During those dreams I clench my teeth. I don't mean I grind them, I mean I clench them like I'm trying to make diamonds from coal.

Due to the clenching, several of my molars were cracked. Before we went full-time, my dentist recommended I have a custom night mouthguard made after I broke two teeth and needed a crown on one. I agreed, even though it wasn't cheap. I wore it every night and hadn't broken any more teeth. But I didn't have it while we were snorkeling and didn't realize I was clenching my jaw again. It's something I've learned I must stay cognizant of at all times now

Luckily, we have dental insurance. When we got back to the RV I went online and called every dentist in Pensacola that accepted our insurance. I found one that could get me in that day and made the appointment.

We were very lucky because the dentist I found had been working on teeth for 30 years. To top it off, he had much lower crown prices than my old dentist in Kansas. That was good, because after the X-rays he determined I needed a second crown.

One of the molars I'd crushed before the custom mouthguard was rotting under a filling and needed a crown, or else it had to be pulled. I agreed to the two crowns of course. What choice did I have? Not eating on one side of my mouth for the rest of my life isn't a rational decision. We made an appointment for the next day to start the process.

When we got home, Laura said she wanted to get her teeth checked out as well, one of hers had been bothering her. I called the dentist back and they said they could squeeze her in the next day at the same time.

It turned out Laura also needed a crown. Great, because we'd totally planned on needing three crowns that week. We just had to pull more from retirement again.

But wait, there's more! When you order in the next ten minutes, we'll throw in a root canal at full price!

Two weeks later, when I went back to get my permanent crowns placed, and one of the nubs was still hurting badly. I didn't just need two crowns, I also needed a root canal. Oh goody….

At least the tooth was already ground down. I was told that was the best, and cheapest, time to do a root canal. So, I had that going for me.

To make matters even worse, we were in the middle of trying to leave Florida early. We'd planned to stay in Pensacola Beach for four months, but Laura's grandpa in Houston wasn't doing well again. We decided to cut our time short and leave after only two months.

We ran into a small problem, though. Before Laura could get her permanent crown placed, our month at the RV park was going to end. They charged $50 per day if we stayed without a monthly rate. We had to find a different park to stay at for the extra few days, one that wouldn't charge us as much as a fourth crown.

Two friends we met at the Pensacola Beach RV Park had moved to a park an hour away in Foley, Alabama. We found a much cheaper KOA near them and moved. We got to hang out with them for several days, which was a lot of fun. They showed us around the town and tried to help us find a park we could workamp at the next winter. We knew we wanted to come back and were trying to figure out how to afford it. Workamping was the best option.

If you haven't heard of workamping, it's a simple idea. An RV park, or other business, allows you to stay for free if you and (usually) your spouse will both work a certain number of hours per week, typically it's 15-20 per person for a few months. Sometimes they also offer a small stipend as well.

146

We found a good option the day before Laura had her permanent crown placed. We spoke with the people managing the resort and got the paperwork we'd need to fill out. We couldn't wait to workamp for them and stay a few months for free.

We planned to leave for Houston directly after Laura had her permanent crown placed. Unfortunately, the dentist appointment was an hour in the wrong direction and had her returning to the KOA after their checkout time. So that morning she drove the SUV to the dentist, and I moved the RV to an empty lot and waited for her to meet me.

By the time she made it back to the RV, bad storms were beginning to build in the area. We decided not to leave that night and risk driving in 60mph winds. The lot didn't allow overnight parking, so we moved across the street to a Home Depot. It was a good thing we stayed. Shortly after we moved, a tornadic storm hit the area with winds so high I had to put all the jacks down. Of course, I called the Home Depot and asked if it was ok first.

A small tornado actually touched down only a few miles from us. We had to grab the animals and run into Home Depot when the sirens went off. That was some of the hardest rain we'd ever seen. That's after I lived in Kansas for 10 years and Laura grew up there. We saw our fair share of severe thunderstorms.

You never know when something will happen that could wipe out your emergency savings. You must have something set aside for emergencies if you plan to full-time RV. There are too many things that can go wrong on the road, and depending on where you are, you may have to pay a steep "middle of nowhere" or "tourist" tax.

I wish I could say we always followed that advice, but we lapsed due to the cost of getting our small business on its feet. Of course, we should have planned better, but we didn't know what we didn't know.

CHAPTER 17

A New City and New Adventures

———~~~———

We said goodbye to our new friends in Alabama and left for Houston. Although we didn't take I-10, the direct route there. Laura had read many bad reviews about I-10, specifically the portion that runs through Louisiana. People who had driven to Alaska said that section of I-10 was worse than the Alcan Highway. Since we were already having enough problems with the RV, bypassing that road sounded like a great idea to us.

We decided to go north first, then took a west hand turn at the next major highway. That roundabout route may have added a lot of miles, but we skipped arguably the worst road in the country. We overnighted in Walmart's for the whole trip.

When we arrived in Houston, we went straight to the RV park we'd reserved on the north side of the city. We chose it because it was only 15 minutes from her grandpa. We didn't go to see him that first day as we got in late, but we did go the next.

That first night was brutally cold, especially for Houston Texas. It got down to about 10 degrees. The next morning, as we were walking out the door to go see Laura's grandpa, she slipped on the icy steps. Her feet flew out from under her and she landed on the metal steps HARD. The joy of seeing her grandpa for the first time in 20 years was painfully cut short as she lay there crying. She was very lucky that nothing was broken, but the areas on her back that hit the steps were knotted and hurt for a month.

Once we realized that she didn't need to go to a hospital, we decided to continue on to grandpa's house. Laura hadn't seen him in so long because there had been some "family problems" when she was young, and she hadn't seen him since. Anyway, he was the one that had taken Laura on RVing road trips around the country when she was young. She was so happy to tell him all about our new lives since he had been her main inspiration.

The videos from Chris & G showed that we could live and work on the road, but without the epic trips with her grandpa, she wouldn't have had the fond memories of traveling which made her want this lifestyle.

We spent several days with him, his wife and his son, Laura's uncle. Laura really enjoyed her time catching up with her family. We even took her grandpa to doctor appointments at the VA hospital and tried to help him any way we could while we were there.

We would have spent more time with him, but I had to work. While in Houston, I spent about 40 hours a week driving for Uber. The population was immense compared to Pensacola. My nights of sitting around for an hour or two waiting on a passenger were basically over. Houston's pay rate wasn't as high, but I made up for it with double the fares. I did have to learn a new city though, and there were several rough nights getting lost in that massive city.

> *I talk about some of the crazy Uber stories in depth next chapter.*

During my time Ubering in Houston and Florida, Laura was glued to the computer. She was researching everything about starting and building a YouTube channel, blog, Instagram, and Twitter accounts. While we were in Houston, she completely overhauled our website. Before, it had looked fairly basic, but it worked. Then she made it look professional.

Sure, it took a little longer than hiring someone, but she did a marvelous job and now knows how to run the back-end of our site. I've never once been embarrassed to tell people about our site. For being so new to the social media game, she had our site looking and working like we'd been doing it for years.

It got to the point where she'd learned so much about website creation and social media that she was getting angry with me because I couldn't relate. Laura wanted someone who could answer her questions and be a sounding board for her ideas, and I wasn't up to the task.

I knew that Uber was taking me away from Laura and that wasn't helping us start our online business and brand, but we needed money. Luckily for us, Laura is a tremendous researcher, and she started our channel off on the right foot.

Even though we were small, Laura's research had us seeing steady growth. By the numbers, we weren't doing very well. However, when we analyzed it by percentages, we were surpassing every other RV YouTube channel.

For me, the best part about Houston was reconnecting with a friend from the Army. He didn't live too far from where we were staying, and he came over one night. We sat and swapped stories about my third deployment, but his first, for hours. It was the most fun I'd had in a long time. I wish I could have spent more time with him, but we were both too busy.

I was working so much that Laura and I hardly had any time to go out. Laura did some research and found two things in Houston that looked really fun and we planned two-day trips. Sure, we filmed videos about them, but they were more mini vacations so we could spend time together.

The first was the Houston Museum of Natural Science. I didn't appreciate places like that when I was young, I hated museums and would throw a fit if I had to go to one. I guess I grew up because I love them now. I just think it's really neat to look at the past up close and personal. It's not something we think about often, so when you're standing in front of some 20,000-year-old relic it brings some perspective about our existence.

The second was the Johnson Space Center and Neutral Buoyancy Lab. Purely by accident, we happened to go during some sort of special weekend and the Lab was included in the regular entry fee. Regular tickets don't usually include that building. Considering it's one of the largest swimming pools in the world we thought we'd struck the lottery. After Laura's years of swimming she was thrilled to visit it. They had a life-sized recreation of the International Space Station (ISS) in the pool with astronauts in the water training.

We spent hours at the complex and saw everything there was to see, including an entire Saturn V rocket. The same rocket that did the moon missions. After we'd been gone for seven hours it was time to head home and let the dogs out. We try to let them out no later than eight-hour intervals. Unfortunately, we hit traffic on the way back and the dogs had to wait nine hours.

The next day, we encountered a small problem. Somehow all the footage we'd filmed at Johnson Space Center was gone. It had been accidentally deleted. One of the main reasons we went to the space center was to film a video. I was thinking about all the money and time we'd spent trying to make that video when I suddenly remembered data recovery software.

Laura looked it up and found a good software that was somewhat affordable for a one-time use, and we were able to recover about 75% of what we'd lost. We couldn't have been happier! Laura made the videos for the museum and space center, and we sat back, positive they'd go viral. After all, people like museums, don't they? Sadly, neither one did well, but we learned several valuable lessons through making them.

We Make New Friends, Again

When Laura was in college, she met a guy online. They never met or dated, but they talked periodically over the years and stayed friends. Laura was excited to meet him when we realized that we were going to Houston

I'll admit, I thought it was a little weird we were meeting a man she'd only known online, but she swore he was a great guy. He'd been married for a few years and had kids, so I agreed, and I'm glad I did. We had so much fun with them that first night that we went back for a second dinner and game night.

They turned out to be wonderful people and we still talk to this day. We're actually responsible for planting the RV bug during those game nights. They bought a 30' travel trailer and a new truck for a several thousand-mile road trip the year after we met. Now they're talking about possibly going full-time for a while before their kids start school.

If we keep recruiting people to the lifestyle, we may have to start handing out t-shirts.

Time to Move

Houston is one of only a few cities that required Uber drivers to have a license and insurance from that state. The city waived the requirement during the Super Bowl to accommodate out of state Uber drivers for the huge influx of tourists. Once the Super Bowl was over, and since I didn't have a Texas license, we decided to leave the area.

Even though I had a friend, and Laura had family in Houston, the traffic in the city was wearing on both of us. Even going to the grocery store was a chore. The constant city noise of traffic, gunshots, sirens, loud car stereos and low-flying aircraft was the final straw. We needed to leave.

Laura found us a nice little park with full hookups near Canyon Lake, TX. It had an affordable monthly rate, and it was only a few hours away. We needed someplace to spend the rest of winter before we began our trip north to tour the popular national parks. It looked like a beautiful area with many things to do, so we agreed to stay there for two months.

CHAPTER 18

Tales from an Uber Driver

———— ❧ ————

When I tell people I was an Uber driver, they always ask if I have any crazy stories. People love hearing about the weird things others do. Here are the strangest things that happened during my 2 ½ months of driving for Uber.

My First Passenger

The first night I drove for Uber began with a passenger I'll never forget.

I was in the RV with Laura wearing my Uber polo, excited about the prospects of my new job. Her Escape was fueled up, I had cleaned it spotless inside and out, there were extra phone chargers, gallon

Ziplock's in the seat backs for sick bags and a new air freshener in the vent. Laura even found me little signs for the headrest backs that asked passengers to please leave me a five-star rating and a tip if they thought I deserved it.

With everything ready, I turned on the app and sat back waiting for it to signal when I had a potential passenger. The RV park seemed like a great place to begin a night from. There were several large hotels across the street, hundreds of vacation homes and a monstrous set of five high-rise condos on the island. I figured my chances of being pinged were great there.

Just a few minutes later my phone went off and I ran out the door. The directions had me driving to the end of Pensacola Beach, where the expensive high-rise condos are.

After passing through a security checkpoint I found the correct condo building and parking in front of the elevators. The instant I stopped I selected that I was at the pickup location and sat back to wait for my first fare. Almost 15 minutes later, a couple in their 40's exited the elevator.

As they were getting into the backseat, I realized they were each drinking something from red plastic cups. They were planning on drinking red wine while I drove them to dinner. I regretfully informed them that not only did I not allow any drinks without lids, but it's also illegal for passengers to drink in Florida. The driver is who will receive the very large fine, not the drinking passenger. I looked it up beforehand because I thought it could be an issue.

They instantly became extremely rude. They had a conversation about requesting a different driver or taking the wine back upstairs since it was apparently very expensive. The conversation took place a foot from my head, but they acted as if they were the only people in there. They decided that waiting for another driver would take longer and took the wine back up to their condo. Fifteen minutes later they returned, and we finally set off for downtown Pensacola. I should have just canceled.

Typically, I can talk to anyone about almost anything. Four years of commission-based retail sales taught me that skill. That night I learned some passengers just didn't want to talk. Well, talk to me anyway. Mr. Big Shot was on the phone most of the time talking about closing some giant real estate deal that he would make a $50,000 profit on. I thought it was odd how loud he was talking about that deal, almost like he was trying to brag. In contrast, when he spoke with his wife they whispered.

On my third or fourth attempt to strike up a conversation Mr. Big Shot finally bit. I was excited about the job and asked them about their experiences with other Uber drivers, I was looking for the likes and dislikes of passengers. I guess he was still mad about the wine, because he took the opportunity to educate me. He told me that every Uber driver allows them to drink in the back seat, and that if I didn't change that I wouldn't ever make any tips. I say he educated me because he was talking down to me as if I was a child that needed to be taught to never touch a hot stove.

Shortly after that little gem of knowledge I dropped them off at the restaurant. Sure enough, they left without leaving a tip. I didn't change the open drink policy though. Upholding my agreement with

Laura to keep her SUV clean was much more important to me than making a rude braggart happy.

I'm Not an Ambulance

Shortly before we left Pensacola, I was pinged to pick up a passenger at some very rough looking apartments. When I pulled in, the 20 or so guys sitting around the front door eyed me like a fresh steak. After a few minutes without the passenger coming out I called. She had walked out near the road so I could pick her up faster but hadn't told me.

Anyway, I left the guys who may very well have been discussing how much money Laura's Escape was worth in a chop shop. I was in for another surprise when I located my fare. She was probably in her early 20's, and she had in infant in a baby carrier.

When I selected that I'd picked up my passenger the Uber app then showed me her drop off location, the children's hospital emergency room. Immediately I asked her if she needed an ambulance instead. She downplayed it and said her child was just throwing up a bit, and she didn't have a car. I don't know much about babies, so I took her at her word.

However, a few minutes into the drive I learned that she probably did need an ambulance, but she couldn't afford it. Her baby hadn't kept any food down for a day, wasn't sleeping and was feverish. She explained this all to me very matter-of-factly. That was right about the time I decided to risk a speeding ticket. Even if I was pulled over, I think explaining the situation would have likely resulted in a police escort to the hospital.

Thankfully, we made it to the hospital without incident. I don't think I could have handled a baby dying in my back seat. I'm pretty sure I'd need a decade or three of therapy after that.

It's Hard to Be Scared When You're Laughing

I think the most memorable event was the shooting.

It happened during my first night driving in Houston. I'd been pinged and was on my way to pick up a fare when I stopped at a red light. Looking at the opposite corner of the intersection, I saw a man standing on the corner at a gas station. By the way he dressed and carried himself, it was obvious to me that he was a gang member, or at least wanted to be.

To my extreme surprise, he suddenly pulled out a pistol, and struck a pose. While holding it almost upside down above his head, he proceeded to dump his magazine as fast as he could pull the trigger, hit nothing but air, pull his pants up and run away. Well, run the best he could wearing that ridiculous outfit. It was like a scene straight out of cheesy comedy movie.

It was one of the funniest damned things I've ever seen.

I understand that most people won't find any humor in a shooting. You must understand my background though. I joined the Army with an Airborne Infantry contract pre-9/11, I was trained for combat, deployed three times, two of which were the Afghanistan and Iraq invasions, I lived three years of my life in combat zones, reenlisted for the same job twice, and even spent a year of my career attempting to join the Green Berets.

160

Unfortunately, I wasn't able to function on four hours of sleep and couldn't pass the training, so I was kicked back to the regular infantry. After I retired, I even worked at a gun store and range for a year where I taught people how to shoot.

So, when I watched a walking gang banger stereotype obviously fire a gun for his first time, I couldn't stop laughing. It was the kind of uncontrollable laughter that makes you worry about how much you're breathing.

After those three years in combat, that was hands down the most piss poor attempt at killing someone I'd ever seen. Clearly the safest place to stand was in front of him. My only regret was not being able to film it to show all my army friends. Good humor should be shared.

I was laughing so hard I didn't even notice the light had turned green until the car behind me honked. I'd been a little stressed and that good laugh really cheered me up. I was wiping tears from my eyes as I drove away.

I would have called the police, but I was working and wouldn't have been able to stick around to file a report. On the way back, after I picked up my passenger, I saw an officer at the gas station casually talking to someone. It seemed obvious to me that no one had been hurt as no EMS personnel had responded.

I've Still Got It!

Due to the city's nightlife, there was a ridiculous amount of money to be made. As long as I worked past 2 am though. Laura and I hammered out a new agreement pertaining to how long and late I

161

would work each day. It was even less desirable hours for our relationship working later, but I worked a day less per week.

One night, as I was making the closing rounds picking up drunks, a woman around my age got in the backseat. She was very intoxicated. She wanted to go to another bar nearby, but instead of dropping her off in front, she asked me to drive around back. Fine, whatever. I received odd requests fairly often and didn't think much of it. When I stopped, she didn't want to get out of the SUV. Great.

She wanted to talk. Great, again. Yeah, I've got time to talk and not make money. It's cool. Sigh....

She was sitting directly behind me, and I learned very quickly that she didn't just want to talk when she began to rub my shoulders, which I stopped immediately. I don't know what was going on in her life, but she was desperate.

I don't even remember what she said, probably because I wasn't really paying attention. I kept mentioning Laura every chance I had to respond. She mentioned she was a veterinarian, so I told her Laura, MY WIFE, was a vet tech, which she promptly scoffed at. The strangest thing was that she didn't seem the least bit deterred by my being MARRIED.

She was very pretty, and I'm sure she wasn't used to being shot down. After a few minutes of striking out she became extremely angry. Before she got out, she had some choice words for me, my sexuality and my anatomy. Then she got out with a huff, stormed away, and all without leaving a tip.

That's the only reason I entertained the conversation in the first place, because without tips, Uber drivers barely cover their expenses.

Thankfully, that was the only time something like that happened. I'd like to think any other women that were interested backed off when they saw my ring, or when I mentioned Laura, or maybe she was the only one.

Guess I'll never know. Oh, shucks.

Sleep It Off, Just Not Here

Late one evening, I arrived at a restaurant to pick up my next passenger. A man helped an extremely intoxicated woman into the backseat, but he didn't close the door until they made out for a minute. I assume her friends had called for a lift, shoved her in the back seat, closed the door and went off to enjoy the rest of their night. I still think it's odd that her kissing friend didn't come with her.

Anyway, the woman was around 40, fairly attractive and dressed to go clubbing (use your imagination). She was conscious and somewhat coherent for the first half of the trip. But then she passed out.

I realized she was asleep and let her be, hoping a nap would make it easier to get her out of the SUV later. Boy, was I wrong. As I pulled up to her condo building, I announced very loudly that she was home.

She didn't even stir, great.

I pulled up to the front doors, put the SUV in park, got out, opened her door and again, loudly told her she was home. Again, no response. I was becoming nervous by that point. She was breathing and still alive, I had that going for me at least.

I decided to escalate and yelled at her that she was home. I wasn't going to have some passed out passenger hold me hostage the rest of the night. Thankfully, she somewhat regained consciousness then, but what happened next was worse. She couldn't get out of the backseat by herself. Although watching her try for a few minutes was pretty funny.

She was so drunk she'd lost all motor control. I really thought about calling the police, but for a non-emergency call on a weekend night at 2:30am, my chances of someone showing up within an hour were slim. So, I rolled the dice and grabbed her arm. I helped her out and onto her feet, but that still wasn't much better. She couldn't stand on her own.

UGGHHH....great....again. Sigh....

I got a tight grip under her right upper arm, almost in the armpit, and halfway carried/guided her into the lobby, just like a POW (prisoner of war). I guess some of my training stuck. I walked into the lobby desperately searching for a doorman or someone I could pass her off to, but we were alone. I did see security cameras, which was good for me. They could back me up if she tried to claim anything inappropriate happened. That's what I was really afraid of.

I pulled/carried her to the elevators where she tried to push the up button. After the third or fourth failed attempt, I reached around her and pressed it. While waiting for the slowest elevator in the world, she tried to face plant a few times. Good thing I decided to stay with her.

When the doors finally opened, I let go of her arm so that she could walk in. She promptly attempted to meet the tile face first. Lucky for me she was small, I snatched her up by both upper arms in mid-fall. Still holding her arms, I picked her up off her feet, carried her into the elevator, put her in the corner, turned around and left.

On the way out, I made a point to look directly into one of the cameras and hold my hands out as if to say, "I wash my hands of this tomfoolery." She must have made it into her apartment, because I never heard anything about it.

Now, after the fact, I realize that I should have called in the incident as an "unresponsive person." EMS would have likely responded, and she may have even needed them. I'll never know.

Who Calls an Uber After Surgery?

I arrived at some sort a clinic for this passenger. After a few minutes a man in a wheelchair, his wife and small boy came out. My best guess is he'd had some sort of elective surgery. Maybe butt implants? I say that because he wasn't at a hospital, and his butt, or something back there, was bleeding. Also, his wife had multiple...cough...obvious elective surgeries.

At least they had stacks of pads for him to sit on, and he was fully bandaged, but a little still leaked from....thank God for the pads. They were using Uber because they had flown into Houston for the surgery and didn't have a car. They needed me to take them to the pharmacy to pick up pain medication on the way to their hotel. He needed several days of bed rest in their hotel before they could fly back.

I was used to people asking me to help them run errands, but this took half the day. His Doctor wrote a prescription for a highly controlled pain killer but had prescribed it in the wrong quantity. No pharmacy could fill it. I know, because we tried like four pharmacies.

Finally, someone told the wife no one could, or would, fill it because the quantity was incorrect. This was after an hour or two of having Mr. Bleeder in my back seat. Finally, they got the Doctor to call something else in, we picked it up, and I headed to their hotel.

Oh, but the story doesn't end yet! Where would the fun be in that? As I was pulling up to the hotel, the wife asked me if I could wait, because she needed my help with a grocery run. She promised me a good tip.

Ok, fine. It was either that or waiting for a new passenger, and a guaranteed fare was better than waiting or driving around looking for one. Luckily, they took the bloody pads with them and I didn't have to deal with those.

After 10 minutes she came back out with her son, and I plugged in the new address and took off. Unfortunately, I'd just begun driving in Houston and wasn't used to their highway system. Whoever planned the highways there likes to place two exits right next to each other, and I ended up taking a wrong exit. Then I got so flustered I did it again.

After an extra 15 minutes of driving in circles, I finally got them to the store, then had to wait almost a half hour more while they shopped. I finally got them back to the hotel and she gave me a $40 tip, which was nice, but that trip took several hours of my life.

PTSD Triggers, and an Ambush?

I had some bad days driving for Uber, this is one of them.

On the day of the Super Bowl, I picked up three average looking middle aged guys who wanted to be taken to a hotel near the stadium downtown. As I was pulling into the parking lot, a group of men and women that had been sitting around the entrance suddenly sprang into action. It really felt like an ambush, enough so that my pulse went from 80 to 200 in a heartbeat.

Several of them jumped in front of the SUV to block me, while simultaneously several others ran up on either side of me. All of them were yelling. One of the men in front started beating on the hood. I was boxed in, as there was steady traffic behind me. Boxed in by people clearly presenting themselves as hostiles.

After my three years in combat, I was a little burned out on people trying to kill me, if you can imagine. Even as I write this, I can barely write two words without a typo. Thinking about that situation again brought back some of the same feelings.

While keeping my eyes on the potential attackers I immediately reached for the gun under my seat. I know carrying a gun is against Uber's policy, but screw their policy. My mind began to race analyzing the situation and strategizing multiple fight-or-flight scenarios.

1. I couldn't back up because of traffic.
2. I could have run over the people in front of me, but their friends could still attack me and there was no guarantee that I could exit anywhere else.

3. I could have presented my gun in hopes they would back off, but that's a huge gamble. It could prompt someone I couldn't see to fire at me and my passengers.

4. Were the passengers in on it?

5. Was it a kidnapping or robbery attempt?

6. How many targets were there? How many could I shoot before they would return fire? Would I need to reload?

7. Were there others I couldn't see that would return fire even if I neutralized everyone I could see?

During the few seconds it took me to strategize the scenarios, I observed that all of the potential attacker's hands were empty. That helped me back down a bit, since they weren't armed that I could see. Once I composed myself, I rolled my window down to see what they wanted. They had boxed me in and were yelling at me because I couldn't park there. The stupid hotel had actually hired a goon squad to keep people from parking there during the Super Bowl.

I told them I was an Uber driver just dropping off passengers, but they didn't care. They started grilling me about my passengers, while still surrounding me, and still not completely out of traffic. "What room are they in? Let us see a room key. How long are they staying?" ETC, ETC, ETC.

I was still very much on edge, but I kept my composure and tried to answer their questions. I basically told them "Why would I know any of that?" That just pissed them off more. Then my passengers started chiming in and answering questions. It turned out they weren't staying at the hotel. They just wanted to go to the hotel bar, drink and watch the game.

The "goon-squad" wouldn't let me in. So, with the car hanging halfway out into traffic, my passengers were forced to get out, and I had to back out into traffic to leave. Fun times.

I immediately called Laura and told her what happened, and she helped me calm down. Then she promptly wrote a review on Google explaining what happened, and how lucky they were that I'm not trigger happy. The review was some sweet revenge. The pro-veteran crowd wrote so many reviews and called the hotel so much that they had to stop answering them and also turned off commenting on their Facebook page. They tried standing their ground at first, that was fun. I'm always down for a good fight.

Thinking back on it now I'm kind of surprised there wasn't some cheesy comic book villain standing in the shadows, cackling with laughter shouting "GET EM' BOYS MWAHAHAHAHA!!" Humor helps me cope with triggers. Trust me, it's better than anger.

There were many, MANY, other noteworthy stories. However, these were the most memorable, and this isn't a book about Uber.

CHAPTER

19

SURPRISE! We Bought
A Lemon RV....

————∾∾————

We left Houston for Canyon Lake, TX hoping to have an
uneventful two months while we waited to begin an epic
National Parks road trip on our way to Washington. That whole
uneventful thing was doomed from the start, we just didn't know it.

The Cedar Creek Saga Continues

While we were in Florida, Cedar Creek was supposed to send us
our reimbursement checks for the warranty work which had been

completed. It took them so long to send the checks that they never arrived before we left.

When they missed us, we told Cedar Creek to send replacement checks to my family in Washington, so it wouldn't matter when they arrived. Cool, everything was fixed we thought. My family received the checks, sent them to us and we deposited them. Everything would have been just fine, except that Cedar Creek had canceled the Washington checks, as well as the Florida ones. Our bank slapped us with three fees for depositing bad checks.

We contacted Cedar Creek again, angry as hell that time. They never apologized, and instead, they tried to talk their way out of their own mistake. Our mistake was calling them in the first place. What was said on the phone was forgotten, which allowed that debacle to happen. We should have stuck with email.

The check situation was the last straw, and we refused to work with the same customer service representative again. Our file was passed to her supervisor who seemed more competent. Thankfully, the supervisor was able to get the checks figured out.

Cedar Creek refused to refund the bank fees, but they did finally issue one check for the entire total they owed us. When we deposited that one, we hoped it was the end of dealing with them.

We were so naive.

More repairs

The day we pulled into Canyon Lake, I discovered a fairly serious problem when I opened the RVs sewer cap. Grey water poured out and splashed all over me, which immediately alerted me to something else needed to be fixed. And to how terrible that stuff smells a foot from your face.

I called Cedar Creek and received permission again to use a mobile repair tech. The catch was the same as before, we had to pay the tech upfront, submit the receipt to Cedar Creek, then wait a month or two for a reimbursement check. We figured that was better than putting our house in a shop for a month. So, I found an RV repair tech who said he could fix the dump valves, and who wasn't booked up for two months.

I should have known something was wrong when I had to lend him my tools and let his wife/girlfriend/whoever use my hotspot to work. After a quick inspection he discovered that one of our grey tank valve cables was broken and the other two valves also needed to be replaced as they were about to break.

It turned out that whoever originally installed the three dump valves had wrapped the cables around each other several times, TIED THEM IN A KNOT (I wish I was kidding) and finally the cables were bent at a 90-degree angle where they opened the valves. When I looked at it, I was amazed they lasted as long as they did before breaking.

I contacted Cedar Creek and they overnighted three new dump valves to me free of charge, which was very nice of them. When the tech came back to install the new valves, he broke a piece of our plumbing removing one of them. He said his only option then was to remove our entire sewer system, rebuild it, then install it as one piece.

Before he left that day, I asked him to look at a few other things. Might as well ask while I have him there, right? I showed him several problems that had come up since Florida and he said he could fix them all, he'd just need parts. That is, until I showed him the wavy exterior wall near the door.

He looked at it from multiple angles, beat on the wall with his fist in several spots, and knew what was wrong. He called it adhesion separation, basically the adhesive that holds the wall to the studs had failed causing the wall to separate. I asked him what could cause that, and he told me there's a few ways.

1. Not enough adhesive was used. He said sometimes the spray nozzles can clog preventing the full amount from dispensing. Or they went cheap.

2. There's a structural problem that allowed enough twist to force the separation. He said that was highly unlikely because we'd have cracks in our walls if that was the case.

3. The adhesive used was a low enough quality that it failed on its own.

He was very sure that only the factory would be able to fix it. He also said it was such a rare issue that he'd only seen it happen a handful of times in 20 years of working on RVs.

The tech was a bit strange but had been very helpful. The first major problem we encountered with him was purely by accident. I was still talking to him after he'd inspected the wall while he was working (I try to learn every chance I get). When I asked him if he accepted credit cards, he became visibly agitated and said no, he only took cash or check A little odd, but not a huge problem. I told him I could get cash from my broker in a few days.

Immediately after that conversation, he said he needed to take all my plumbing home to put it together. He lived nearby, and I didn't see anything wrong with it, so I agreed. As he was putting away his tools, he told me he'd be back the next day.

Well, the next day came and went. And the day after that, and the day after that and....you get the picture. He wouldn't answer the phone or return my calls. He was holding our SEWER SYSTEM HOSTAGE until I could get cash! During that week, we had to wash dishes outside and exclusively use the campgrounds bathroom and showers. We couldn't use any water in our house, unless we wanted it to dump out into the underbelly of the rig.

During that week while we waited for the Brown Bandit to return our plumbing, I received a very interesting call. It was from the technician's wife/girlfriend/whoever. She called me madder than hell, thinking it was a girl's number, and that Ken, the Brown Bandit, was cheating on her. I didn't have to act confused because I didn't know what she was talking about. In retrospect, I realize now that she was probably high on something. I felt bad for her.

After washing dishes outside for yet another day, we were finally fed up. I came up with a simple plan and tricked him by calling from Laura's phone instead. Surprise, surprise, he picked up when he didn't take the call from my number a minute before. When he answered, he promised he'd be there the next morning. We were highly doubtful but decided to give him one last chance.

The next day, when he was an hour late, I called again and left a message. He wouldn't answer either number that time. I told him that if he wasn't there in 15 minutes, he'd never get a dime from me. I said that I had another tech lined up to finish the work if he wouldn't. I don't like lying, but sometimes it's necessary. Ken was there in 14 minutes.

He did finish the work, and he properly diagnosed some other problems on our rig including the wavy wall, but I didn't get some of my tools back. Amazingly, he had figured out how to accept credit cards at last (is it really that hard?) and we said good riddance to the Brown Bandit.

The Wavy Wall That Started It All

It's funny. If we had bought any other RV, you probably wouldn't be reading this book. Sure, we had dreams and aspirations of making it big, but the "how" is where everyone struggles. We were struggling too, until this point.

The instant the mobile tech told us about the wall, we emailed Cedar Creek. We explained what he'd said and sent them pictures. That was the point when communication began to deteriorate. After the whole check and reimbursement debacle, Cedar Creek was already on thin ice with us.

During the sewer problem, the communication wasn't fabulous, but it was tolerable. However, when we told them about a possible serious structural issue, the wall, the games and excuses began. To protect ourselves, we decided to film some of the problems we were having. That was another genius Laura idea. The result was our first Lemon RV video. We posted it on YouTube and emailed Cedar Creek the link. Then we waited.

Cedar Creek responded by saying we needed an inspection from a Forest River authorized repair center before we could move forward. I guess an inspection by Joe Shmoe RV tech didn't cut it. That's when the fun began because there were very few Forest River authorized service centers near us.

Being in Texas, an RV dealer can't legally work on an RV unless they sell that brand. At least that's what several Texas dealers told us. The closest Forest River dealer was an hour away, the next was 2 ½.

When I called the closest dealer, I received some bad news. Their body tech was out for two months recovering from cancer surgery. Of course, we were happy he made it. But I was forced to call the next dealer, hoping they would have someone who could inspect the wall.

On top of everything, we had our backs against a wall again (wall puns haha). The factory one-year warranty was only weeks away from expiring. If we didn't get that inspection before it expired, Cedar Creek could, and likely would, deny any warranty claims.

The second dealer was also very sorry, but they were booked for months. I then called the third, fourth, etc. and all had the same response. No one could inspect it before the warranty expired. I'm no quitter, so I called the second dealer back. I explained the situation we were in and even offered to pay them. I was willing to haul the rig out there and wait for days, just in the off chance someone would cancel, and the shop could get us in. The situation was so stressful that Laura and I were having difficulty sleeping.

The service manager must have felt bad for us, because he told me to come out the next day and they'd squeeze us in. We packed up that night and were ready to go before we went to sleep. With the 2 ½ hour drive, we wanted to hit the road early to give the shop as much time as they needed.

When we arrived, I met the service manager I'd been speaking with and he sent one of his inspectors out to meet us. After she finished, there was only one line left on the three sheets of inspection paperwork she'd brought out.

During the inspection she even found several things we didn't know about. While she was looking at the bedroom slide, the storage tray under the bed fell apart, dropping its contents all over the floor. The tray damaged the base the mattress sits on while the slide moves in and out. Luckily that happened during the inspection because those both made her list. Also, two of their techs came out to fix the underbelly paneling since it was falling down. Turns out, Ken, the Brown Bandit, hadn't put it back on correctly.

After the inspection, the service manager said he felt so bad for us, that he wouldn't even charge us. He confirmed the wall could only be fixed at the factory. The manager said he wouldn't even attempt it, and also stated that any other shop would likely say the same thing.

We emailed Cedar Creek again and told them, again, that it was recommended by the inspector to go to their factory for repairs. Their response was laughable, at best. We were told that any Forest River authorized repair facility could fix it and to simply make an appointment with one.

Fine, whatever. Even though we had just been told the exact opposite, we started making calls. Every shop I spoke with said the same thing, they wouldn't touch that wall.

The repair facilities were worried about being able to fix it correctly. A term we used in the shop I worked at when we had to work on an old beater was that we didn't want to be "married to it." The idea is if you fix one thing but something else goes wrong the customer will claim it was your fault and you'll have to cover it out of pocket. And that can just go on forever. Because of that, some shops would rather not take on risky projects.

Again, we requested Cedar Creek to take our rig to the factory for repairs. Once again, they denied our request. Well, it wasn't really a denial as much as it was a game. They said it couldn't be fixed by them until November, and it was only March. Then we explained why we kept asking them to take it back, no one else would take it.

Cedar Creek responded with a list of EVERY SINGLE Forest River repair facility in the country. It was only a list of over 350 names. We didn't even know where to start. Gee, it sure would have been nice of them to narrow that down a hair first. Maybe by who's actually capable of fixing it? Just a thought.

After Cedar Creek sent the list to us, they immediately began stonewalling us. I highly suspected they knew it would have to be returned to be fixed. My hypothesis was this: they avoid and ignore the requests hoping the pesky customer will give up, go away, let them off the hook, and then never follow up again. Well, clearly, they hadn't been paying attention earlier.

We're probably two of the most stubborn people they've ever dealt with. After a few years in combat, I'd lost every ounce of tolerance for bullsh!t I was born with. Laura has a very strong never-say-die attitude from years of saving hundreds, if not thousands, of Fluffies and Rovers. I don't think we could have rolled over if we'd wanted to. (Seriously, our bodies may have protested with seizures or heart attacks if we'd tried.) We're nothing if not persistent.

Cedar Creek clearly underestimated our resolve. We knew they were ignoring us. Just a week or two earlier, when we were dealing with the sewer, we'd been talking by phone or email every few days. Then we reported the wall and they clammed up. Even worse, they clammed up when we only had about a month of factory warranty left.

Well, that was just fine with us.

Our reaction went something like this. (The following events have been dramatized for the purpose of entertainment, and because it's hilarious)

> *After the 20ᵗʰ time of trying to call Cedar Creek without anyone answering, we'd had it! We decided that drastic measures had to be taken so Laura grabbed her phone and called a friend in the White House.*
>
> *I went right to the kitchen where I cooked and ate two pounds of bacon while drinking a gallon of coffee. Why? Cause, 'Merica! Then I went outside to blow off some steam by arm wrestling a grizzly, and winning. To*

celebrate the win, I fired off a few thousand rounds while wearing an American flag as a cape.

The flag was blowing in the wind as Marine one landed behind me and it looked super cool. Trust me, I was there. Of course, killer rock music was playing from somewhere the whole time.

Actually, being that this is my fantasy, Metallica was there playing live. After the third encore they agreed the RV industry should produce higher quality rigs and have better customer service. Smart guys.

While I was talking to James, Laura was sitting down with the President to talk about the shoddy state of the RV industry (he came to see her of course). She convinced him to drop us off at the factory for a face-to-face on his way back to the White House.

We walked outside, through the field of brass, past Metallica (still playing of course), stepped over the crying grizzly cradling its broken arm and we all high fived on the way into Marine One.

During lift off, I saw the grizzly limping away into the woods. On our way to Indiana, we helped the President figure out some things with foreign policy, trade, immigration, taxes and I gave him some pointers about fighting in the Middle East.

When we arrived in Indiana, we had a sit down with the President and board of Forest River. We reminded them to focus on the customer instead of the shareholder. They agreed and gave us a new fully loaded RV for our troubles.

My memory may not be the best, but I'm pretty sure it went something like that...

Well, back in reality where none of that happened (too bad), we were freaking out a little. We were extremely worried the warranty would expire before we could get the wall, and several other items fixed.

Viewers Contact Us

After we posted the first Lemon RV video our views went through the roof! We'd never seen views or subscribers anywhere close, and we were inundated with comments from our new viewers. Most of them were angry for us or sharing their own horror stories. It turned out we weren't alone. Hundreds, if not thousands, of other RVers had been, or were being, taken advantage of by dealers and manufacturers, just as we were.

We learned so much, so fast our heads may have literally been spinning exorcist style. We're both typically skeptical people, but when so many people were telling us the same things over and over, we decided there may be a kernel of truth to their claims. Of course, I can't prove what those viewers told us. But if any of their claims were correct, then a lot of strange things about the RV industry begin to make sense.

Here are the main points:

- Warranty work can be written off as a loss on taxes for the manufacturers. But spending more money to build a better RV is just lost profit.

- Most manufacturers eliminated their quality control position on the factory floor after the market crashed in 2008. Apparently, it was slowing down production too much and costing them money. I guess building quality RVs was too much of a hassle.

- The average new RV owner only spends 28 days using their rig in the first year. It drops to 14 days for every year thereafter. If that's true, it leads me to believe those one-year warranties are a gamble. The manufactures gamble that no major problems will occur during the 28 days of use. Then, if something does break, the industry has some standard tactics to keep from having to fix it.

- The tactics we were told about.

  I. Say whatever's broken isn't their responsibility. They only installed the part (third party) and you have to talk to who made it.

  II. For motorized RV's, it's common to hear that you have to speak with whoever built the frame, drivetrain, living area, etc. No one will want to take responsibility.

  III. Manufacturers saying it's a dealer problem, and vice-versa. We spoke with one person who was forced to trap them, just to get her RV fixed. She called the manufacturer, then walked into the manager's office at the dealership. As both were simultaneously lying to her, saying it was the others responsibility, she put the call on speaker. The problem was fixed.

- RVs with obvious known problems will be rolled out of the factory and sent to a dealer for them to fix before selling. That was one tip where people didn't want to give their real names because they still worked in the industry. Given the quality issues with new RVs, I'm inclined to believe this may occur.

- Manufacturers only pay a percentage to dealers for warranty work. Those aren't non-profit shops. Dealers want to do the work that pays the most, which can put warranty work at the back of the line.

- Managers and executives at the manufacturers will often shuffle around every few years. Supposedly, it's so customers can't pass around their contact information easily.

- When you buy a new RV, the paperwork you sign waives your right to a court trial if there's a problem. You legally agree to not sue them in court. By signing your paperwork, you agree to arbitration. This one is REALLY sneaky. Arbitration keeps everything out of the public eye, lets them set the rules for how it'll be handled, and usually allows them to pick the arbitrators. I wonder who's side they'll be on? (Obviously contact an attorney if you have any legal questions. They can likely provide more clarity on this point.)

- There isn't a federal lemon law for non-motorized RVs. For motorized ones, it only covers the drive train. We were told by viewers that the RV industry spends millions of dollars on lobbyists to ensure that no lemon law is ever passed federally. However, there are a few states that have passed RV lemon laws, Texas is one of them. If you buy a lemon fifth wheel or travel trailer, don't expect legal help unless your state has a specific lemon law. We were told the manufacturers know this and build accordingly.

- There's no training standard for RV technicians like there is with vehicles. Most vehicle techs are Automotive Service Excellence (ASE) certified. RV repair centers can, and often do, hire people with no prior experience because they're cheap. Then the lack of required training keeps them cheap but undereducated. People wonder why repairs are often done poorly, and why there are often new problems when they receive their supposedly "fixed" RV.

- Techs at large national dealers were only given 1.5 hours to complete a PDI (pre-delivery inspection). There's no way they can check everything in that short time. Another reason to hire your own NRVIA certified inspector.

- One viewer who'd worked for a large national chain wrote in and said something to the effect of "to be a technician at **** you legitimately need NO certification and only minimal 'handyman' experience. While we did have a few trained/certified techs, many were not. We also had a high turn-over rate."

- Apparently, dealers know a lot of the RVs they're selling aren't in good condition. Then they say it'll take months and months to fix them after the purchase, which it could. All in the hopes the consumer will trade in their new RV, with a large depreciation, and buy a more expensive one. We've spoken with hundreds of people that have done just that at the recommendation of a dealer. Why does this scenario bother me so much?

    I.   The dealer gets two new sales and another used sale by being dishonest.

    II.   The average person buying a new RV is a senior citizen using their retirement and savings to finally travel after working 40 odd years. I hate it when people take advantage of the elderly.

    III. Several senior citizens told us they felt they had to trade in a new RV that needed many repairs. They didn't want to waste the time they had left to travel while they were still physically or mentally able to do so.

    IV.   Dealers are incentivized not to fix the broken RVs they're sent because of this whole mess. Which potentially leaves more people buying new broken RVs.

    V.   We were also told the broken RVs traded in often aren't fixed before they're sold. I wonder if those customers are told to trade in also? Finally, dealers often won't disclose why an RV was traded in, which can perpetuate the cycle.

Here's some homework for you. Go to a local dealer and ask how many 1-2-year-old RV's they have for sale which were traded in. Go look at the rigs to see if there's any obvious signs of use. I'd be willing to bet they're hardly used. Ask the dealer why they were traded in. I'll bet they say something like the people just didn't want them or they traded up to a more expensive rig. I'd also be willing to bet if you hired an inspector, he'd find major problems with most of them. Even if the problems were known to the previous owner, I highly doubt the dealer will disclose them. Used RVs are almost exclusively sold "as is," leaving the new owner to deal with any potential problems. This is why we tell people to hire an independent inspector.

- Lemon RV's can and may be replaced, at no cost to the owner, under the right circumstances. But it depends on whether or not you can make the stars align.

I want to expand on that last point. Approximately ten people contacted us using fake names (they told us such), all with nearly identical stories. Their RV had been a lemon, either the dealer or manufacturer couldn't or wouldn't fix it, the dealer/manufacturer messed up somehow (such as refusing to fix it or they tried and failed), each blamed the other, the owner hired a lawyer and went to arbitration. Step one of the resolution, signing a non-disclosure agreement (NDA) so they could never tell anyone what happened.

Suddenly we understood why we NEVER heard about anyone having a lemon RV replaced. The people in charge didn't want anyone to know replacement was even an option.

After hearing all these potentially terrible things about the RV industry we didn't know what to think. It all sounded terrible, but what could we do about any of it? If what we were told was true, then there wasn't anything we could do.

Obviously, we're not the types to roll over and take it. Instead, we went online in search of other owners that could possibly confirm what we'd been told.

When we first began talking about our problems online, we went to the Forest River Owners Group (FROG) website. We quickly found that any comments they didn't like, such as talking about our lemon, the terrible customer service, or poor build quality, were quickly deleted. I don't know why we ever thought bringing up those issues on a forum run by the company was a good idea. When we realized how they'd been controlling information with an iron fist, we decided it was a good time to crash their party.

We realized that, like us, other potential customers likely couldn't find honest reviews or find the help they needed. To fix the glaringly obvious problem we decided to start the Forest River Cedar Creek Owners' group on Facebook. We wanted a group where people could find the help they needed without their questions being deleted just because it looked bad for Forest River or Cedar Creek.

Little did we know, but there's a Cedar Creek cult following. The instant we said anything they viewed as negative, which was anything other than raving about how amazing Cedar Creek's are, they trolled us mercilessly. We were forced to kick out about 30 people in the first two months.

Every time we posted about a new thing breaking, which was almost weekly, they would come out of the woodwork. They had a standard list of comments for tearing down anyone who spoke up. Here are some of the more memorable comments:

- "You must new to RVing, better get used to things breaking."

- "I love my (fill in the blank), I've never had any problems with it." This would always be in response to someone asking how to diagnose or fix something. Rather than being helpful, the trolls felt compelled to harass someone just for trying to fix their RV. They would also clog up the response feed making it harder for the person trying to fix something to find the answer they needed.

- "You must not be maintaining your RV correctly. I've never had a problem with that."

- General vague derogatory remarks about our age. Apparently if you RV and you're under 40, your RV will break easier? We never understood those comments, but it was clear they were trying to insult us. Funny thing about that, to insult me, I must first value your opinion.

- "You'd better learn how to fix things yourself." It was under warranty, no I shouldn't be fixing it myself. Why would people be so quick to let the manufacturer off the hook?

We didn't let the trolls stop us from sharing our story though. The group has been fantastic ever since we cleared out the cult. Many owners have found the help they desperately needed to diagnose or fix their own Cedar Creek.

Around that same time, a man sent me a private message saying he was in the middle of winning a battle with Forest River. He was successfully suing them and wanted to help us. He wouldn't give me his personal information due to an NDA, but he did give me a list of personal phone numbers for several Forest River executives. His lawyer had received them, and they were absolutely not public knowledge. He was very specific about that last point.

He was so incredibly nervous when we spoke on the phone. It was clear he wanted to help us, but he also didn't want to jeopardize his deal. After profusely thanking and promising him that I wouldn't tell anyone who gave me the information, I called the first number on the list.

On the third call, someone answered. Although I'm sure he wishes he hadn't. I quickly gave him a brief description of the problem and how the warranty was about to end. He was very polite, agreed it was a problem, took down my information and said he'd have someone get back to me the next day. Right before we ended the call, he asked me a question.

"Where did you get my number from?"

I made up a story about finding it in some nameless online forum that I couldn't remember. He bought it, I think, and we hung up. I called that number again a few weeks later to thank him for his help, and it had been disconnected. That smelled fishy to me, like perhaps they don't want the little people to know their real numbers, so they don't have to deal with them. Guess I'll never really know.

Cedar Creek Calls Us!

The day after speaking with the mystery executive my phone rang. It was Cedar Creek's customer service manager. We'd spoken though email before, but this was different. He called me out of the blue for a little chat. I put him on speaker, so Laura could join in. The customer service rep we'd been trying to work with was with him taking notes, so that she could better help us later on.

I explained our concerns about completing the work before the warranty expired. That was all we really cared about. He promised us they would fix our current list, and anything else that came up before we could get it into an authorized Forest River repair facility. What was really telling about the surprise call is what he said before we hung up. It was something to the effect of, "please only call us to deal with this."

That statement really tipped their hand. Whoever that executive was I'd called likely wasn't happy that I'd called him. I suspect he hung up from me and made a few calls telling people to make us happy, so we'd go away.

The customer service rep said she'd begin working more closely with us. As for any new problems, we just needed to email her pictures and descriptions of them as she was going to start a running list.

After hanging up, I think we hugged and even cried a little, I don't really remember. Anyway, once we knew they'd cover it we went back to calling shops. We wanted to do a national parks tour ending in Washington state to see my family, so I began by called shops near them.

When I called the Camping World near my family, they said they could fix the wall, and everything else on the list! They could get us in mid-June, three months out. We made the appointment and probably cried some more.

It couldn't have been more perfect. The timing was correct for us to do the trip we wanted, and it was exactly where we were headed. Then my mom said we could stay in my Grandma's house while the RV was being repaired. The "Hebard Luck" had struck again in a BIG way. Everything lined up so perfectly it's almost as if we had someone looking out for us.

I emailed Cedar Creek and told them about the appointment. Our rep said she would update the Camping World service manager about our list during the coming months so that we wouldn't have to deal with multiple parties. Our warranty had been effectively extended by two months. Apparently, all our problems had been solved!

Our Lessons Learned from Having a Lemon RV

If you have an RV, you know things break. If you don't own one yet, you will likely learn this lesson soon after buying one. Sadly, most owners learn the hard way. After living in it for 10 months, but only being on the road for five of them, we never thought so many things could go wrong.

Before we bought our fifth wheel, we'd seen very few videos of people talking about how all kinds of things were breaking and needing repairs. Also, we'd only read a few blogs about how new owners need to expect things to break, or to not even work at all. Because we only saw a handful of people talking about it, we thought it wasn't a common problem. And having never owned an RV before we'd never experienced it firsthand.

Inevitably, whenever we posted something about it falling apart or having problems the trolls would chime in. Those comments always rubbed us the wrong way. How and why can that mindset ever be normal?

HOW!?!?!

Imagine if buying a new car, refrigerator, computer, or hearing aids was the same. If they just broke or fell apart for no reason after a few months, or were commonly constructed poorly? There would be riots in the streets and I believe the rioters would be justified. But for some ungodly reason it's just accepted that RV's fall apart or are poorly built. I believe if people stopped accepting poor quality as "normal" things would change.

We thought we were going into RV ownership with our eyes wide open. Oh boy were we WRONG! Remember what I said about learning the hard way? Well let me explain. We had this ridiculous notion that if we were just careful that everything would be fine. We knew the build quality wasn't the same as a home, and that you can't be rough on things. However, we never considered that no matter how careful we were, it wouldn't matter.

No amount of being careful would have prevented a weld in our kitchen slide from breaking, or most of the LED lights from burning out in the first couple of months, or an exterior wall separating from the studs.

I have several points of advice that could save RVers a lot of headaches.

1. If you're buying an RV, DO NOT plan on moving straight into it. Just in case that wasn't clear, never ever, unless a natural disaster destroyed your home, move into an untested RV. I don't care if it's custom ordered from the factory or if it's your best friend's and he takes perfect care of it and stores it in a big RV garage. You need a buffer, of preferably a few months, to find the kinks. I promise you there are kinks. But people will say, "It's new and everything is under warranty......" That's them trailing off when they realize that it can take months, MONTHS, to get parts. It's not like cars where you can buy parts from 20 stores in town. And if it's your friends, either there's stuff wrong he doesn't know about, or there's something about to break. You need someplace else to sleep in case your new home on wheels isn't so homey right away. Several people have told us they sold their home with no buffer and were forced to stay with family, friends or hotels for months until it was fixed.

2. Yes, everything can, and could very well, break. But fear not if your RV is under warranty. There's this handy device most of us have in our pockets or purses that takes pictures. These pictures are what's going to save your wallet. With them, you can prove to the manufacture/dealer that what you say is broken, is actually broken. We commonly hear people say they took their RV into the shop and the techs couldn't find the problem. If you see a problem don't assume it will be the

same or even present when the tech inspects it. Same goes for your car.

3. You don't have to put your RV in a shop for months (usually). Email the manufacturer, show them what's wrong, directly request authorization for a mobile tech to come to you and do the repairs. This is what we did, and it kept us from having our house in the shop for months at a time. That authorization process is vital. Without having that upfront, they can possibly choose to not reimburse you. It's basically the equivalent of a bad date "going to the bathroom" and leaving you to foot the bill.

4. Options for warranty repairs:

   - Taking it to the dealer and leaving it there for a good portion of the year so your brand-new home can sit on the lot and rot untouched while they wait on parts and fail to update you on the non-existent progress. Of course, not all shops are like that. That's more of a worst-case scenario. Sadly, we've heard that exact story from viewers so many times there's no way it's the exception.

   - Find an independent shop to do the work. The speed difference between independent shops vs dealers will be the rough equivalent of a Ferrari vs a Prius. There's just one little issue with getting that fast work, the independent shops want to be paid upfront. They don't want to deal with the manufactures several month delay for reimbursement. That's fine if you're retired and have a sizeable bank account you've built up over 40 years. Unfortunately, for many of us that's not the case. Repairs go on whatever credit card isn't currently maxed out, and we hope and pray the manufacturer sends the reimbursement check before we get sent to collections. That fast work is like a bad ex. You know it's fast and fun, but you'll pay for it. That crazy ex may even try to take your dog.

- The third option is to have a mobile tech come to you. Again, make sure to obtain prior authorization. The difference is they come to you and repairs will likely be completed even faster. Although, mobile techs won't be able to repair as much as a shop due to the limitations of what they can bring with them. Again, they expect you to pay upfront because they know the RV warranty reimbursement program works at a snail's pace.

5. Regardless of what breaks, who fixes it, or how minor the problem is, DOCUMENT EVERYTHING. You need a cache of pictures, video, and documents that would make the NSA jealous. Manufacturer warranties usually last just one year, although some companies give two or three years. If you have a problem outside of that period, and think they're responsible, you'd better be able to prove it.

6. TEST YOUR RV!!! Test it the first night you get it and test it often. If you haven't set foot in it for months and then suddenly take it out for a week, that's when you're going to find your

problems. Periodic dry runs can save you a lot of headaches, and let you enjoy your vacation. Take your RV out often and try to find the problems, especially if it's under warranty. Check everything like you're buying it again. People buy RVs to get away, to actually enjoy life and not just stay chained to a desk. They want to experience something other than over-hyped tourist traps on their two weeks of vacation a year. People buy RVs to make the boring parts of life bearable. So, the last thing they need is to finally get that three-day weekend, escape from work a few hours early, throw the family, dog, and some firewood in their RV, get to the campground only to find that something's broken, and they get to spend their precious vacation trying to fix it. That's how people get addicted to Xanax.

7. Remember to stay calm. Unless an electrical short burns it down, a slide falls out, or the black tank overflows inside, it's probably not a vacation killer. Build a campfire, make s'mores, have an adult beverage or two, and schedule someone to look at it when you get home. You're on vacation, remember? Hopefully nothing on the above list ever happens to anyone, ever. Not even if they're in your opposing political party.

If you buy an RV and expect everything to break, you'll be happy when only a few things do. But the flip side is getting angry over everything that goes wrong. Pick your battles and remember to have fun out there. Isn't that why you bought an RV in the first place?

20

How We Kept Our Sanity

If you read that last chapter and wondered how we didn't literally go insane, I'll explain it now.

Even though we were dealing all the ridiculous warranty and repair problems, we were still living the full-time RV life. And remember, we'd only been on the road a few months. So, we still wanted to go adventuring every week and enjoy our new-found freedom. We were constantly making plans to go do and see things.

1. We planned our National Parks road trip.

This was our main sanity retainer. We spent weeks going through national parks books Laura had bought in preparation for the trip, blog posts and various YouTube videos. We planned the kind of trip most people only dream about. We had about two months of travel time before we had to drop the RV off. That gave us all the time we needed to go and see what we wanted to. We thoroughly enjoyed the planning process, and it gave us a break from the issues we were dealing with.

2. We explored the local area at least once a week.

Sitting around waiting for the epic trip to Washington was torture. We had serious cabin fever and we couldn't leave until April when the weather was better. The next best thing was exploring the area around us. Aside from finding a lot of interesting places it also gave us plenty of opportunities to film and learn more about filming. Granted, we burned a lot of diesel with all that exploring, but it was worth it.

3. We went to the lake and let the dogs play.

This was part of our exploring. We went to the lake several times and the dogs loved it. They're very different swimmers though. Bullet is a lab so he's technically a fish out of water. When you let him off leash, he closes the distance between himself and the water as fast as physically possible. Kimber, on the other hand, is quite dainty about swimming. She never wants to get her face wet, and she just wants to stand on the rocks and watch the water. She'd rather walk or swim from rock to rock.

4. We took the dogs on daily long walks.

That was good for them and us. Part of the reason we did so much walking was because we were trying to get back into hiking shape. We knew we'd want to go hiking during our national parks trip and we were nowhere close to where we needed to be to hike any meaningful distance. Thank God we did prepare a little, it ends up being very important later.

5. We went sightseeing at local caves and a safari experience.

They were so much fun! I'd never been in caves before. There's something mysterious and almost magical about them. Your imagination can really run wild underground. I'll bet I could come up with some excellent fiction plots if I went and just sat in a cave for a few hours.

The safari was so much fun we drove through it twice. When we bought our tickets, they gave us a bag of food to feed the animals. Then we drove through a park full of African animals that all know vehicles mean food. Have you ever had a full-grown ostrich stick its head though your window? We have, and that head really filled the space between me and the windshield. It was incredible. Well, except for the ostrich drool. At least that cleaned up easily. We enjoyed making that video.

6. We found a fabulous restaurant, thanks to a viewer's recommendation.

At the time, we only had around 200 subscribers on our YouTube channel. It was the first time anyone had written in and suggested we go somewhere or try something we were actually close enough to do. They'd seen a few of our videos around Canyon Lake and knew the area well. They wrote us saying that we needed to eat at a restaurant called Granny D's.

I'll admit, it was a little strange having a fan that wanted to tell us about their favorite place to eat, and we could go eat there too. Thankfully we listened to their advice. The food was so good it was hard to comprehend why the prices weren't several times higher. We ate there 4-5 (or 10, I don't know) times before we left. We tried breakfast, lunch and dinner and never ordered anything less than outstanding. We still talk about it.

7. We conducted our first round of downsizing since we'd been on the road.

We went through literally everything we had, made a sale pile, and I set up a yard sale in the RV park. We needed to shed a lot of weight, and items we simply didn't use. We had been storing things in the back of Laura's SUV and the backseat of the truck and it was driving us both crazy. We had decided to sell her SUV and had to clear out enough space so the dogs could ride in the truck.

The yard sale didn't fare well, so we Ebayed and pawned the leftovers.

8. I got to meet up with another friend from the army.

This friend was the driver in my truck for the last 4-5 months of my third deployment. We probably sat together in that truck for over 1,000 hours. It was the first chance we'd had to see each other in 10 years. He drove down, and we hung out for a day, I wish it could have been a week.

People say you make lifelong friends and form a bond in combat, and they're right. Your background, color, religion, political affiliation or any other stupid qualifier didn't matter. We bonded in combat because we had to. But beyond being forced to live and work together, we shared so much.....LIFE together that it was hard not to become friends. I love how RVing has allowed me to reconnect with some of them.

Meho, Torres, Nunez, if you're reading this, I'm SO HAPPY we got to meet up. I can't wait to do it again. To all the guys I've missed so far, I hope we can hang out soon.

9. I finally learned how to use our filming gear, mostly.

I got a lot of drone practice in and finally began to feel comfortable flying it. Also, Laura bought me a set of neutral density (or ND) lens filters for the drone that made the footage look much better. I also began to learn about angles, lighting and setting up shots. Although, we still didn't learn how to use the DSLR. That mistake bites me in the butt later. Don't procrastinate, learn how to use your equipment.

10. I found and split about a cord of firewood and we had tons of campfires.

The RV park had cut down a tree at some point and left the rounds lying in the grass. I asked and found the park management didn't want it and didn't care if I took it. I bought an axe, hauled two truckloads back to the RV, and split wood for several days. I ended up with a wood pile probably 4' tall and 8' long when I finished.

My dad owned a tree service. So, I grew up with a wood stove and splitting wood. There's something very therapeutic about splitting wood, it's hands down the best stress reliever for me. The wonderful side effect is the exercise, hand eye coordination, and the fires of course. I was dumping the ash out of our fire pit every other day. I sold some of the wood, gave some away, took some with us and left the rest behind to fuel someone else's vacation.

I sold my dad's axe during the estate sale before we moved into the RV. It's one of the greatest regrets in my life. If you bought an axe with a red head on a light wooden handle from an estate sale during May 2016 in Overland Park, KS I'd really like to speak with you. Please email me.

11. We sold Laura's Escape to fund the trip up north.

We knew we had to sell her SUV to fund the trip, but Laura wasn't happy about it. It was the first nice vehicle she'd ever had, and she loved it. If she kept it though, we couldn't ride in the truck together or film on travel days, we would have to continue finding extra parking in RV parks, and it was adding 30-40% to our fuel costs on travel days. We finally decided that selling it was the best option. Although it needed some work before we could list it.

Driving it for Uber had taken a toll. It needed new front brakes, even though I didn't realize it. Laura had been complaining about a high-pitched squeal when braking for a while, but I couldn't hear it. That's when I learned that I did, in fact, have some hearing loss from combat. I had no idea what "squeal" she was talking about. I wonder how many Uber passengers were cringing every time I braked?

Anyway, I put new pads and rotors on the front, cleaned the fuel system, fixed some cracks in the windshield, changed the oil and listed it for sale. After a few horrible low-ball offers we were running out of time and began to think we'd have to take it with us again. With only a few weeks left, a young woman contacted me out of the blue wanting to look at it. She lived over an hour away and was willing to meet halfway, which was very courteous of her. She brought the standard, "I know cars" friend to look it over. He gave her the OK and she wanted to buy that day.

I wish we'd known she was that motivated because I left Laura and the truck at the RV. I had to go back, get Laura and the title, then we both drove to San Antonio and met her at her bank where we received a cashier's check for just $500 less than our asking price. It worked out so perfectly that it could possibly fall under Hebard Luck.

12. We stepped up our YouTube channel by making several videos per week.

During our time in Canyon Lake we made some big changes to our YouTube channel. Thanks to all the research Laura had done while in Houston she was full of ideas for YouTube and the blog. We began to put them into play and saw some nice growth in return.

That was the first time we tried to implement a filming schedule. We decided to put out 2-3 videos a week. In reality it wasn't that clean, but we began to finally feel like we were getting our feet under us filming-wise. We paid for Adobe Premiere Elements 15 video editing software and Laura's editing skills took off like a rocket.

We'd suspected the laptop wasn't cutting it for video editing, but when we got the new software it was confirmed. Every time we tried to make a video, it would crash several times. Through some research, I determined the main cause was slow disk speed. After watching some YouTube videos, I cracked a computer open for the first time ever and replaced the hard drive with a solid-state drive (SSD). It worked much better after that

> *I wrote this book on that same computer. Upgrading the hard drive taught me there's nothing scary about opening a computer. I had to open it again and replace the fan a few months after installing the SSD. I felt completely confident the second time.*

Suddenly our videos began to look much more like the other YouTubers we were watching, instead of like home movies from a 90's camcorder. We felt we were learning new lessons and improving on every video we created.

I still remember those filming lessons today. Well most of them anyway. I think filming is called shooting for a reason. To be good at either there's a list of things you must know how to do, and know how to do them simultaneously, if you want to be any good at either. It's easy to forget a step and receive subpar results, I still do it sometimes. For some stupid reason I keep forgetting to adjust the white balance more often than not.

13. We attended our first large RV show.

We'd been to the small RV show in Overland Park, Kansas before we bought ours, but it was nothing like the Austin show. Austin was easily 20 times larger.

The show was an hour away so that only gave us six hours to look around before we had to head back for the dogs. Six hours wasn't nearly enough time, but we still enjoyed it. We'd never had the chance to walk through so many different RVs before, especially without a pushy salesman hounding us the entire time. Sure, there were other people walking through them, but we had the freedom to browse at our leisure. If we found one we liked we could just sit down in the recliners and talk about it.

Here are some important things we learned while there.

- Dealers are highly motivated to sell the units they take to shows. After all the foot traffic through them they'll be very hard to sell later. So, you can possibly negotiate a fantastic deal.

- If you do find one you like, request to buy the same model at the show price, but not the one at the show. You don't want to buy one that's just had 10,000 people walking through it breaking stuff. Maybe they'll agree, maybe not, it's worth a shot.

- You'll find the best deals on the last day of the show because they don't want to take them back to the dealership. Although you'll likely have to buy the RV at the show, you could, again, get a great deal.

- You can meet a lot of wonderful people. Don't be afraid to strike up some conversations and see where they go.

- If you want to film review videos, RV shows are a great place to do them without a salesman hovering over your shoulder the whole time. You won't get a ton of uninterrupted time, especially if it's a popular RV. We did find it easier than filming at dealerships though. We filmed several different rigs in one day and had videos for a few weeks.

14. Bullet went cliff jumping.

This only made the list because it was too crazy to leave out.

Now it's not like we took him to a cliff and pushed him off, far from it. We were walking the dogs on a path around the lake because we were trying to find a way down for them to go swimming. At one point we came to a ledge about 4-5' tall with no clear path around it. It looked like people had just been climbing up and down. We were trying to figure out how to get Bullet down when he apparently became impatient and found his own way down, by way of going airborne.

I didn't have his leash locked because why in the world would he jump off the cliff? He'd never done anything like that before, so it didn't cross my mind as a possibility. He's not a puppy anymore, but don't tell him that. He put his knees in the breeze and took a flying leap of faith off that cliff like he'd be landing in a 1980's ball pit.

He hit the ground several feet away from the base of the ledge. When he landed all his legs collapsed, and he slid another foot on his chest and chin in the dirt and rocks. We climbed down as fast as possible, seriously worried about him.

Laura checked him over but couldn't find any signs of injury, luckily for him and us. We didn't exactly have the money to pay for surgery if he had seriously injured himself. He was stunned, and slow to get up, but thankfully didn't have to be carried back. He looked more confused than anything. I can imagine him asking why he can't just jump off a cliff. We called off swimming that particular day and went back later. I'm happy to say that time Bullet made it swimming with no cliff jumping.

I think the main trick to not losing our minds was simply keeping busy. We hardly had a spare minute those two months, during the day at least, to sit around and worry. We packed our days so full of adventures and work that we were beat by the evening. And with all the firewood is was easy to relax around a fire.

21

The Adventure Begins

The plans for this trip were exactly what we had envisioned RVing would be like. We scheduled the trip perfectly. We had planned multiple stops, near or in, national parks from Texas all the way up to Washington. We calculated mileage to determine how long drive days would be and planned our stops accordingly to keep drive days less than six hours. We reserved RV parks at each place we wanted to stay. We calculated the costs of fuel and RV parks to ensure we had enough money to complete the trip.

All this planning was completed before we left Texas. We'd been wanting to take a trip like it for over a year and could barely hold back our excitement. So, it should come as no surprise to hear we chose to leave a day early again.

The departure date was set by when the monthly rent at the RV park was up, just like in Kansas, but when we were sitting there with everything ready, why would we stay the extra day? So we just left. We considered swinging through Big Bend National Park on our way out of Texas. However, after doing the math, we realized it would add a few hundred dollars in fuel to our trip, so we scratched the idea.

We stopped at a Walmart in Fort Stockton, TX that first night. We chose it because there's not really anyplace else to stop on I-10 in western Texas, plus that's where our route to New Mexico detoured north from I-10 as well. What followed was one of our most interesting Waldocking nights ever.

Shortly after I returned from speaking with a manager to ensure we could overnight, a small S-10 truck pulled up next to us. Considering we were on the edge of the parking lot, and a long way from the entrance, we both thought it was very odd. Oh, but it gets better.

The kid in the truck immediately began removing several storage totes from the bed. Next, he unrolled a tarp, laid it out on the pavement in front of his truck and set totes on the corners to hold it down as it was windy. He'd clearly done this before. Then he pulled a tent from one tote and set it up in a few minutes. After it was up, he moved all the totes inside the tent, probably to hold it down. Finally, he pulled an army cot out of the truck, assembled it, and put it inside the tent.

Yes, it was very strange. But the annoying part was that he set up directly next to the bedroom window at the foot of our bed and didn't close the tent flap. It was warm that night, so we needed the window open and max air ceiling fan on to make it tolerable inside. When the slides are in the only place we can sit together is the bedroom. But every time we started talking, he'd stare at the window. It was kind of creepy.

After a bit he went inside Walmart, so I fired up the truck and moved us back as far as I could, about 10 feet. I didn't want to be rude and ask him to move his whole set up away from our window, so I just moved the window. When he returned, we had to hold back our laughter. He just stood there looking back and forth at our rig and his tent for a solid two minutes. I don't know what he was thinking, but he finally went back in his tent. Maybe he set up so close to use us as a wind or light block? If that was the case, he still had the truck next to him. I don't know. He was still in the tent the next morning as we left.

We took Highway 285 NW from there towards Carlsbad. That was one of the roughest roads we've ever been on. The entire Texas section we drove was terribly beat up, probably because it's oil country. We were passing massive oil operations, and trucks hauling their giant machinery, all day. To top it off, it was a 65mph road with hardly any shoulder and oncoming traffic in the next lane.

I had been feeling confident in my towing skills before that road. Within a few hours my nerves were fried, and Laura was ready to quit for the day, but there was no place to stop until we left oil country. Although, we were forced to find a place to stop when Laura's bike fell off the roof.

Yeah, I wish I was kidding.

While going 60 mph, her bike fell out of the rack and slammed into the side of the truck. It was a wheel-off rack, meaning the front wheel is removed and the bike is held by the front forks. Without the tire to cushion the blow we were very lucky it didn't break Laura's window, but it did scare the hell out of us.

I immediately pulled over onto the "shoulder" as far as I could, but it still left a solid foot of the RV and truck in the lane of traffic. After several minutes there was a break in traffic and I jumped out. Laura couldn't really open her door because of the whole "bike hanging off the side of the truck" thing.

Thankfully, Laura had insisted on using bike locks around the racks and bikes to prevent theft. Well, turns out it also prevented the bike from falling on the road and getting run over. I undid the lock and pulled the bike down. Immediately I saw the front forks had bent and I knew I couldn't get it back on the rack. So, I chucked it in the fifth wheel, we got back on the road and off the edge of it.

When we got going again, Laura surprised the crap out of me by telling me how she'd had a nightmare the previous evening of the bike falling off the roof of the truck. Luckily, when it actually happened, it didn't smash the window and kill Kimber like in her dream. When we finally arrived at the RV park outside of the caves, we received another surprise.

Carlsbad, New Mexico

Our first destination was White's City, just outside of Carlsbad, New Mexico. We made that the first destination because of the Carlsbad caverns. We'd called the park the day before to ensure we

211

could arrive a day early. I was told to just show up, no reservation needed, and that they were never full. That was obviously too good to be true, I shouldn't have trusted it.

When we pulled up, the signs were terribly confusing. After figuring out where the "office" was I got another surprise. It was actually a gift shop. The girls running the registers were also the people that checked RVers into the park, and they didn't know anything about the RV park. Fun times.

The girls didn't know which spots were vacant, or even which ones had full hookups. After they'd pulled out several maps they couldn't read, I finally told them I'd just drive around the park, find a spot, and come back to tell them which one I picked. They agreed to it and I happily left.

I walked back to the truck and told Laura what was going on, then I dropped the trailer in the parking lot and we scouted the park. I'd say it was tight, but that's a terrible understatement. I had a hard time on a few turns with just the truck. When we realized we couldn't get our trailer in there Laura began calling other parks in the Carlsbad area, about 30 minutes away. Luckily, she found one before I was even done hooking back up.

It turned out to be a brand-new park named Bud's Place, only open a few months. Not surprisingly, they were almost full. It's the only park we've stayed in where every single spot was an easily accessible pull-though, had free actual high-speed WIFI, there was enough space between RVs for everyone to put out their awnings and every turn was built for long trailers. If only more RV parks were built with RVs in mind, hmmm.....

I spent most of our first day there on the phone trying to get the bike warrantied or fixed, all to no avail. The bike's manufacturer chalked it up to user error. The bike rack manufacturer also claimed user error. They both said the cross pin that clamped through the front forks wasn't tightened down enough. That allowed for vibration which eventually led to the fork bending and pulling off the pin. The pin was still locked in the rack when the bike fell. I'm sure all those oncoming semis hitting us with their wind didn't help.

Since we couldn't do anything else with the bike, we continued on with our road trip of a lifetime. The next day we went to see Carlsbad Caverns. We'd done a lot of research and had planned what portion of the caves we would visit. I highly recommend doing the same, you could easily spend two days only walking through the touristy areas.

While there, I finally got my National Parks Access Pass. Since I'm a disabled veteran I took my paperwork with me and one of the rangers was able to issue the pass. I'd called ahead to ensure they could issue it first since not every national park can. With that pass I can now enter national parks, monuments, etc. for free. Camping isn't free in most of them, but it's usually heavily discounted. At least I won't get charged an entry fee for the truck, RV, or anyone in the vehicle. It's saved us a lot of money so far.

We decided to skip the 1.2 mile walk down the natural entrance and opted to take the elevator down the 750'. Riding an elevator from the 50's down 750' kinda felt like we were going down into some old fallout shelter or secret government facility. Then walking out of it into a dimly lit giant cave complex just reinforced that feeling.

I really think I should sit in a cave and write someday.
Something about it just ignites my imagination.

We briefly considered walking down the natural entrance, but we knew that if we did then we wouldn't be up for another few miles of walking the big cave rooms. Also, we couldn't leave the dogs long enough to do it all at once.

The elevators are really neat. There're two sets that were built 20 years apart. The primary set was built in 1932 with the secondary set built in 1955, both sets were overhauled in the 70's. Little did we know when we planned our trip, but they had been having problems with them. From November 15 through May 16 they had no working elevators.

When we arrived, they'd had the secondary set running for maybe a week. The rangers were clearly excited about them working again. I'm sure they were becoming tired of walking the natural entrance every shift. They told us there was no end date to have the primary set running. They've since fixed them.

Neither of us had ever been in a large cave before. The one near Canyon Lake could have fit in there several times over. If you've never been to the Carlsbad Caverns there's miles and miles of paved paths, ceilings so high you can hardly see them, and breathtaking views every few feet. There are even several sections you can only view on ranger led tours to protect the delicate formations. We learned they're still exploring the cave complex after almost a century of it being a national park. They still don't know how big it is.

We really want to go back someday and see the other portions we missed. We also need to go back during the right time of the year to see the sunset bat flight. The rangers told us it's the largest in the world. They even have amphitheater style seating built all around the cave's entrance so that people can watch the bat flight. Oh well, next time.

The next day I was walking the dogs in the RV park near sunset. It was a fairly warm and windy day and there was a lot of sand in the air which makes for beautiful sunsets. While walking them to the edge of the park I was thinking about how it felt very reminiscent of the Middle East. Then out of nowhere a gust of wind blew through the park pushing a little wall of sand ahead of it. As the sand reached me, I was suddenly transported back to Iraq.

Great, another flashback. Because that's what I need while standing in the middle of a road. Sigh....

I knew I wasn't really in Iraq, I knew it was a flashback, but that didn't change anything. I stood there a few minutes, looking around me, because I no longer saw the RV park. Instead, I was seeing some random street in Iraq. It was even complete with the one-foot margins of trash smashed up against each curb. There were walled off cinder block homes lining both sides of the deserted street. The trash was even moving a bit in the wind. After several minutes of standing alone in the middle of that Iraqi street wondering how long it would last, I finally snapped back to reality.

The dogs were both still standing next to me just sniffing the wind. We finished the walk while I tried to ground myself in reality. It had been several years since I'd had a flashback and it caught me off guard badly. But I just stood in the same spot and waited for it to pass, which luckily it did.

> *I think the key to dealing with flashbacks is to stay calm. I've had a few over the years and did the same thing every time. I stayed calm, reminded myself that what I was seeing wasn't real, and waited for it to pass. I know they don't last forever, or even very long usually. I feel it's important to stay calm and stay put. You don't want to go walking out into traffic or something. I'm probably lucky that I don't relive anything traumatic during flashbacks. I know not everyone is.*

While in Carlsbad we also visited the Living Desert Zoo and Gardens State Park. It's on top of a hill that overlooks Carlsbad, and the view is spectacular. We really wanted to film a sunrise time-lapse from up there. Unfortunately, every morning after that until we left was cloudy. I'm always hunting for cool time-lapse opportunities.

But back to the zoo...you need to show up early, like when they open. The employees at the zoo confirmed what we'd read on Google, the animals don't like hanging out in the afternoon heat. We arrived right as they opened and saw about everything: eagles, hawks, bobcats, elk, bison, wolves, snakes, black bear, a fox, prairie dogs, antelope, even a mountain lion. They chose animals that are all indigenous to the area.

Along with the animals there's also the Living Desert side of the park. Everywhere you walk there are different species of desert plants, and they're not all just cacti. The crown jewel of the park is the

Succulents of the World building. Inside you'll find a pleasant 120-degree environment filled with thriving desert plants. You really should brave the heat and go inside. They have a hibiscus that's half the size of our fifth wheel! And it smelled AMAZING in there. I wish I could have bottled that smell.

White Sands National Monument, New Mexico

After our week in Carlsbad, we spent a few days in Alamogordo, New Mexico, or as we like to call it, Pistachio Land. Directly across the street from our RV park was the world's largest pistachio. It wasn't real of course, but it's almost two stories tall and an easy landmark. There were several pistachio farms and wineries within five minutes of where we were staying so we stocked up on fresh pistachios and some excellent small batch wines.

During our time there we spent a morning at the sand dunes. I bought a sled at the visitor's center and......tried to sled the dunes. After several failed attempts, and a lot of wax, I realized I was just too heavy for normal sit-down-and-push-off sledding, so I got smart. I cooked up an idea so brilliant I should have asked someone to hold my beer. I placed the sled at the edge of a tall steep dune, walked about 20' back, got a running start, leapt from my feet, aimed my butt at the sled, perfectly made contact, promptly bounced off and flew over the edge of the dune, and then I uncontrollably rolled halfway down. Thank God no one was filming, oh wait....

We made a video about it if you really want to watch me fail miserably. I think that part made it in.

217

After I realized that I was too heavy to sled the dunes we found some kids without a sled, and a very exhausted looking mother, to give the sled to. That was far more valuable than the $5 return fee. The mother was incredibly thankful. I'm sure the kids were too, and I just couldn't hear them as they were already flying down the dune before I had even walked away.

On our way home from the dunes we saw signs for the New Mexico Museum of Space History. Well, we couldn't pass that up and decided to stop. We learned about how the American rocket program was pioneered in White Sands and how they tested the first nuclear bomb near there. If you get the chance to go, it's a small museum, but very informative. They also have a planetarium and IMAX with several excellent space shows.

While doing some Google Earth research on the dunes, Laura found something strange just north of them. There's a long black strip of land. We couldn't figure out what it was at first until Laura discovered an article about a 5000-year-old lava flow north of White Sands. And our route to Albuquerque was going to take us right through the middle of it. We could see on Google that there were pull-offs on each side of the road. So, before we went to bed, we charged up the cameras, GoPro, and drone batteries for a long day of filming.

We left early the next day and gave ourselves plenty of time to explore the lava flow. We stopped for an hour or so and had an experience I thought would never happen. We got to walk through a field of lava! I put the drone up and shot about 20 minutes of video then grabbed the DSLR and walked out into the lava field to try and capture the stark beauty of the area. I was surprised to find beautiful flowering plants growing out of the lava. We didn't see them anywhere else in New Mexico. After we had our fill of lava we got back on the road.

Albuquerque, New Mexico

I have many relatives in the Albuquerque area, and we were able to stop over Easter weekend and see them. That excitement was reigned in quickly though. Halfway through the day's drive there, Laura began to feel sick. She looked up the symptoms and they perfectly matched altitude sickness.

Laura grew up in Kansas where the average elevation is around 1000 feet, and she'd rarely traveled anywhere with higher elevation. When she found herself at five times that height her body just couldn't adapt. All weekend her lips were blue, she was exhausted, had a terrible headache and no appetite. She could hardly get out of bed.

We researched how to get over altitude sickness and found a few simple things we could immediately implement. WebMD recommended acetaminophen or ibuprofen, plenty of water and rest, and no alcohol.

The worst part of her being sick was missing Easter dinner. My uncle is an excellent cook and certainly didn't hold back that evening. I took Laura a giant plate of leftovers.

I had a lot of fun visiting with my family that weekend. We had lunch Saturday and dinner Sunday night. I spent the rest of the time at the RV taking care of Laura. I'd experienced a little bit of altitude sickness before, but nothing like what she was going through.

While there, I picked up a new accessory for the RV, an external pull-handle waste valve. That's because when I pulled the sewer cap off at the RV park a bunch of black tank "stuff" spilled out. The new black tank valve was already failing. Luckily, there was a Camping World a few minutes away and they had the external valve in stock.

If you don't already have an external valve, I highly recommend it. If you have an internal valve fail the external will allow you to still remove the cap and hook up a hose, all while preventing a mini biohazard at your campsite. Well worth the $20.

Taos, New Mexico

In light of Laura's altitude sickness, going to Taos was probably a bad idea. However, she was feeling better by the time we left Albuquerque, so we stuck with the plan. We didn't want to stay there longer anyway. Albuquerque has the highest vehicle theft rate of any city in the country. Considering we can't move our house without the truck we were right to be cautious.

In one day, we drove to an RV park just outside of Taos, another 3000 feet in elevation, and all Laura's progress was reset. We chose to visit Taos because my cousin, from the same family in Albuquerque, lives there with his family. It had been several years since I'd seen him. Sadly, I don't think his kids remembered me. I need to spend more time with family. RVing has a strange effect with family. We spend less time with our immediate family but more time with our extended relatives.

Laura's altitude sickness was far worse there, she was forced to spend the first few days in bed. It was affecting me slightly as well, and I noticed I needed to drink more water and sleep a bit longer. I felt bad about leaving her, but I hadn't seen my cousin in years, so I spent a few days with him and his family.

We cleaned out some prairie dogs on his old property, I fixed something on his truck, and we just caught up on each other's lives. We've always gotten along well, but never lived close. So, catching up every five years is normal for us.

When Laura was finally feeling better, we visited the Taos Gorge. At 800' deep it's tough to comprehend what you're seeing at first. What really surprised us were the anti-suicide signs and emergency phones located along both sides of the bridge. Apparently, it's a problem there.

The next day Laura was feeling even better so we decided to drive the Enchanted Circle. It's an 83-mile loop that circles a large cluster of mountains, mesas, valleys and national forests. We saw truly breathtaking scenery on that trip, and tons of wildlife including a group of Bighorn Sheep within a few miles of us starting.

There was some poor planning involved for that trip though. We weren't using the RV GPS because of all the RV restrictions programmed in. Instead, we were using google maps and we lost signal right around the time we needed to turn. I don't know how far north we accidentally drove, but we saw a sign for Colorado before we finally turned around. Oops.

Other poor planning took place as well in the form of me not thinking the elevation may change during the trip. There was a small, tiny, almost imperceptible elevation gain of a mere....5000 feet. Even I felt that one, especially since we went up and down in a matter of a

221

few hours. I felt so bad for Laura. She seemed to be doing ok, but I know she was just putting on a brave face. I was having a hard time breathing at the 12,000' mark. I could only imagine how she was feeling.

Some of the roads in the Circle are quite curvy and narrow. If you have an RV over 25' you'll be much better off parking it and driving something smaller. There were a few corners I had to use half of the other lane with just the truck.

Laura was finally on her feet and feeling fairly well the day after the Enchanted Circle trip, so we had a big dinner at my cousin's before we left. We also gave him all our heavy Pyrex cookware and storage containers. I'll bet we shed 30 pounds from the RV. We replaced them with a set of Rubbermaid stackable containers that might weigh two pounds. Weight is something you must consider in an RV.

Then the morning we planned to leave he invited us to have breakfast with his family at a restaurant named Michael's Kitchen he does social media work for. Normally we won't do anything the morning of a travel day, but he insisted.

That may have been the largest meal I've ever had before a travel day. Afterwards we understood why he was SO insistent we eat with them before we left. That was the best breakfast we'd had since Granny D's. I can't say which place was better considering they served different kinds of food. But Michael's had these cinnamon rolls I couldn't have finished by myself when I was 17 playing football. They must have weighed several pounds. I'm so happy I bought one to eat later, in a few sittings of course.

Mesa Verde, Colorado

The cliff dwellings at Mesa Verde were high on our must-see list. Neither of us had ever seen them in person, so we made sure to include them.

We sure had an interesting day getting there. We went over our highest pass yet with the RV at about 11,000'. We stopped at the top and let the dogs play in the snow. Although they wore out very fast in the thin air. The views were incredible, we just stood there and looked out over the landscape for several minutes. The air was so clear we could probably even see the western border of New Mexico.

After several minutes of difficult breathing we decided to get back on the road. After the bike incident and altitude sickness we were happy to have an uneventful travel day. Not every day on the road needs to be an adventure worth writing about. Right?

The road down the other side of the pass was something like an 8-10% grade for miles and miles with several 180-degree switchbacks and more than a few 90 degree turns. With the exhaust brake on I coasted down in 2nd or 3rd gear going about 30-40 mph for an hour. I was much more concerned with safety than speed. It's difficult to stop at higher speeds while towing, especially while going downhill. I didn't want to risk my brakes failing.

The road was basically empty. We only saw another person every 15-20 minutes, it was very peaceful. However, during a longer stretch of steep downhill I saw someone in a pickup truck towing a long trailer in my mirror quickly catching up to me. We were in a passing area, so without slowing down one bit, he flew around me. He must have been doing 80mph.

As he passed, I saw he had two expensive custom rock crawlers on a flatbed. Right behind him was another truck pulling a massive toy hauler going just as fast. This is where things became interesting.

The mostly empty road just happened to have an oncoming car as the second truck pulled out to pass us. You know how you can judge distance and speed to get a feeling for whether it's safe to pass or not? Well, I guess this guy either couldn't, didn't care or was dumb enough to think he could make it.

With the oncoming car clearly visible he pulled out to pass me. I instantly told Laura to grab the camera. I didn't know if anything would happen, but if it did it would be bad. The truck floored it trying to pass me, rather than pulling back behind me and waiting for the ONE CAR to pass. I stood on the brakes while also down shifting. I really thought he would hit the car head on, and I'd drive through whatever was left of the toy hauler. That's if it didn't roll off the cliff and take us with it.

The oncoming car must have also hit the brakes because they miraculously didn't crash. However, the toy hauler literally slid sideways back into my lane, maybe a half second before the car would have hit it. The trailer tires kicked up enough smoke from sliding that it was visible in the pictures.

While it was sliding, I had this gut feeling that it was going to roll. It was only a few feet in front of us and I knew I could never stop in time. I've never seen a trailer lean that badly. It was worse than the Class A after the hit-and-run when he was running from me. By the grace of God, it didn't roll, and the two adrenaline junkies disappeared around the next corner never to be seen again.

See, it went well. We didn't die!

Luckily neither of us needed to change pants, so we continued on to Mesa Verde. Right before we passed the entrance to Mesa Verde National Park there was an old gas station on the opposite side of the highway. You'll know it if you ever see it by the skull and crossbones flag and the sign declaring, "Massive petroleum spill TOXIC SITE."

It's an old Sinclair station covered in graffiti and signs. We looked it up and there's a crazy history behind it. Apparently one of the underground tanks was leaking after the station was closed. Supposedly they drilled trying to get the gas out of the ground but broke into the water table spreading it instead. According to what we read, it was then abandoned, and all clean-up operations ceased. If that's true, the signs make sense. We didn't stop to verify the information.

The next day we got up early to go tour the national park. Entry was free again thanks to the Access Pass. If you haven't been to Mesa Verde give yourself a lot of time to explore. From the entry gate to the cliff dwellings it's a 30-45-minute drive, and a few thousand feet up in elevation.

Sadly, the main cliff dwelling site was closed to tourists. A ranger told us the cliff above was cracking and could possibly fall. Naturally, they weren't letting anyone go down to that site. He said it would be something like 8 million dollars to anchor the cliff and keep it from falling.

I hope they're able to come up with the money. It would be a terrible thing to lose those 1,000-year-old dwellings because they're some of the best preserved in North America. It's not like we can just get a 1,000-year-old civilization to come back and rebuild them.

We drove the loop around the mesa and stopped to look at everything. There are multiple pit dwellings they've found and restored on top of the mesa, it's not all cliff structures. I was very happy we'd invested in a 300mm lens for our DSLR before the trip. It wasn't the highest quality lens, but we needed it. Many of the cliff dwellings are only visible from across canyons and you need a long lens if you want to photograph them.

Whenever we're able to go back we'll sign up for some of the ranger led tours. We didn't know about them before we went unfortunately. On those tours Rangers will take you up close and personal to several of the cliff dwellings, and you'll get a history lesson along the way.

We were only there two days and got back on the road.

CHAPTER 22

Arizona and Utah

———— ∿ ————

Page, Arizona was the first location Laura said we had to visit. I didn't understand why until she showed me pictures, then it went right to the top of our list for several reasons.

- Lake Powell is there, and if you don't know what that looks like stop reading this and go Google it. The landscape is so stunning that multiple box office hits have been filmed there.

- The Antelope Slot Canyon is nearby.

- Horseshoe Bend is only a few minutes away.

- The Grand Canyon is day trip distance.

We made a two-week reservation at the Wahweap RV park. It's still on the top of our favorite campgrounds list. The RV park sits on a slight hill which gives you breathtaking panoramic views of the lake and the surrounding scenery. We spent several nights sitting outside watching the sunset.

Our only gripe about the park was no T-Mobile service, we had to drive into town to work.

Laura's bike saga resumed in Page. When the front fork on her new Cannondale bike bent, we thought for sure that it would have to be replaced. The only problem was finding a Cannondale dealer on our route up to Washington. We were hopping around national parks the whole way there. That route kept us away from large cities, which is where you usually find Cannondale dealers.

Just as we were coming to terms with Laura not having a usable bike for the next two months, I got my hair cut in Page. As with any hair stylist or barber, they'll talk your ear off while they work on you. Luckily for us, the woman who cut the little hair I had left was no different. I was telling her about our crazy RVing journey, and when I mentioned what happened to Laura's bike, she said there was a small bike shop named Rim Trail Bike and Hike just a mile away. I'd already driven past it a few times, guess I wasn't paying attention.

We didn't even have our bikes with us at the time, but we figured it wouldn't hurt to pick someone's brain for a minute about them. Laura had been kicking around the idea of converting her crossover bike to more of a mountain bike style, and with the fork bent we thought that would be a good time to do so. A conversion would entail a new fork with suspension and larger tires with better tread.

Since we thought the fork needed to be replaced anyway, I asked the owner of the shop if a conversion was doable, or even a good idea. He explained that just buying a mountain bike would be much better for what Laura wanted. but he was willing to look at hers. He asked me to bring the bikes in and said that he'd do some research on parts that night. When I dropped the bikes off later that day, he shocked me by saying he might be able to fix Laura's.

The next morning, we went back to see what he'd found about the cost of converting her bike. Instead the owner shocked us again by presenting us Laura's bike with a fixed front fork! He'd bent it back into shape perfectly. Not only had he accomplished the impossible by bending that aluminum without breaking it, but he only charged us $15 to do it!

He also tuned up both bikes, and they badly needed it. After a few months of rusting to death on Pensacola Beach, and a few thousand miles sitting on top of a truck, they were in rough shape. The chains were so rusted we thought we'd need new ones. My brake cables are exposed so they'd rusted badly, and I thought they'd also need to be replaced.

The owner gave us more good news, nothing had to be replaced. He had cleaned the rust off everything, the chains, brake cables, suspension tubes, and gears. He also cleaned the bikes and got all the dirt, road grime, and bugs off.

We'd both had "tune ups" at big national chain bike shops before. For about the same cost, they only checked our brakes and gears, that was it. This shop went so above and beyond our expectations that I went straight home to write a blog post and make a video about him.

It's not every day you find someone who actually takes care of their customers.

Our First Truck Problem

The day after the bike shop, we had our first "breakdown" since we'd hit the road, if you want to call it that. We were driving into town to work and I saw a message on the dash display I'd never seen before.

The dashboard displayed an "engine power reduced" message and the check engine light came on. Right before that message popped up, the display showed that the truck needed to run a regeneration (regen) cycle, that cleans out the diesel particulate filter (DPF).

Then a few minutes later, AHNJ did something we'd never experienced. No matter how much I pushed the throttle, or what gear I was in, I couldn't get over 32 mph. That was even going downhill. The instant we had signal I stopped and started researching.

I learned that "limp mode" is the common usage term for what we were experiencing. I also learned that it's incredibly common in our truck. To fix it you must get over 35mph and drive 30 miles for it to complete a full regen cycle. However, I was really having trouble getting over 35mph. I could reset the speed limiter by turning the truck off, but if I couldn't reach 35 mph within a few minutes it would go into limp mode again. Getting out of the campground to the highway was a long road with a low speed limit. That made the problem more difficult.

Around that time, I remembered my tuner had a variety of functions other than tuning. I began to scroll through everything and found an option to force a regen cycle. Once I finally left the campground area, I was able to reach the required 35 mph and finish the regen. We drove the full 30 miles just to be sure. At least I didn't have to reach 88 mph.

AHNJ ran and sounded much better after the regen completed. As an added bonus I also got a lot of power back I didn't even know was missing. It must have been building up for some time. We were just lucky we could find signal to figure it out, and that it didn't happen on a travel day. Being forced down to 30mph on the highway sounds terrible.

Back to Adventuring

During our time in Page, we explored all around the great state of Arizona. Lucky for us, our RV park was on the shores of Lake Powell. So, we had to pull out our new inflatable kayak for the first time. If the views are spectacular, why not get up close?

Using the inflatable kayak for the first time was quite the experience. I hooked up the fancy electric pump wrong and so I also had to use the hand pump, which took forever. I'm honestly surprised I didn't have to take a break and put Laura on it. I wasn't in very good shape. Ugh, I'm still not. Don't think you'll magically get back into shape just because you start RVing. I think in some ways it's more difficult while traveling.

Anyway, did I mention it was a tandem kayak? Que the hilarity, or possible divorce, whatever. We were hitting each other's paddles every other stroke since we didn't buy one actually long enough for two people. I was sitting in back and Laura was in the front, and I was also drenching her with my paddle, oops.

If it was said once it was said 50 times, "Paddle left, we're going the wrong way! I am paddling left, you're not paddling left!" It was a lot of fun, but we still need a lot more practice, or a longer kayak.

The next day we hiked Horseshoe Bend. After all, it was only a 20-minute drive from the RV park, we'd be crazy to skip such an awe-inspiring place. A word of caution when going there, it's a huge international travel destination. The parking lot was totally packed with rental RV's and tour buses. We were lucky to have AHNJ, he didn't mind parking in the dirt and rocks on the side of the parking lot.

I said we hiked there because there's a decent walk from the parking lot, Maybe 1.5 miles roundtrip, I'm not really sure. Remember what I said about not being in good shape? Yeah, that walk wasn't as fun as we thought it would be. All the foreign tourists were flying past us and we realized we'd become "average Americans" around the third time we had to stop.

But once we reached Horseshoe Bend, all our aches and pains were forgotten. We filmed and photographed the area for an hour before heading back to the truck. Sadly, it's one of those places that's awe inspiring, but after a while there isn't anything different to look at. On the way back I thought about the lack of safety railing. We saw several tourists climbing out to dangerous places trying to get better pictures. Although, I may have done the same 15 years ago, before I realized I wasn't invincible.

We decided the Grand Canyon would be a good follow-up visit after Horseshoe Bend. Considering it's only two hours southwest from Page it was an easy decision. Of course, we drove down to see it, it's one of the Seven Wonders of the Natural World. Seriously, how could we skip the Grand Canyon!?

We usually leave the dogs in the RV while we go exploring, but not that time. We can't leave them for more than 10 hours, and we didn't want to only spend three hours at the Grand Canyon. We got up at the crackish of dawn, or thereabouts, threw the pups, water, and food in the truck and hit the road.

I'll remember this trip for the rest of my life as I'd never seen the Grand Canyon in person. Laura went when she was young and had very fond memories from that trip. It had been with a church group and they even hiked to the bottom of the canyon. We didn't attempt that hike because we knew we weren't in good enough shape, and neither were the dogs. I guess we'll just have to get in better shape and go back. Oh shucks.

Several memorable things happened during the Grand Canyon trip. We got to take a selfie on the edge of the Grand Canyon (kids these days). We also got to watch a thunderstorm roll through the canyon. We had to stop and watch it, neither of us had ever seen anything like it before.

I can't remember any other time I've had the chance to watch a thunderstorm from an elevated position several miles away. Typically, you only see a dark cloud on the horizon. From our vantage point we watched the cloud form and shift and observed the bands of rain falling at an angle from the storm's own wind. The unfortunate part of the storm was it dropped the temperature almost 20 degrees. We decided to pack it up and head home at that point. We hadn't brought coats along because it was 70 degrees when we left that morning. We were cold the entire day, but the storm froze us out.

As we were leaving the Grand Canyon it began to snow, in the last week of April. We sure didn't see that coming. It snowed enough, and was cold enough, that it accumulated on the sides of the road. The elevation was around 8,000', and the weather can be a bit testy there. We have to go back and boondock near there so we can explore it more. A day trip just didn't cut it.

The day before we left the Page area, we went to the lower Antelope Slot Canyon, another huge international tourist attraction. There were so many people on the tour the guides were packing everyone in shoulder to shoulder.

If you're claustrophobic at all skip this tour. We waited in line for an hour to get into the canyon. At least the tour guides told us the best camera settings while we were waiting in line, which was helpful. It was another hour to get through the canyon. If you have a panic attack and need to leave, you won't be able to quickly, we could barely turn around in there.

Be prepared for a lot of time standing around, the tour moves very slowly. On a positive note you have lots of photo opportunities.

If you do decide to brave the hordes of tourists and pay the steep ticket prices, you'll get some breathtaking pictures. I would recommend not changing lenses while in the canyon though, it's very dusty. The surprising part was our phones actually took better pictures than our DSLR because they had such a wide field of view. I know I know; a different lens could give me a wider field of view. It's on the very long list of things we want and can't afford.

Torrey, UT and Capitol Reef

After leaving Page we made the long six hour drive up to Torrey, Utah. We stayed there for a week and spent more time relaxing than exploring. Following our busy schedule in Page, we needed some down time to catch up on work. Although we did rent a jeep from the RV park for a day of off-roading.

Before we thought about doing any hikes or exploring, we drove out to the Capitol Reef Visitors Center to find maps and speak with rangers to research the area, then we drove some of the park for an idea of where we'd want to go later. Our scouting mission took a bit longer than anticipated since we didn't know how big the park was until we drove it.

On our way home we stopped at the visitor's center again to use the restroom. While there I saw four people standing in front of an older Class B camper van with the hood up. I asked what was wrong and learned they'd thrown their serpentine belt and were stuck. Luckily, I had the necessary tools to get their belt back on and save them from calling for a tow in the middle of nowhere. They were so incredibly thankful. I just hope it stayed on long enough to drive to a shop.

The next day we decided to rent a Jeep and go exploring on the north side of Capitol Reef, which is only accessible by dirt roads. AHNJ can handle dirt roads just fine, however a jeep is much narrower, and not responsible for towing our house. Sadly, the rental jeep wasn't in good condition. The steering, suspension, and air conditioning were all in need of repair or service. The shocks needed to be replaced.

We quickly learned that our one ton dually rode better on dirt roads than the rented Jeep did. But we'd paid for it and were stuck with it for the day, so we tried to make the best of the situation. We drove about two hours out on the dirt road north of the park. We stopped often to look at things and enjoy the scenery. We only encountered one other person all day, after the super touristy sites in Arizona that was a welcome break.

Unfortunately, the Jeep's suspension was so terrible that Laura's back began to hurt terribly. When we finally went to do some hiking, she was hurting too badly to even try. Luckily, we'd parked next to the shortest trail, so I grabbed the cameras and ran down and back for a quick video. We decided to save the hikes for our next stop at Arches National Park. We'll go back to Torrey some day and see the rest of it.

I squeezed in some truck maintenance before we left Torrey. I ordered oil, filter, and catch pan to the RV park. AHNJ was overdue for an oil change, and I wanted to upgrade to full synthetic for a few reasons. Since a shop would charge about $200, I figured why not just do it myself? I knew how.

When it all arrived, I threw on some old clothes, drove AHNJ's front tires up onto some RV leveling blocks and crawled under it. After two years of changing oil for Tires Plus it was like riding a bike. Even with greasing all the suspension points I was done in an hour or so. I dumped the old oil in the new jugs and dropped them off at a shop that would take them.

I'd never had full synthetic oil in AHNJ before and couldn't believe the difference. Of course, some of it could be that the old oil was, well old. There was a noticeable power increase and mileage gain. I watch my mileage like a hawk and can say it absolutely made a difference. I won't run anything less now, unless it's free.

Something funny happened the morning before we left. We were walking the dogs at the RV park and saw a long blue ribbon of plastic caught in some sagebrush blowing in the wind. As we approached, I realized it was unrolled dog poop bags. Some idiot must have dropped them and not realized it. I walked over to them thinking I could get a free roll of poop bags when Kimber tugged back because she was doing her business that would require a bag.

We keep bag holders zip tied to the retractable leash handles so we can always pick up after them. I reached down to grab a bag and saw the screw on cap was gone, and it was empty. I looked over at the bags blowing in the wind and realized who that idiot was. I rolled up my lost bags and found the end cap. Oops. I gave Laura a good opportunity to give me some crap from that one.

Moab, Utah and Arches National Park

We planned to stay a week in the Moab area. We liked to schedule by the week at each location because most RV parks cut a weekly deal which makes the last day or two free compared to their nightly rate. I haven't written much about the other parks we stayed at much because there wasn't much notable to write about. However, this one was different.

When I tried to check in, I found a very serious problem. Even though I'd told them our trailer was 41' they'd booked us in a 35' pull through site. Meaning, we could get hit in the front or the back, and we couldn't park the truck with us. Of course, I told them 35' just wouldn't work for us. That's when I was informed all their long sites were full and they didn't have anywhere else to put us. Great.

I went back to the truck and told Laura. She called the other RV parks in town and no one else had availability. If you want to go to Moab make your reservations a few months out to be safe, it's a popular tourist destination.

Anyway, I went back to the office and told them they had to fix their error. I didn't care how they did it, but it needed to happen immediately. She called another woman in and they went over the schedule to see if they could move anyone around to find us a longer site. At first, they said we'd have to move three times in the week. I refused to accept that. They made the mistake, so they had to make it right. That's just good customer service.

There was another aspect to our engagement that really rubbed me the wrong way. The whole time they were working on finding an appropriate site they were complaining about some mysterious "girl" who had made our reservation. Apparently, she had made many mistakes and had just been fired. Even though the mysterious "girl" seemed like an all-too-convenient scapegoat, I was willing to accept their story. However, I did have one question for them, what was her name? My suspicions were confirmed when they both preceded to trip over their tongues trying to give me different names.

Eventually they found a few reservations they could shuffle around to get us in a 38' site for the whole week. It was the best they could do. After standing there for almost two hours I told them I also needed a discount. That had been the worst experience checking into a park we'd ever had. They did manage to give us a free night, which was nice. On a positive note, no one hit the trailer, even though we were sticking out in the road.

Our first day at the park was spent working on videos and blog posts. That's usually how our first day goes after we travel. We thoroughly enjoy traveling and exploring, but work must be done first if we want to eat. We tried to meticulously document the entire journey as we thought it was going to be our big break. We started the trip thinking it would finally put our channel on the map.

The second day we drove into Moab and explored the town. We were both struck by how busy it was for such a small town. We didn't have a minute without heavy traffic and the amount of people on foot was staggering. There must have been thousands of people walking around. After a while of small towns and middle of nowhere's, seeing the hustle and bustle of a popular tourist destination shocked us.

That night we went home and planned to tour the National Park the next day. We did our usual routine. We spent hours watching videos and reading articles about the park. Then we hammered out a route and plan of what we wanted to see and how long it would probably take. We began planning in that manner for several reasons.

1. To make it back to the dogs in time.

2. Choose between attractions, areas, etc. to see what we want on the first trip which saves time and fuel.

3. Plan what we want to film, so we get what we want on the first trip (it took as a while to figure this one out).

Even though we had sold Laura's SUV to help fund the trip, we were still on a strict budget. After the aimless driving and tanks of diesel in Pensacola we learned our lesson and began planning better. Also, we had a finite amount of time at each location during the trip. Time management was essential if we wanted to have time left to produce what we filmed after we spent a whole day filming it. Pre-planning has saved us a monumental amount of time and money while allowing us to be more productive.

Neither of us had been to Arches National Park before, so we asked a few locals in town about it. One man told us to get in line at the gate early to beat the tour buses, which was great advice. We learned the buses get there around 8-9 a.m. and clog up the line badly. Of course, it was all buses with Chinese tourists. That becomes important later.

To get into the park you must drive up several switchbacks and ride a cliff edge for a while. We saw several people bringing their RVs with them, and we consider that a very bad idea in that park. The roads throughout the park are all very narrow and there's rarely a shoulder. Also, there are very few places to park something that large and the Chinese tour busses take most of the large spots anyway.

If you enjoy beautiful scenery and/or geology, this is a park that needs to be on your bucket list. Within minutes of leaving the switchback climb Laura was getting after me. There were so many amazing things to see that I couldn't keep my eyes on the road, oops. Finally, we just started pulling off every chance we got so I could look at everything safely.

We had a strange experienced at the first parking lot we pulled into. AHNJ isn't exactly a small truck and sometimes needs a readjustment to fit into a parking space. That lot was fairly small, and I couldn't get into a spot on the first attempt. Within just a few seconds of trying to readjust, a tour bus behind us laid on his air horn. Of course, it shocked the crap out of us, we weren't expecting an air horn 10' behind us. I quickly finished parking and the bus driver whipped into the space right behind our truck and offloaded his 50 or so passengers.

As we got out to take pictures, we saw the buses driver standing next to his door staring and giving us a dirty look! It really put us back on our heels. We entered the park that day ready to see a lot of cool stuff and have fun, not to be harassed. Anyway, we took our pictures and moved on to the next cool thing to see.

After an hour in the park we were having a blast! We'd seen all kinds of amazing things and were filming a pretty good video we thought. On the way to see our first arch, the Double Arch formation. We were going just under the speed limit so that Laura could get pictures while I was driving when a tour bus suddenly flew up behind me. He must have been going 15-20 mph over the posted limit.

Right about then I saw there was a line of traffic ahead of me waiting to get into the parking area. The road was a dead end with everyone going to the same place, so I kept going the same speed. Why would we want to race to the end of the line just to sit there and wait? Well, I guess it only made sense to us. The bus began to lay on its horn like we were in New York traffic.

So, I have this thing from my time in the army where I don't care to be pushed around or told what to do by anyone not in charge of me. My reaction was the same as it is with tailgaters, I hit the brakes. I didn't stop, but we took our time getting to the end of that line. I don't care for bullies or trolls and I relish the chance to stand up to them.

The reactions from the driver and tour group leader standing next to him were priceless. First, when they tried tailgating me within inches of our bumper, I slowed down more. When they backed off, I sped back up and they kept their distance. Good, first lesson learned.

Second, they started flipping us off. I stuck my phone out the window, so they would know I was filming them. They stopped making obscene gestures. Good, second lesson learned. But then they started filming us too, that was fine with me.

When we both finally parked the situation took a turn. I was over the whole thing and ready to go see my first arch ever. However, the tour group leader that had been flipping us off wasn't even close to being over it. I learned this as he actually ran up to AHNJ and began filming the truck, license plate and us. Two can play that game pal.

I grabbed the gimbal with GoPro and filmed him back, in case he tried to do anything dumb. When he finished, I walked over to the bus and filmed it, the companies name, the DOT numbers and plate as well. I also took pictures of the same with my phone. Oh man he lost it when he realized that he couldn't bully us and scare me off. I had a VERY difficult time holding back my laughter when some scrawny guy a foot shorter than me tried to get in my face and intimidate me. I may be out of shape, but I'm still a decently sized guy at 6'2" 220ish.

The group leader was so angry that he couldn't bully me into backing down! As a last-ditch effort, he pulled out his phone and pretended to report us to the rangers. (I can't make this stuff up!) I knew he was faking it because he didn't look up their number, call it and have someone answer in less than 10 seconds. There wasn't any cell signal there anyway! I just stood there, staring at him, listening to lies about our supposed road rage.

I thought his little act was hilarious. I was waiting to find out what he'd try next as he was becoming quite entertaining. I didn't know we'd get a free show along with the cool scenery.

However, by that time, he'd stressed Laura out so badly she couldn't handle him anymore. When she told me, she was already shaking. That REALLY pissed me off because I was sure her reaction was exactly what he was trying to elicit. I wonder how many other tourists he's bullied and harassed? Rather than putting Laura through any more I let him win that round. And right when I was beginning to have fun, oh well.

I simply turned around and left while he was still "on the phone." Holding Laura's hand, almost dragging her, I plowed a path through the gawking mob of Chinese tourists that had gathered around us. We left to go see the arches. There are four arches that surround the Double Arch parking lot and we picked one the tourist group wasn't going to.

Walking through arches for the first time was an experience we'll never forget. We were absolutely blown away, not just at their size, but at how they were able to form and stay standing. I never climbed on top of an arch, but I did climb all over that place in search of the best camera angles. I even climbed up underneath the rear arch in the Double Arch pair, it's not too difficult if you have decent boots. I shot some great pictures sitting up there. Laura didn't join me because she didn't feel up to climbing steep slippery rocks. They're worn smooth in many places from all the foot traffic.

While straddling that sliver of rock I was reminded of visiting the Paradise Glacier ice caves in the 1980's with my parents. I clearly remember walking through the two largest caves and getting down on my hands and knees to look into the third. They'd been melting for half a century so the fourth was already gone and the third almost was. The caves were on Mt. Rainier, until the glacier finished melting in the 1990's.

You know how every now and then you see something that's so incredible, it's instantly permanently burned into your memory? The ice caves did that when I was six. Thirty years later, I sat under that arch reflecting on how we were having that experience almost weekly during the trip. As if I'd needed confirmation that I'd picked the right path in life, God gave me an arch to sit under and ponder life.

I was in for a shock when I climbed back down to Laura though. The tour guide had gotten in her head so badly that she'd been experiencing a mild panic attack since we'd walked away from him. She'd just been holding it together for me. I felt terrible, especially since we could have gone home and come back in a day or two. Instead, I was off climbing stuff and having fun.

As we were driving out of the park, I decided to stop at the entrance to speak with a ranger. That tour guide giving Laura a panic attack had REALLY pissed me off, I hadn't been that angry in a long time. I went into the visitor's center and asked for an LE (law enforcement) ranger. It took a few minutes for them to find one, but I wanted to wait for someone who had true legal authority.

I told him what had happened and showed him the pictures of the bus. He sincerely thanked me for reporting it. He said they had problems with the bus companies on a regular basis, but no one ever provided the evidence needed for them to do anything about it. He asked me to fill out a report so that he could revoke their tour company license for the park which I happily did.

I didn't and still don't care how they drive in other countries. Treating people like that just isn't acceptable. I was happy to do something about it. Hopefully they won't ruin anyone else's day.

The next day we didn't go back to Arches. Instead, we did some research because we'd noticed almost everyone in the RV park had an ATV, side-by-side or dirt bike. Of course, we were intrigued. We quickly learned that Moab is the off-roading capital of the world, shows what we knew.

Naturally, we thought an off-road adventure would be a lot of fun, also it would make a good video. We looked up rental companies in town and discovered there's a lot of them. I also asked an employee at the RV park what company the locals like and it matched with what we'd seen online.

One company was a clear front runner from the reviews and apparent professionalism. It may have also helped that their posted prices weren't terrible. It was going to be expensive for our budget, but we figured we could swing it. After the Jeep debacle we still wanted a fun off-road experience, so we went straight there hoping to rent a side-by-side and play the rest of the day. We were in for a big surprise though.

We learned they didn't post the deposit fee and gear rental fees online. The deposit was almost as much as the rental, and the safety gear was another $100. It was going to be almost $1,000 to rent one, for half a day. Sure, we'd get the deposit back if nothing went wrong, but I couldn't gamble with $400 at that time. It turned out all of the shops had an expensive deposit, so we were forced to shelve that idea for a later date. I figured it would be like renting a car, you prove insurance and there's no deposit. Now we know better.

The following day, we decided to try Arches again since we hadn't seen most of the park before. We went on several hikes that time and had a much better experience. We learned the large tour groups don't do the miles long hikes. We'd finally found a way to enjoy the park without being mobbed! We had so much fun hiking all over the park seeing the lesser visited arches.

After walking several miles, in the desert sun, still above 5,000' elevation, we were exhausted and had to call it quits. On the way home, Laura remembered that one of our viewers had recommended a pizza place in Moab named Zax. There was still some time left before we had to let the dogs out, so we decided to finish the day with a late lunch date.

We don't eat out often, so we try to pick good places when we do. When the pizza arrived at our table, we instantly saw why Zax was so highly recommended. Sure, it's possible we devoured it just because we were wiped out. But we both remember it being some of the best pizza we've ever had.

Dinosaur National Monument

After leaving Moab we spent two days driving north to Dinosaur National Monument, located on the border of Utah and Colorado. That drive was wonderfully uneventful. We were very thankful that neither of us became sick, nothing broke and no one tried to kill us. It's those little things in life that make it enjoyable. Although it did feel a little strange.

We stayed at a small, almost empty, RV park in Jensen, Utah. There are three entrances into the monument, two in Colorado and one in Utah. We chose the Utah side because that entrance has the large visitors center and the Quarry Exhibit Hall. The Hall allows visitors to see over 1500 dinosaur bones, and there is an 80-foot long mural, showing the history of the dinosaurs found in the region.

I don't know why other people would visit the monument, but we went to see the fossils. If you want to see the fossils you need to go to the Quarry Exhibit Hall. Sure, people still find fossils around the park. Although we didn't have time to go fossil hunting, we wanted to what other people had found. I don't have anything against fossil hunting, I've done it before, we just didn't have the time.

Due to bad weather in the forecast we chose to visit the monument the day we arrived. Usually we don't do that, but a nasty winter storm was being predicted and we only planned to be there one full day. The visitors center and the quarry were both closed by the time we got there, but the monument wasn't. We grabbed a map at the gate and just found other areas to go see.

It turns out there are hundreds or thousands of petroglyphs scattered around the monument. We drove to a remote area on a sketchy dirt road in search of them. We stopped at multiple locations marked for petroglyphs and took many pictures. When we parked at the last location, Laura saw a small herd of Bighorn rams up on a ridge.

I put the 300mm lens on the DSLR and snapped a few pictures before they moved off. I put the camera back in the truck afterwards since I still wasn't used to using it so rarely carried it. We then set off on a path that lead up to a cliff face to view another collection of carvings. There, we found the lizard carvings the monument is famous for. Aside from the mountains of fossils, the lizard carving is probably the next big it's known for. As we were standing there taking pictures with our phones, I heard something scrape a rock behind me.

I turned around and saw a Bighorn ram standing on a boulder, staring at us, maybe 20 yards away. It was more than close enough to charge, and I REALLY didn't want to give him a reason to. Laura hadn't noticed it yet, so I whispered to her to turn around slowly, she was as shocked to see it as I was.

The ram was so close we could see the amber color of his eyes and its light brown fur softly blowing in the wind. We all stood there for a minute having a visual Mexican standoff. After that minute we realized it wasn't acting aggressive, and it probably realized we weren't a threat, so we both began taking pictures.

We figure they're very used to tourists because it didn't seem to care we were there. It walked off the rock, towards us, and began to casually eat some flowers. After a minute another ram joined it. It was a once in a lifetime opportunity and I've kicked myself ever since for leaving the DSLR in the truck. This is why I say to learn your equipment.

We took the best pictures we could with our phones and logged another amazing memory in our lives. After watching the rams for about 15 minutes they wandered off, probably in search of more flowers. We talked about the experience the whole way back to the truck.

The snow barely missed us the next day and we were able to visit the monument again, while everything was open. In the visitor's center we learned the Colorado entrance received 8" of snow that morning. Lucky us, we only got the cold.

I just have to say the pictures of the quarry we saw beforehand didn't do it justice. Even though we'd seen complete fossils in the Houston museum just a few months prior, the quarry was a completely different experience. These were fossils still embedded in the dirt and rock where they'd fallen eons ago.

Obviously, we photographed and filmed the entire place, but then we stood there for a while just soaking it all in. After we stared at one area a few minutes we'd move over and stare at a new section. We then went upstairs and did the same thing. We were totally nerding out and loving it! I'm not entirely sure how long we spent in there, but it didn't feel long enough.

During the two days spent visiting the Monument we saw few other people. If you want someplace unforgettable to visit, but can't handle crowds, you may want to consider Dinosaur National Monument. From our experience it's a lesser known and visited National Monument, but it's really a hidden gem and worth visiting. A few months before standing in front of those fossils I hadn't even known it existed. It's another example of why we love the RV life.

The Blizzard!

Was that dramatic enough? I hope so because we endured INCHES OF SNOW!! You read that right, entire inches. Oh, but I'm getting ahead of myself. Let me start at the beginning.

Our next destination was an RV park on the banks of Colter Bay in Grand Teton National Park. It was a two-day drive which we hoped would be uneventful. Sure, there was a bad winter storm named Janice forecast for Wyoming and Colorado, but it was supposed to hit a few hundred miles east from us. None of the weather models we found showed it coming anywhere near our route.

Since we felt safe from the storm we left on schedule. Our route was Highway 191 north to Rock Springs, we planned to overnight there at a Walmart. When we turned north out of Vernal there was a very steep climb with a few switchbacks that took us up about 1,000' in a few minutes. At the top of the hill we saw our first flurries.

Laura pulled up the weather again to see if we needed to turn around while we could and call the day. However, the forecast and radar showed nothing even near us and it still predicted a clear travel day. We figured it was a fluke and continued on. As we increased in elevation the flurries became a little stronger. The snow wasn't sticking to anything though, and it was forecast to get warmer throughout the day. So, we continued on.

Within an hour of leaving Vernal we realized the forecasts had all been horribly wrong. Snow was sticking to everything but the road. The worst problem was that we were in the middle of nowhere. There weren't pull offs, rest areas, cell service, or anywhere to turn around. We realized we were stuck. So, we continued on.

Back when I met Laura, I'd purposely take my Tacoma out if it snowed to drift around corners in 4x4, just to see how much snow I could kick up. Before the Tacoma I loved nothing more than snow donuts in my 350Z at the barracks parking lot. I've never feared driving in the snow. Although, I had zero experience towing our home through snow, and that did scare me.

Sadly, driving in snow is one of Laura's greatest fears. She spent the entire day with a coat over her head too scared to watch. And with no cell service she couldn't see what the weather was doing, look up a place for us to stop, or find anything to entertain herself with.

The entire route was up and down passes through mountain valleys. About two hours in, the snow began to stick to the road. It wasn't bad at first, but it quickly became worse. I only saw a handful of other vehicles the entire day, and not one was a snowplow. Most of the snow I drove through was untouched. Maybe it was just snowing hard enough to cover the tracks? It sure felt lonely out there.

Oh, I forgot to mention the nearly suicidal deer. They sure kept me on my toes, as if I didn't already have enough to worry about. I'm guessing so many deer were near the road due to the lack of traffic, but who knows. What I do know is those assholes scared the crap out of me more than a few times. Because towing our house over unplowed snow-covered passes wasn't bad enough, the deer decided to crank up the stress level a notch.

Considering we didn't have any sort of deer guard or bumper on the truck, I was very worried. A deer strike could disable the truck and strand us hours from anywhere. That's best-case scenario. If I'd hit a deer, I may have lost control.

Every hour or so I'd see a deer a few feet off the road. As I approached EVERY SINGLE ONE OF THEM looked at me, turned towards me, took a step towards the road, contemplated ending it all, then turned and ran off into the woods. What's the record for surviving the most heart attacks in a day?

In each instance I envisioned us sliding off the road, rolling off a cliff and dying. I was fairly certain we were going to die for several hours that day. Every now and then Laura would ask if it was safe for her to look. She must have felt me tensing because she always asked right when things were the worst.

I typically don't like lying to anyone, especially Laura. But I lied my ass off that day. Each time I tried to keep my voice calm and just said "not yet, I'll tell you when you can look." That day sucked enough for both of us already without Laura having a full-blown panic attack.

I'm really glad she listened to me. Otherwise she may have seen the time I came around a corner and found a double trailer FedEx semi stopped in our lane at the bottom of a….I don't know what percent grade hill. It was steep and COMPLETELY snow covered. There weren't even tracks in the snow for me to follow.

The driver had stopped to put on chains. When he saw me coming, he ran around his truck to check for traffic, then he waved me around. I put the truck in 4x4 high as I pulled into the oncoming lane to pass. He ran to the front of his truck and waved me on again. Nice guy, I wish I could have stopped to thank or help him. Although I was certain if I stopped on that hill, I wouldn't be able to get moving again, probably why he helped me. I downshifted and focused on keeping my speed up. The rear tires slipped a bit once, but AHNJ crushed that hill. Laura felt them slip and asked what happened, I made something up.

Because the nerve-wracking drive wasn't enough on my plate, I was also trying to film it, because that's just what we do. So, when I say the worst part about the day was the GoPro overheating, I hope you can understand how angry that made me. It was mounted on the dash and would overheat once an hour or so. I'd have to pull the battery out and lay them on the center console to cool before it would turn back on.

Shortly after I passed the semi, I heard the GoPro beep as it turned itself off from overheating. So, only me and God saw the next part. I wish it had been in the video, it would have shut the trolls up, oh well. We hit the core of our storm and it was coming down HARD.

Rounding a corner, still in 4x4, I saw nothing but an empty white field in front of me. Let me be clear, obviously the road was still there somewhere, I just couldn't see it. All I could see were the reflective plow markers on each side of the road. I'd noticed them a few hours before and they ended up saving our butts. The plow markers were the only way I knew there was a road still under us. Without them, I may well have driven off into a field and got stuck. Or drove into snow-covered water, which would be a bit worse than getting stuck.

We were still going up and down steep hills in and out of woods full of suicidal deer, and I couldn't see the road. I tried to keep my speed around 25-30 so that I wouldn't stall on the hills, but I could hopefully stop if needed. Then, on that snow-covered portion, another deer tried to kill us.

Maybe they were homicidal deer? Either way I pumped the brakes for deer life (puns) and it decided to let us all live by running off like the others. Or maybe it was a coordinated effort by a group of deer sick of people driving through their home? It could have been a deerspiracy to make us wreck and then rob us or hold us hostage for ransom. I'll bet they would ask for a pallet of deer corn.

That's the kind of ridiculous stuff my imagination comes up with. I've got some really good fiction ideas. Maybe I'll get around to writing them someday.

That day was a little reminiscent of climbing the switchback hill our second day on the road. I just kept reminding myself of all the ridiculous stuff I'd lived through. If I learned anything from my time in the army it's that you can do anything if properly motivated.

254

Staying alive is sometimes the proper level of motivation needed to accomplish seemingly impossible tasks.

The relief we felt as we finally pulled into the Rock Springs Wal-Mart parking lot was palpable. Laura came out from under the coat and I pried my fingers from the steering wheel, I'm surprised I didn't leave grooves. The lot was almost empty, and we found a great spot on the outer edge. After the manager gave us permission to overnight, we settled in for a long cold night. That wasn't the end of our day though.

Winter storm Janice shut down I-80 shortly after we stopped. That resulted in every open square foot of Rock Springs filling up with semis and other RVs. It was sad watching people drive through the full parking lot a few hours later. When I walked the dogs that evening, I saw there wasn't an open shoulder anywhere. Every road was reduced to a single lane with semis crammed in on both sides.

It only snowed a few inches on us that night, thankfully, the bulk of the storm hit to the east. We left early the next day since it was going to be a long travel day. The roads were treated and clear by then, so we were able to continue on to Grand Tetons National Park. As we drove out of Rock Springs, we didn't see a single open spot where a semi or RV could have parked. The entire town was packed. Even the pull-offs 30 minutes outside of town were full of semis.

CHAPTER 23

Wyoming and Washington

Grand Tetons National Park

This location was tied for first on our list. Laura had gone there for a week with her grandparents in their RV about 25 years before. She had many fond memories of that trip, it motivated her to go RVing in the first place. I'd never been to that area of the country before, so it was all new to me.

Grand Tetons National Park is very well known for its abundance of wildlife. We had our first wildlife encounter before we could even get to the campground. I drove around a corner to find a mob of people and cars on both sides of the road. All the people were running to the right side of the road. Most of them had professional camera setups I could drool over, so I figured it had to be something good.

Laura grabbed our little Nikon and stuck it out the window. We didn't know what was going on, but apparently, we needed to take pictures of it. I slowly drove by the crowd, and it turned out to be a moose with a calf about 40 yards off the road. We got one decent picture and were introduced to the wildlife jams.

A ranger later educated us about wildlife jams. There are bison jams, bear jams, elk jams etc. They happen whenever there's wildlife visible from the road. People hit the brakes to get pictures. Sometimes they'll just slow down, some pull over, others just stop in the middle of the road.

It's really important to pay attention while you're driving through national parks with a lot of wildlife, otherwise you may rear end someone sitting in the middle of the road taking pictures. I had a few close calls where people slammed on their brakes or pulled a U-turn with no warning.

The check-in process at that campground was the longest I'd ever experienced. I'm surprised Laura didn't come in to see what the holdup was. I received a 15-20-minute educational course on campground and national park rules considering bears and bear safety. I was also given a stack of paperwork on bear safety, just in case I forgot the briefing I guess.

They went so far as to say that if we left any of the prohibited items outside (grills, food, lotion, etc.) they would be confiscated without warning. I left there feeling like they had bear safety well under control. I should hope they do anyway, they deal with tens of thousands of tourists every year.

I feel that even if you don't get the in-depth instructional tutorial as I did, you should still know not to feed the bears, right? Isn't that just common knowledge these days? I was glad they said something about the grill and lotion, though. I hadn't thought about the grill and didn't even know lotion was a problem.

Bears are very good scavengers. If they think there's an easy source of food they won't hunt or forage. Instead, they'll troll your campsite and pick up anything left out or left behind. There's a problem with this, as they'll start to associate humans with food. Guess what happens when they're hungry, see a person, and the person doesn't have food....they can become the food. I know not everyone understands why they shouldn't feed the bears, but I'm willing to bet everyone's been told a time or two not to do it.

The RV park was heavily wooded and beautiful, we had a spot on the edge nearest to the lake. We couldn't see the lake, but we had a wonderful view of the woods. It was much better than the views at most RV parks. We booked two weeks there and couldn't wait to relax and enjoy the outdoors.

After we finished setting up, we walked the campground and the surrounding areas. It was a lot of fun listening to Laura recount memory after memory of the area. Although, the campground had a view of the lake when she was young, the trees had grown up and blocked it since then. The shore was about 100 yards from us, and we could see water sparkling through the trees when the sun was at the right angle.

We didn't have enough cell signal in the RV to get online, so we went to check out the Colter Bay Lodge the next day and get some work done. The lodge had very fast WIFI, it was much better than we were used to. We posted the video about the blizzard while we were there and had enough signal to share it and respond to all the comments. That was nice, we weren't expecting good internet and the ability to work in the middle of nowhere.

A few nights later an RV parked behind us in the next row's end spot. I remember watching the wife outside with a flashlight trying to guide him in around 10 or 11pm. I even had a conversation with Laura wondering why anyone would choose to tow that late.

Two days later, I saw the new neighbor outside, so I went to go meet him. We were still new RVers and I liked to meet people and try to learn from them. He was an interesting guy, but a little odd. I learned that he'd planned on getting in after dark but had a blowout which pushed him back even later.

When I asked him how fast he'd been going he claimed to not know. Maybe he didn't want to say? Driving faster than trailer tires are rated for is a great way to make them blow. We seriously question why people choose to tow late and fast. Too many things can go wrong and it's harder to get help at night with most businesses closed.

Later that morning, I was looking out of the living room windows when I saw a large white fox in the road next to us. I said something to Laura about it, grabbed the camera, and snapped a picture. After all, it's not every day you get an opportunity like that. Seriously, foxes are usually very skittish animals. Why would one be in a campground swarming with people? There had been kids playing outside not long before.

After it left, I went outside to see if I could find it again for another picture. Instead, I found my neighbor and we got to talking. He'd been fishing that morning and was cleaning a bunch of trout on his picnic table in a five-gallon bucket.

Cleaning fish in your campsite is a big no-no in the bear safety world. I mentioned the fox to him, and he seemed pretty happy about it. He also happily reported that he'd seen a grizzly there the evening before. I didn't realize how odd his excitement was until I thought back on the situation later.

I quickly learned that he loves wildlife, maybe a little too much. Then the conversation turned weird. He said he'd fed the fox, and that he'd been doing it for 30 years in that campground because he loves seeing wildlife up close. That's when I ended the conversation, I had no want to befriend such a reckless person.

His actions explained why the fox had been there though. I'd been very curious about it because they're normally skittish animals that actively avoid humans. Except that particular white fox had been running around a campground full of people, in the middle of the day with kids playing in the streets.

I still wanted more pictures of the fox, so I set up the tripod in the living room and stood there looking out our big passenger side windows waiting for it. I had a conversation with Laura while I was waiting about our neighbor and what he'd told me. It was very worrying, but we didn't know for sure if he was telling the truth and had no evidence, so we decided there was nothing we could do.

It's a good thing I was watching for the fox because I happened to see our neighbor walking into the woods with the five-gallon bucket, so I grabbed my phone and started filming him (I still didn't know how to film with the DSLR then). We have a YouTube channel after all, and you never know when you'll find the next viral video.

At first, I thought he was just dumping the water from cleaning the fish. I actually said on camera "that's dumb, he'll attract bears. He should dump it down the sewer hole." I filmed him dumping the bucket and walking back out of the woods.

Very shortly thereafter, the fox came back, except it was in the woods that time. I tried and tried to get a good picture, but it was moving quickly with too much brush in the way. After several attempts I took the next logical step and went outside to get closer.

I followed the same path as my neighbor, and about 50 feet into the woods I saw something that didn't make any sense. There was a pile of fish on the ground. There was a lot of brush between me and the pile and I couldn't see it very well, so I walked around. As I was going around, I pulled out my phone and began filming again. The video was too shaky for YouTube, so I stopped recording about the time I walked up on the fish.

I'd been standing in front of the fish for maybe half a minute when I heard growling in the brush behind me. I jammed the phone in my pocket and spun around reaching for my gun! I had a carry permit that was legal in that state, and it's legal to carry concealed in national parks if you have a permit for that state.

My first thought was "it's only a .380 and nowhere near powerful enough for a bear, I'm screwed." I hadn't brought my usual carry gun, so it was all I had. And like an idiot, I'd left the bear mace you should never go anywhere without in bear country, inside next to the door. I found myself doubly under prepared, expecting the grizzly from the night before to have returned for the fish. All of this raced through my head in the amount of time it took me to turn around.

I knew I was in trouble.

Just as I was pulling the pea shooter out of my pocket, I heard my neighbor start laughing. The idiot had followed me into the woods, apparently thinking it would be a hoot to start growling to scare me. Actually, he did a decent impression. I understand that he didn't know me, however, I happen to be a retired infantryman with three tours between Afghanistan and Iraq.

He'll never understand how lucky he was that he pulled that stunt on me instead of anyone else, because I'm trained on how to NOT be trigger happy. Ammo conservation is actually very important in combat, regardless of what Hollywood will have you believe. Also, the rules of engagement were quite strict, something else Hollywood often gets wrong.

Mr. Suicide Wish walked out from behind a tree all smiles, as I was trying to put my gun back without him seeing it. He walked right up to me, way too close for comfort, and just struck up a conversation. I was having a hard time concentrating on what he was saying though. Besides feeling his breath on my face, my pulse was still through the roof.

The chat quickly took a turn towards Weirdville though.

He proceeded to show me pictures he'd taken THE NIGHT BEFORE of a full-grown male grizzly standing in front of our RVs, the same one he'd previously mentioned. He swore up and down that he hadn't fed the bear. However, it seemed a little too coincidental after he admitted to feeding the fox. I asked him when he'd taken the pictures, and it was at the exact time Laura and I were taking a walk through those very woods to go see the lake. We must have missed the bear by minutes

I walked out of the woods with him, said goodbye, and went back inside. I was still on high alert from the potential attack, I was furious at him for being a willful idiot, and I was scared for the kids and other campers he'd endangered. I told Laura what happened, and we debated what to do.

Within minutes of me coming back in Laura saw him load something in his truck and leave in hurry. So, I went back out in the woods, better prepared that time, because he clearly didn't want me to see what was out there.

I returned to the same spot and found the pile of trout. There were about seven full size fish left after the fox had already made several trips. They were gutted and cleaned, but NONE of the meat had been taken. Now I challenge anyone reading this to give me another reason for him to have dumped all his freshly caught fish in the woods, without keeping any of the meat, other than to bait the local wildlife. I'll wait.

I shot a short video of the fish, explained how close they were to the campground, and I covered what else had happened. Laura and I were both extremely bothered by the whole situation. Especially since there were lots of children playing all over the campground. Pretty much the worst place to bait in carnivorous wildlife, such as a grizzly bear.

After stewing over the situation a few minutes, I decided to tell the rangers. Knowing the fox was making quick work of the evidence, I jumped in the truck and quickly drove up to the front office, so they could call a ranger. I parked, jumped out of the truck, and was halfway into the building when I realized my neighbor's truck was parked in front of it.

OH NO!! He knew that I knew, and he'd beat me there.

I couldn't report him and ask the office to call for a ranger with him in there, so I got back in the truck and just started driving. We didn't have enough cell service to use the internet, so I drove around, hoping to flag down a passing ranger. Luckily for me, I found a nearby ranger station. I walked inside, didn't see anyone, so I called out, "Anyone here?"

A ranger responded in a nearby office, so I proceeded in. He looked like he was just about old enough to carry a gun, but I went ahead and told him the story. About a minute in he stopped me and said he needed to push this up to one of the LE rangers. He had me wait and went in the back. After a few minutes a man old enough to be my dad walked out. He asked me what had happened, and I told him everything.

I could tell he'd been at the job a long time, and that he knew what he was doing. I'd been worried I'd get the kid who may not understand the severity of the situation. Being a criminal justice major helped us fast track through the Q&A. I must not have explained the time sensitive evidence well enough because he gave me a witness statement to fill out. I then showed him the videos and reiterated there was at least a fox eating his evidence. That did it, and we took off for the campground.

When we arrived, I took him straight out to what was left of the fish pile. The fox had been busy while I was away, only a few fish were left. He took pictures, asked me a few more questions, and gave me the witness statement to finish.

While filling out the statement my neighbor returned. The ranger went over and they had a fairly long conversation. They walked out into the woods, came back and talked some more at his RV. Eventually the neighbor's wife brought out binders of paperwork and they went through them for some time.

After almost an hour we finally saw the ranger hand the neighbor something, then walk back to our camper. I gave him the finished witness statement and an extra 8 GB SD card with copies of the videos and pictures.

The ranger told us he had in fact ticketed our neighbor, for feeding the wildlife. Although he didn't say how much it was for. He did say the neighbor had to return to that county to appear in court. The ranger said there was no way to handle the ticket by mail. So that was also a punishment in itself.

The ranger then said our neighbor had lied through his teeth by claiming he'd only thrown one fish out, accidentally with the water. He also claimed to have a traumatic brain injury that seriously affected his judgment, that's what the binders were about. Apparently, it wasn't bad enough to stop him from hauling a 40-foot camper around the country though. What? That seemed a little….fishy.

So, you remember how we turned off to Weirdville earlier? Well, I took a stroll down main street this time, quite involuntarily though.

The ranger proceeded to inform us that he couldn't kick our neighbor out of the park unless he was being arrested, and he wasn't being arrested. WHAT!?!?!?!? The guy that likes to bait grizzlies now knew we turned him in, and he couldn't be forced to leave?

We fully expected retaliation, something bad like a pile of meat on our front steps. With the ranger's help we immediately began to look for someplace else to go as his phone worked there. We couldn't find anything available within an hour and it was already getting dark. After the ranger left, I called the office and asked if they could, or would, kick out the bear baiter. (We could make calls though. Weird, I know) To our extreme surprise they said no as well.

Apparently, I'd stopped for lunch in Weirdville, great.

Even though our neighbor had broken park rules and FEDERAL LAW no one could, or would, do anything. The "office staff" (I won't say what I'd like to call them) in the office actually said, "You have insurance don't you?"

Great, so if that clown was angry (which I'm sure he was), and slashed our tires, I guess it's just on us then? Since we couldn't find anywhere to go, we stayed put, and I pulled one-man guard duty most of the night.

The next morning, barely awake, we went to the office to speak with the manager and get some damned answers. The manager started right off by informing us that she'd known our neighbor for 30 years. Oh crap. She then defended him by telling us he was at her place the previous night giving her…. wait for it….FISH! So, he couldn't have possibly thrown out as many in the woods as I said he did. He actually had dinner with her after speaking with the ranger.

UGHHH!!! When did I rent a room in Weirdville? I couldn't seem to escape the place!

The man fed her the same lie he'd told the ranger, the one where he'd only thrown out one fish "by accident." That old chestnut. She bought it hook, line, and sinker (fishing puns haha). She insisted over and over that he was such a nice man, she'd known him for years, he'd never lie to her, and there was no way he'd ever retaliate against us. We didn't buy a word of it. After all, the only things we really knew about him was he liked to break the law, endanger others, lie to law enforcement, and lie to his friends.

Well, I can be a "bit" ornery when I'm upset, just ask Laura. The manager refused to listen or back down. So, while she was in mid-sentence, I took out my phone, pulled up the video of the fish pile, and showed it to her. I then proceeded to inform her that her "friend" was lying to her and that he'd only run over to her place with fish the previous night to grease the wheels, because he'd been caught.

It's amazing how fast the excuses disappeared once she saw the evidence. I wanted to scream "Do you really think I'd have ruined our vacation over one stupid fish?!?!?!?" Suddenly, she was much more willing to work with us. She still insisted she couldn't have him removed, however, she did quickly find us another spot we could move to.

It wasn't a perfect fix, but it was a lot better than the "sucks to be you" they'd been giving us. We happily took the new spot, packed up and moved in 30 minutes, and never dealt with the bear baiter again.

So, what's today's lesson kids? If you do need to report someone for breaking the law in a national park, make sure that either:

1. You're leaving immediately.

2. They're leaving immediately.

3. Law enforcement assures you, ahead of time, the offender will be removed.

4. Or, just keep your mouth shut.

We sure learned some interesting things about our nation's parks, the people that visit them, and the wildlife that lives there. It turned out not everyone follows the rules, especially friends of the park manager. I still can't comprehend the level of stupidity we encountered there.

Since the people in charge seemed incapable, or unwilling, to protect the law-abiding citizens, it was apparently up to us to protect ourselves. Thank God for video evidence. If you're like me, and you care about a little thing called safety, don't assume others share your sentiments.

When we posted a video about this, we actually received a fair amount of hate and trolling. I guess some people think it's totally cool to bait grizzlies into campgrounds. After the trolls, I felt like I was buying property in Weirdville.

Lucky for us the bear baiter story ends there.

Our time in the Grand Tetons wasn't over though. We still had a week left and planned to have some fun dammit! We took several long drives around the park, roaming aimlessly looking for wildlife or amazing photo opportunities. Sadly, all the hiking trails leading into the Grand Tetons were still snowed in. We were there a few weeks too early, so we couldn't go on the nicer hikes.

I wasn't dissuaded from hiking though. I grabbed hiking maps from the lodge and looked up several trails I could walk during that time of year. We were back up to 7,000' and Laura wanted nothing to do with hiking at that elevation, and I didn't blame her. The elevation was still mildly bothering her. She didn't want to get a few miles into a hike and run out of steam when she needed to get home.

I found a trail with some interesting things to see, packed a bag, wrote down where I was going for Laura in case something happened, and grabbed the bear mace and my other carry gun. See, I learn from my mistakes.

When I arrived, I found the trail impassable due to spring runoff and was forced to pick another. However, due to lack of cell service I couldn't tell Laura about the change in plans. I was also in a hurry so that I wouldn't run out of daylight and didn't want to drive all the way back to the RV.

I found the new trailhead and took off. I'd walked a few thousand miles in the Army, and it was like reconnecting with an old friend. I'd forgotten how much I loved walking through the woods alone. I very much enjoyed my time preparing for, and going through, SFAS (Special Forces Assessment and Selection). That's the selection process soldiers must pass to be accepted into the Green Beret training program. It entailed a lot of time walking alone in the woods.

Knowing that walking was the bulk of the schooling, I spent many days doing the same in preparation. I was stationed at Ft. Lewis, Washington back then. Washington has beautiful woods to walk through. I figured out where some apple trees and blackberries were naturally growing and would always plan my route to go by them to load up on snacks. Sadly, I didn't find any snacks walking the Grand Tetons.

I brought the GoPro and Nikon along, since I planned on making a video out of the hike. Everything was going very well until I made a critical error. The trail signs and the map had very different verbiage. Also, the map wasn't topographical, it was an inaccurate touristy map. I wish it had been topographical because I can read those easily. Then the trail signs were different at every crossing. I was having a difficult time knowing if I was even going the right direction. Since I couldn't figure out if the trail signs or the map were correct, I picked one and went with it.

I picked wrong. In hindsight, I should have found a list of trails online and researched them for primary and secondary routes before I set foot on a trail.

I meant to walk a shorter loop, around four miles. Instead, I walked a nine-mile loop. Of course, I didn't realize the problem until I was halfway into the long loop. I wasn't out there on a land navigation course, so I wasn't checking the map regularly. I was just following the trail signs since I'd realized the map was less than reliable.

I had a stroke of luck though. I was standing on a peninsula jutting out into Colter Bay thinking over my situation and I checked my phone. Amazingly I had service! I didn't think it would be enough for a call, so I wrote out a text to Laura explaining what had happened, where I was, where I was going and when I thought I might get back. It sent, and she promptly called me.

Surprisingly, we both happened to be standing in just the right spots for our phones to work at the same time. She was obviously very worried about me, especially since she was expecting me home any minute. But there was nothing we could do about that. Either we could waste some poor ranger's time for a non-emergency, or I could just keep walking. Laura's main concern was whether I could make it back to the truck by dark.

I knew I was starting to wear down though. I'd just walked four miles at a good pace, with only a few short breaks to film, at 7,000'. I was making decent time, but I hadn't been conserving myself for another 4-5 miles. Especially 4-5 miles of needing to push myself.

I did some quick math and figured what pace I'd been walking at, which was pathetic for me, and figured I might get to the truck 30 minutes before dark if I was lucky. That's dark, not sundown. I had my usual flashlight with me, and I was on a well-established trail. Even if it got dark, I could still easily make it out. After explaining all that to Laura she calmed down.

I'd already started walking before we hung up. I had a goal, getting to the truck before dark. After we hung up, I found a log to sit on. I pulled up my socks, tightened my boots, grabbed the snacks from my bag, and took off with a little pep in my step. During the second

271

half I focused much less on photography and a lot more on maintaining pace. Until that point, I was more focused on setting up shots, enjoying the scenery and the woods.

Unfortunately, I'd only packed a few snacks for a few miles of walking. Knowing I'd need the energy to make it back in time I scarfed them all. I was already running out of energy which meant I'd waited too long to eat; my body was going to be playing catch up the rest of the way. Great.

An interesting thing happened while I was booking it back, my imagination began to wander. I've always had an extremely active imagination. Just ask my mom and every one of my teachers before college. Maybe it's from being an only child?

If I'd written down all the crazy stories that have run through my head, I could likely be a professional writer by now. Sadly, I was always too busy, or distracted, to focus on them. ADHD is both a blessing and a curse. But now that I have a little more time maybe I can finally knock out one of the 10 ideas I have in the chute?

An active imagination can be nice sometimes, I can make my own entertainment when I'm bored or on a longer-than-expected hike. Although it can be double edged sword. After combat, it took a turn. Hardly a day went by in college where my imagination wasn't running wild strategizing what I would do during an active shooter scenario. I had a plan for every room, every class, every time.

Anyway, I came up with a wonderful story idea about someone who takes the wrong trail on a hike, gets chased by a wounded pissed off animal and somehow figures out how to survive. I don't want to give it away, but if I can ever find the time to write it, I think it'll be a good story.

Back to the botched hike where I had a very nice story outline in my head. I was pushing myself hard. The sun wasn't far from going behind the mountains and I knew it would get dark VERY quickly once that happened. I was so out of shape that it was the first time I'd been out of breath for a continuous hour in a few years. I was feeling the elevation too, I'd burned through my snacks and could feel my energy dropping fast, and to top it off I was almost out of water since I wanted it in me for the final push.

After I'd run through the bear story in my head a few times I switched back to thinking about the video. I was losing light, and I hadn't finished it yet. I decided to round it off with some comedy and quickly put together an idea I thought would be hilarious. I filmed a series of shots showing me lost in thick brush, panting hard pretending to be lost, crawling past the camera, and finally laying in the woods talking about how I couldn't go on.

I thought it was a very clever way to round out the video and the day. It wasn't raining or snowing, I wasn't injured, nothing was chasing me (that I knew of) and I was still in good spirits. Even with taking the wrong trail I was having a good day. I'd found several beaver huts, saw a beaver just a few yards from me, and I accidentally surprised some elk scaring the crap out of them.

Something wonderful happened while I was looking for places to get the shots I wanted. I came upon a trail fork. It was the first leg I'd walked, I was finally on the home stretch! When I'd finished up with all the shots I wanted I took a short break. I peed, tightened my boots again, killed my water, and checked the worthless map for the final time. If what I was seeing was correct, I only had about 1.5 miles left.

The sun had been down for a bit by then, it was quickly getting dark and cold. I'd already cycled through focusing on using different muscle groups several times and they were all near failure. It's a trick I learned during timed rucksack marches. For instance, by focusing on pushing with my glutes I can give my quads a little break, and vis-a-versa. But I was out of time, out of shape and all out of tricks.

No matter how much I just wanted to put my head down and push through to the end, I knew I couldn't. Dusk is prime time for wildlife to be roaming around and I was there during spring, which is also cub time. I had to focus on my surroundings to ensure I didn't get myself un-alived by surprising a momma grizzly.

I missed my deadline, but I only had to use my flashlight for the last 10 minutes or so. As soon as I left the woods headed for the parking lot, it got light enough for me to turn my flashlight off. It was even still light enough for me to film the closer. The woods can mess with your head, I was glad for having spent so much time in them before.

I dug my keys out of my pack while I was still walking. I hobbled up to AHNJ and had to use the grab handle to get inside, it's a bit tall and my legs had decided it was quitting time for the day. I remember just sitting there with AHNJ running and the seat heaters on for probably 10 minutes before I tried driving. I didn't trust my legs to push the brake pedal.

Laura was so happy when I walked inside. I vaguely remember putting my boots outside to dry since they were soaked through with sweat. I could barely move the next day, but I finally found that feeling of accomplishment I'd been missing.

A few days later Laura wanted to try a small hike, so we grabbed the dogs and put in about two miles. During our walk we met two girls and started talking. It turned out that one of them used to live near Laura, but she was then living in an RV and workamping at the park. She hadn't done any traveling yet, so when we told them all about what we did, they were enthralled. We have yet to tell someone about full-time RVing and receive a negative response.

We chose to not let the bear baiter ruin our vacation and I'm glad we did. We still enjoyed our time there, even if we were a little early for the season. On another positive note, a few days before we left, the Colter Bay gift shop and restaurant both opened for the season. Laura was able to relive some more of her childhood memories. She told me the restaurant hadn't changed since she'd been there. We have every intention of going back. I just hope we don't see our old neighbor again.

Yellowstone National Park and West Yellowstone

While preparing to leave the Grand Tetons we ran into a problem. Both the Rand McNally RV GPS and the Garmin in AHNJ's dash said we had to travel south a few hours, cut west below the mountains, drive north several hours, then turn east, spending a total of 9-10 hours driving to West Yellowstone around the entire Grand Tetons mountain range. Or we could follow the Google maps route of 2 hours directly through Yellowstone.

After hours of exhaustive searching we found nothing online saying there was anything wrong or unsafe with the direct route. We even traced the route on Google earth looking for a problem. In the end, we decided to roll the dice and ignore the $500 RV GPS we'd bought to keep us safe and to follow Google.

The drive north through Yellowstone was far from uneventful. We drove over a pass with 6-8' of snow piled up on each side of the road. I stopped to use the bathroom and saw a thermal vent with boiling mud on the side of the road, which I filmed of course. We saw a lot of elk and bison and we ran into multiple animal jams, several times I was worried about stopping in time. Luckily, I always try to keep a safe distance.

We also saw the scars left from the 1988 fires that almost burned Yellowstone to the ground. New forests are growing back, but the skeletons of burned trees randomly jut up from the fields of green, almost like bony fingers grasping for the life they used to know. The burned trees must have been 50' taller than the new ones.

We were still curious why both GPS's wanted to route us 7 hours out of the way, so we drove with them on, muted of course. We wanted to see where the problem was, and we were in for a surprise. While approaching the West gate, both GPS's showed the road ended at the gate. As we drove through the gate, which was more than tall enough for us, the GPS rerouted and showed us to be 10 minutes from the RV park. We never did figure out why they both thought the road ended there, but they thought we couldn't drive through the West Yellowstone gate.

We stayed at the park for two weeks and couldn't have been happier doing so. The RV park was very nice and there's a lot to do and see in West Yellowstone. Another bonus of staying in town was fantastic cell service, we'd been missing that.

I think we made four trips into the park. By trips I mean 10 hours of sightseeing, driving and filming. Each day was exhausting. Then we'd have two days of work afterwards editing and posting a video, plus all our other social media work. We also made videos about the town of West Yellowstone and of the RV park we were in. Yellowstone was on the top of my list for the trip. I couldn't wait to go see and film everything, I'd dreamed of seeing Yellowstone most of my life.

We learned a few things you should know if you're wanting to go as well.

- If you have an RV over 35' it will be difficult finding an RV spot inside Yellowstone. Most of the campgrounds were built a long time ago and only have shorter sites.

- If you're staying outside the park, like we did, get to the gate before 7am. Otherwise the Chinese tour buses will beat you there.

- You must plan your days. The park is far too large to just drive around aimlessly if you want to see the main attractions. You can drive for hours between main areas. We split the park into sections and spent a day in each one.

- If you're on a budget pack a lot of food and whatever else you think you'll need. Buying anything inside the park was very expensive.

- Cell service in the park is spotty. Bring a map and plan your stops on it beforehand. Don't expect to use Google maps.

- You may have to pass locations you want to stop at since the tour buses clog them up. We had to try a few areas several times before we could get into the parking lot. There were some we just couldn't see thanks to the buses.

- Watch traffic closely. People do crazy things when they see animals.

On our first day in the park, we learned a hard lesson about the tour buses. If they beat you to the gate, they'll also beat you to every place you're trying to go. Those drivers were parking anywhere they could fit. We commonly saw them park across six spots because all the long sites had other tour buses in them. That's why we couldn't park at many of the main areas and had to go back later. Basically, after 9 am, there wasn't much parking anywhere but the main lodge near Old Faithful.

We also learned that the foreign tourists had no respect for us. They would see us trying to film or take pictures and still walk, or stand, in front of us all day every day. We found the best practice was to just get up early and beat them to the park. We were shocked at how rude they were. Maybe that's normal where they're from? It definitely made us reconsider how we've acted on past vacations. I know we'll be more courteous next time we visit another country.

We had a wonderful time seeing all the different brightly colored pools of water hot enough to boil a person in minutes. Seriously, people have fallen in before and it went very badly. Throughout the park it seemed as if there was a new geyser every time we turned around. Eventually I stopped filming them because I didn't want the videos to look repetitive.

I learned so much about photography during those two weeks. We kept trying to take pictures of beautiful things, but they wouldn't look the same as how we saw them. I spent hours online at night researching and trying to learn how to use a DSLR, I'd been procrastinating. Oh, that's where we finally figured out how to film with it. Thank God it didn't take a year of us owning it or anything, Laura figured that one out.

During our last day in the park we were on the wooden walkways that thread through the area surrounding Old Faithful, marveling at everything there is to see, such as geysers that only erupt every few years, when we were stopped by a ranger. He was stopping everyone on that path because a momma grizzly and her two cubs were roaming the area. We'd been driving around hunting bears for three weeks without seeing a single one. We couldn't believe we'd just walked up on three.

The bears were too close for people to roam freely so rangers were posted up at two locations stopping people from using a large section of the path. That was fine with us as we were trying to figure out our camera.

The cubs were probably around 50 lbs., or medium dog size. They were playing and wrestling around a log for the better part of an hour. It was the kind of situation most people will never see outside of National Geographic. The momma was just eating everything in sight. While standing there the ranger gave us all an impromptu class on bears. He said the momma hadn't been out of hibernation long and the cubs were probably still nursing which would explain her appetite.

It was very interesting learning how the park dealt with bears wandering around the touristy areas. He said they have trackers on all the bears and workers constantly monitor them. If one is getting near a tourist area, they call rangers in to block people from getting too close. It seemed like they'd found a nice balance of bear safety vs tourist safety. Sure, having the path blocked was a little inconvenient, but they didn't have to put a bear down because a tourist got too close triggering a defense response from the momma.

While standing there, we learned about how effective bear spray is. He said you can use so little that a can will usually give you 3-4 uses. I would have never thought about needing to use it more than once. But then again, I don't work around bears. He said it's so effective that most rangers don't even want to carry guns.

We took over 300 pictures of the bears, but only 10 or so turned out. I realized that our entry-level camera, and my lack of knowledge, were holding our photography back.

Eventually the bears wandered off and we all dispersed. We walked over to Old Faithful, watched that erupt, and decided to go home. I don't mean to say that Old Faithful was anticlimactic, far from it, we were just exhausted. We'd walked several miles that day at 8,000'.

When we left Yellowstone, I was more interested in photography than ever before. I wanted to obtain equipment that would capture the correct colors and light that I saw. I wanted a camera body with enough focus points that I could fine tune it for whatever situation I found myself in. The bug bit and it bit hard. In two weeks, I went from having a passing interest to obsessing over it.

> *Of course, due to lack of funds we kept that camera for another year. But I credit that experience, and that frustration, for giving me the passion to learn. That eventually blossomed into me landing the Lead Grip and Third Cameraman roles in the movie RV Nomads. We may not have had many usable pictures of the grizzly cubs, but it worked out alright in the end.*

My wonderful time at Yellowstone was brought to an unexpected halt a few days before we'd planned to leave. I was checking comments on social media one morning and found out a friend from my last unit had committed suicide the previous night.

There's a problem not enough people are trying to fix. The problem is that we have many soldiers making it home alive, but still dying. They survive the war overseas but lose the emotional war within. Just from the guys I knew, we've lost three times as many here as we did in actual combat. I was so mentally wrecked after the news that our fun time in Yellowstone came to a grinding halt.

My PTSD has been a serious issue between Laura and I since we met. The emotional damage has made marriage even more difficult than it should be. During times like that Laura has always been very supportive and loving. Neither of us fully understand my PTSD, but she really does the best she can.

I got lucky, many women wouldn't have put up with a husband that can turn his emotions on and off like a light. The worst part is that's usually not a conscience choice. I've become better at recognizing and stopping it from happening, but I question if I'll ever have full control over it.

Mount Rainier/Mt. Saint Helens

Originally, Glacier National Park was going to be our final stop before turning in the RV, but they weren't open since the snow hadn't melted yet. So, we changed our plans and found an RV park in Washington between Mt. Rainier and Mt. St. Helens. I knew Laura would enjoy the woods of Washington's national parks, they're unlike anything I've seen anywhere else. I consider myself very lucky to have grown up near them. There were multiple camping trips in those woods when I was young.

The trip from Yellowstone to Washington was the longest stretch without a fun stop on the trip. We pulled off at a few different touristy destinations along the way, but we mostly focused on putting in miles. That's not our preferred style of travel, but sometimes it's necessary, unfortunately.

Our final stop before Mt. Rainier was in Moses Lake, Washington. Not only was it spaced correctly for how long we like our travel days, but an old family friend lives there. She had grown up with my dad, later became friends with my mom when they met, and they stayed friends ever since.

I don't remember the last time I saw her before that. Maybe when my dad died? She was one of the friends that drove over to help me deal with his belongings and clean out his place. You know how you meet that handful of people in life that are always willing to help no matter what? She's one of them. I let her know we'd be in town that night and she was free for dinner. It was great getting to catch up for a few hours.

The next day, on the way to Mt. Rainier, I had my eyes peeled for fruit stands. In case you didn't know, eastern Washington is a one of the largest fruit growing regions in the nation. In some areas, there are apple orchards as far as the eye can see. Right after Yakima, and before the pass, we finally found one. Maybe I shouldn't have pulled over there with the fifth wheel, but I made it fit. I wasn't about to pass up my first chance at fresh Washington fruit in years.

Sadly, the cherries weren't even close to being in season yet, but I grabbed a bunch of apples and peanuts. There's this cool thing about fresh apples where they last months instead of weeks. I bought a dozen or two and none of them went bad before they were eaten, I should have bought a box full. I wish I'd bought another few bags of those peanuts as well, they were night and day better than store bought.

Our drive over the Highway 12 pass was the best pass of the trip by far. All the snow had melted, and everything was a bright brilliant green. After our time in the desert it was almost too green, but we couldn't get enough of it. We even had a conversation about how Laura wanted to spend more time with green instead of brown desert, which I of course agreed to. After growing up with it, I sorely missed it.

The RV park we stayed at had been a Thousand Trails park two decades before but had since been sold. They parked us in an area with four long rows of full hookup sites. They could probably hold over 100 RV's but hardly anyone else was there. I guess the rows were for temporary guests. as they also had several loops in the woods with more secluded sites, those were much more crowded than our area. The Cowlitz river runs behind the park and there were even a few spots on the shore.

The week we spent there was right before the start of the busy summer tourist season, so we had most of the park to ourselves. Even though we were early, we had a massive stroke of luck with fantastic weather most of the time. It was uncharacteristic for a Western Washington spring.

The park was so quiet and peaceful, we have every intention of going back. We chose that park because it was only 15-20 minutes from an entrance to Mount Rainier National Park. That entrance is also the location of the Grove of Patriarchs, an old growth forest with some of the largest and oldest trees in the Cascades.

I was excited to see the old growth, so we decided to make our first video in the area about it. I didn't realize it, but I was retracing my childhood vacation steps. About halfway through the park I began to have memories of when I was there 25 years before. There aren't giant trees like that in many places of the world, and I knew I hadn't

284

been to any of the others. I think what threw me off was the difference in perspective. I was viewing everything from a position of being three feet taller.

Trying to jog my memory more, I called with my mom after we finished filming. She told me the campground by that entrance to the National Park was where we camped several summers when I was young. So, on our way out we drove through there. I parked in an empty site and got out to look around a bit. Then the memories came flooding back.

Memories of the giant green canvas tent my dad would set up. Memories of mornings sitting at those same wooden picnic tables eating cereal from Styrofoam bowls. Memories of the green Coleman lantern and cook stove, and watching my dad light them. Memories of running around the campground with my friends like we'd just escaped from prison. Memories of my dad splitting firewood. Memories of my parents still being together.

Those camping trips were probably the best days of my childhood. I sat at a picnic table and took a walk down memory lane for a bit. I wondered if I'd sat there with my parents 25 years before. When I snapped back to reality I got back in the truck and told Laura all about it. I don't remember much from my childhood, it's always very surprising when I have more memories.

A day or two later we planned to drive Loop 3 on the southern side of Mt. Rainier. We couldn't find anything online about how long it was supposed to take so we just planned on it taking all day. I was really excited to take Laura up there and show her some of my most cherished childhood memories.

The loop began at the same entrance we had used a few days prior. We decided to see the old growth forest again since we hadn't given it much time before. It was worth seeing a second time anyway.

Climbing the foot of the mountain felt as if we were going back in time a few thousand years. Other than the road, it was pristine untouched landscape as far as we could see. There were glacier-fed waterfalls every few miles, 150'+ tall moss-covered trees and a sense of serenity missing in the rest of the world. We didn't see a single tour bus or large group of people all day. It felt as if we had the mountain to ourselves.

There are pros and cons to arriving before tourist season. A few hours into the drive we found a big con, the snow hadn't melted from the higher elevations yet. The big visitors center wasn't open yet either, because it was still buried in snow. Oops. I guess we were a little too early. That also meant there were no sprawling fields of mountain wildflowers either. I was really sad when I realized Laura wouldn't get to see the mountain, but that gave us a perfect excuse to come back again.

We found that we weren't the only people taking advantage of the roads being empty. Several cyclists were out enjoying the weather. I can't even fathom how much of a genetic god you must be to cycle up a mountain. The pace they were keeping uphill was about on par with my pace on a flat road. On the way down, we "passed" several more. By "passed" I mean they were doing 30-40mph and I had to wait several miles for a good place to go around. I didn't want the wind from our large truck to knock them off a cliff.

It was a good thing we planned on the loop taking all day, because it did. I'm sure it didn't help that we were stopping every few minutes to film and take pictures. Unfortunately, we started late, and it was getting dark before we were even close to being done. There was no cell service but thankfully we had the GPS in the trucks dash to guide us home. Those deserted mountain roads were pitch black at night. We were worried about elk and took it nice and slow after the sun went down.

We were sad that Mt. Rainier was still snowed in, but it didn't dissuade us from going to Mount St. Helens. We checked the weather forecast and picked the clearest day we had left to see the other mountain. I was planning on taking the eastern entrance into Helens but that wasn't open due to snow. Seems like it's a recurring theme. Instead, we drove an hour out to the highway and around to the main entrance of the park. We were glad to have taken that route, there are some neat things to see along the way.

On the way up, we passed the Buried A-Frame house. Someone was having an A-frame house built near the road, when the mountain erupted in 1980. The house was supposedly days away from being completed when a mud river from the melted glaciers buried several feet of it. It's since been dug out, but the ground around the outside of the house is three feet higher than the floor inside. It sure is an interesting perspective. They also have a 30' tall concrete bigfoot statue and bigfoot museum there. If you're into that kind of stuff.

A few miles later, we passed a restaurant named the Fire Mountain Grill that advertised homemade cobblers. We both decided we were eating cobbler there on the way down. Shortly after the restaurant we crossed a long bridge and the landscape changed dramatically. We'd entered the blast zone from the volcano. Now I don't mean different like it was barren landscape, it had been 36 years since the eruption after all. The forest was growing back nicely, but it wasn't like any forest you've ever seen.

People don't realize that outside of National and State Parks much of the woods in Washington are privately owned, usually by logging companies. They still have to obtain permits from the government before they can cut though. When the volcano erupted the blast leveled 230 square miles of forest. Once the ground was able to support life again, and with government aid, the logging companies undertook a massive replanting operation.

Seeing miles of forest where every tree is not only the same species, but the same height, is a surreal experience. As we continued our climb up the mountain, we passed several different sections of forest. There would be different species of trees between sections, but no diversity within the section. There were signs next to each naming the logging company and the year it was planted.

When we finally got to the end of the road, we found ourselves at the Johnston Ridge Observatory. It received its name because that's the ridge where volcanologist David Johnston was camped the morning of the eruption. He was able to radio in that the eruption was happening right before he was killed. The ridge was directly in the path of the blast. He had been warning people about how dangerous the mountain was for weeks. His warnings may have saved thousands of lives. We learned about him in the observatory.

After an hour or so we decided to head home. The mountain was ringed in clouds and we couldn't get any good pictures. Sadly, the second mountain was also a bust. I'll get Laura to a mountain someday, just not those days.

On the way down, we remembered the restaurant advertising cobbler, or at least my stomach did. The building looks like it was an old Victorian home that miraculously survived the volcano and is now a restaurant. If you go on a nice day there's a large porch wrapping around the back of the house that overlooks the river a hundred feet down you can dine on.

Although we only went in for cobbler, I changed my mind when I saw the menu. They have a food challenge called the Bigfoot burger. I'd never done a food challenge before, we had the camera with us, so why not try it. I had to clear my plate in 30 minutes to get a free t-shirt.

I don't know how they were making a profit on that thing. It had 4 beef patties, a pile of sliced cheeses, enough sliced ham and turkey to make two sandwiches, enough pulled pork for a third sandwich and half a pack of bacon. It also came with half a plate of kettle chips smothered in liquid nacho cheese.

They've changed the whole thing now. While researching to write this I saw they've swapped the slimy chips out for beer battered fries, removed one beef patty, and it looks like there's less ingredients all around now. It's also cheaper by 10-15$, I don't remember the exact price of the one I ordered but it was over $50.

Not only did I finish it, but…..well, nothing. I did finish it, but I was so miserably full I could barely drive back. We ordered cobbler to go because I couldn't even think about more food. I didn't eat again that night, and I wasn't fully hungry for over 24 hours. The experience sure made an interesting video though. Now I can always say I've successfully completed a food challenge and I've got the shirt to prove it!

CHAPTER

24

Time to Move Out

———⁓⁓⁓———

After the day at St. Helens, our time on vacation was rapidly coming to an end. We only had about a week left until the appointment to turn in the RV. Knowing the clock was running down, we'd been making plans to ensure turning in our camper went smoothly.

The Camping World service advisor had told us it would likely take all summer to fix everything on our list, so we made plans to move out of the RV. I know most people don't "move out" of their RVs when they go in the shop. However, almost everything we owned was in there.

After working on cars for two years I understood how much of a nightmare it is to deal with a customer's mountain of stuff. For instance, we regularly had to track down wheel lock keys and they're often kept in the trunk. If the trunk was packed to the brim, I'd have to haul their stuff out, set it on the nasty shop floor, then figure out how to get it all back in. That process could turn a 30-second job into 15 minutes. Now multiply that by a 41' foot RV.

We wanted to get our home back as soon as possible and I knew moving out would allow the techs to work as fast as possible. Plus, we wouldn't have to worry about loss or theft. There was one more reason we completely moved out, we didn't know if we'd even be getting our home back.

Multiple people had contacted us with stories about how their RV went in for major repairs and the manufacturer decided a full replacement was cheaper. We didn't necessarily want a new RV though. The possibility of going through the same ordeal again weighed heavily on our minds.

In order to move out we needed someplace to park near where we would be living for the summer. We'd want easy access to our belongings of course. My aunt lives 30 minutes away from my grandma's house, where we stayed for the summer, and she said we could park on her property for a few days while we packed and moved out. We then found an available storage shed only minutes from her house. Everything was coming together nicely.

Only one thing still stood in our way, the Seattle corridor. If you've never driven through the Seattle area, I'll give a brief description. The city is smashed up against Puget sound on the west and thins towards the east as you get closer to the mountains. Unfortunately, there isn't a good north/south route near the mountains. The only highways are I-5 and I-405, right through the heart of Seattle and its suburbs.

The lack of good highway options is one of the main reasons traffic is so terrible there. They're actually trying to dig an underground four lane highway for a zillion dollars because there's no place left to build a new one.

I grew up driving in that traffic and it's so much worse than it was just 10 years ago. Rush hour is now four hours of bumper to bumper gridlock. I used to put my car in neutral, set the parking brake on the highway and wait 10 minutes until I could move again.

I was afraid of towing through that mess because I know how the people drive there. If I got enough space behind the person in front to safely stop someone would jump in the instant it opened, every time. It's just how people drive out there. You must be a very aggressive driver if you want to get anywhere in that traffic. And it's impossible to drive aggressively while towing, I just can't start and stop fast enough.

I saw three options for getting the RV north of Seattle.

1. Start the drive at 3am.

    - Pros: Potentially miss all traffic and make wonderful time.

    - Cons: Drive in the dark, deal with drunks, drive tired.

2. Start the drive at 9am.

    - Pros: Possibly less traffic than rush hour.

- Cons: Possibly as much traffic as rush hour.

3. Drive back over the pass and go north through eastern Washington then cross back over by Everett.

   - Pros: Bypass all of Seattle's tomfoolery.

   - Cons: Drive an extra few hours and hundreds of miles.

Decisions, decisions…

We chose option number two. I don't do well driving tired, Laura doesn't like traveling in the dark, and we didn't have the money to burn on extra diesel going back over the mountains.

The night before we planned to leave, we did our usual pack up procedure to expedite our departure. Everything was going according to schedule the next morning until a couple walked over right as I was disconnecting the power.

Random people walking over to talk in an RV park is fairly common, so I didn't think much of it. Little did I know, but Laura had recommended that camp ground to someone from our Cedar Creek Facebook page. Well, they listened to her, went there, and wanted to meet us before we left.

Before that day we'd never met anyone that followed us online, it was a strange experience. There we were, talking to people that knew us, and I didn't know a thing about them. They were treating us like we were famous or something, which was weird for us. We sure didn't feel like we were famous.

We quickly learned a lot about them, and they were genuinely very nice people. The only problem was they wanted to talk, a lot, and we had our backs against a wall. We were looking at a 4-5-hour travel day and if we left too late, we'd catch early rush hour north of Seattle. Rush hour that would be going the same direction as us.

Having never met fans before, neither of us knew how to politely break off the conversation. Laura kept looking at me and I knew she wanted me to do it, but I couldn't find a break in the conversation. Finally, I just spoke up and told them we had to leave. I apologized for it, but they'd delayed us about 1.5 hours, and I was becoming worried.

> *I don't want to ever be thought of as a stuck-up Hollywood type, but I'm starting to understand why they're viewed that way. If I gave an hour to everyone that wanted to talk to me, talking would become a full-time job, and we're only known to the RV community. Just last night I met a fan and we spoke for almost two hours. I enjoy meeting people, but it can make balancing work and personal life a challenge.*

We finally hit the road around 10:30 am for our second worst travel day, just behind the blizzard day. It began with us sitting behind street sweepers for 30 minutes that were only going 5 mph. To make matters worse, they were blocking both lanes and we couldn't pass.

For most of the day I couldn't get my speed high enough to use my exhaust brake. I knew the brakes were overheating from standing on them every time someone jumped in front of us, but there was nothing I could do about it. If I wasn't getting cut off every ten minutes, it's because we were sitting at a red light.

Once we made it north of Seattle with no signs of gridlock I started to relax. Then we got to Everett. Someone must have been listening to the Good Idea Fairy because they decided it would be a swell idea to shut down two lanes in the middle of the day. Instead of, oh I don't know....maybe at night? We finally found our gridlock.

Normally pulling an aircraft carrier behind me incentivizes people to move when I turn on the blinker. Sigh....not there. Apparently, my blinker said speed up and cut me off. After a mile or two of trying to get out of a lane that was ending, I could see the cones, and no one was letting us in. That's one of those times I wanted a train horn installed on the truck.

I don't know why I bothered, but I turned my blinker on again, and just began to merge. Laura was hiding her eyes, she was terrified. I remember looking over at the guy in the lane next to me as he was driving bumper-to-bumper with the car in front of him. We made eye contact, he looked away then closed the gap in front of him a little more. Those people genuinely didn't care if I couldn't get in and had to sit there for hours. So, I just kept slowly merging.

There's this great thing called the "rule of tonnage" (well, more like a rule of thumb) another RVer told me about. It states the heaviest vehicle has the right of way. I'd never had to use it before, but I learned that day it most definitely works. As I began to cross the line, mere inches from the vehicles next to us, the red sea parted as they all magically remembered where their brake pedals were. We cleared the cones with a few feet to spare.

The funniest thing happened after I merged, several people road raged around us giving us dirty looks and flipping us off for the next few minutes. Like I was the asshole because the lane was ending.

After we cleared the construction traffic the rest of the day went smoothly. We parked at my aunt's house and immediately went to work. We only had seven days to unload the RV into a storage shed and we couldn't be taking a night off, no matter how tired or stressed we were.

We went straight to Home Depot, only stopping for some food since we missed lunch. There I bought two stacks of plastic storage bins for us to pack up everything inside the RV. All our things in the storage bays were already in totes, so we figured we wouldn't need too many. I hate to say this, but we grossly miscalculated how much stuff we still had.

We jumped right into packing that evening and worked until we filled all the totes we'd bought. We filled them all that night just with the living room. We still had the kitchen, bathroom, and bedroom to go. The next morning, I went back to Home Depot for another stack while Laura continued to work on the RV. The second round of totes was easily filled with the kitchen and I was forced to go back for a third time.

We weren't just slinging everything in totes and calling it a day though, we were organizing them as we went. Since we would have very limited space at my mom's house, we could only take a few totes with us. So, while packing we also had to be cognizant of setting things aside that we'd want with us. My mom's house was 30 minutes away and we didn't want to make multiple trips there because of fuel and time. The items that were going there were set aside until we needed to make a trip up to my mom's.

The packing was going well, but the living room was quickly filling up. We had totes stacked 6' high because we were waiting on the storage shed to become available. I'd called about ten different storage companies in the area, which was all of them, and they were all booked up. Well, unless we wanted a 2x1' or a 50x37' shed, or whatever weird dimensions they had left. The only options we had were paying hundreds a month for a shed we could park the RV in or renting several small sheds and spreading our stuff out between them. Neither of those worked for us, so we were waiting on a normal sized unit to clear out.

A few days before the storage shed was going to be available, we made our first trip up to my mom's house. I pulled the hitch out of the truck bed and we loaded the truck to the gills. The bed was half full of firewood as well as a fire pit, propane grill, and other random stuff that had to be offloaded at my mom's because we didn't need to clog up the storage shed with it all.

We packed the back seat with totes full of our pantry food since we didn't want to put one bite of food in storage and invite mice to snack on our belongings. I fit the fire-proof safe back there as well. We think it's vital to have a fireproof safe in an RV, considering they can burn down in minutes.

We spent a few hours with my mom, it had been over a year since I'd seen her, and we had some catching up to do. After we unloaded everything, we apologized but had to leave and get back to work. We'd be seeing her a lot more in the coming months anyway.

The next morning, I went back to Home Depot for the fourth and final time. I had to get a tamper-proof lock for the storage unit, mouse traps, and maybe another few large totes.....Don't judge me! There were a few bulky items left over.

We were blown away by the amount of stuff we still had. We decided to downsize again before it all went back in the RV.

In the middle of moving out we were still dealing with Cedar Creek. We had some serious questions, and they weren't being answered. Questions such as:

1. If Camping World found anything else wrong after we turned it in would it be covered? Cedar Creek said anything found up until we turned it in would be covered. But I know from my time working on cars that issues are often found after you start working on it.

2. Would we be reimbursed for storage and moving expenses? They never offered, and it was becoming expensive.

3. Would Cedar Creek warranty the repair work for any amount of time?

Even though Cedar Creek had told us they'd be more responsive, they were proving it was too difficult for them. Unfortunately, there was nothing we could do about it, so we just kept working on moving out.

Our scheduled move out day with the RV arrived far too quickly. I'd reserved a 10x10 U-Haul truck to expedite the move out process because I've done the pick-up truck moves before and we couldn't afford the time wasted driving back and forth 20 times. We were waiting in the parking lot to rent the truck when they opened the office. We knew moving was going to take a while and wanted to get a jump on it. Even with everything already packed it still took an hour and a half to load the U-Haul.

I had planned everything down to the day because of our tight schedule. We rented the U-Haul that day because that's when our storage shed was supposed to become available. We arrived with everything packed and ready to offload. I walked into the office, confident that our reservation still stood, gave the woman my name, and was then told it wasn't available.

Huh.....?

She told me the person who was scheduled to clear out the day before hadn't. Apparently, that's a common problem, she acted like it was no big deal. I told her it was a very big deal for us. We had one day left to move out of the RV, and we had everything sitting in her parking lot because her company said we would have a shed available that day.

I suppose we could have tried to find a different company, but hers was the only one I'd found within 45 minutes with availability. We didn't want to store our stuff hours away. We knew we'd be spending a lot of time with it downsizing while the RV was in the shop.

Luckily, she was accommodating and had an idea. She grabbed her keys and said, "Follow me." We began walking through the building looking for any empty units, just in case there was a scheduling mistake and one wasn't booked but showed it was in their system. To my extreme surprise we found one in the first hallway.

We went back to the office and she confirmed it was an error and that it was available. The Hebard Luck had struck again, but it wasn't over yet! Due to the inconvenience, and because it was a size larger than we'd planned on renting, she gave us a 50% discount for the first month. I'd originally reserved a 5x15 but the one she found was a 10x10, which was just fine with us. Having the extra space meant we wouldn't have to move everything into the hallway every time we went there.

We only had the U-Haul for 24hours, so we got right to work. We had an interior unit but luckily, they provided hand carts that made unloading a breeze. Otherwise we'd have been looking at hand carrying everything in, and I know our backs wouldn't have liked that. After we dropped off the U-Haul, we went home to get some sleep before going back to my mom's house the next day.

But the night wasn't over yet!

While Laura was in the shower, she suddenly called out for me because the water pump had stopped. I immediately started checking everything that could have caused it but couldn't find the problem. Meanwhile, Laura was freezing, covered in soap, waiting for me to figure it out. I was running out of things to check and didn't have an answer. The pump is 12v, so I didn't look at any of the 120v stuff first, but when the 12v system checked out I was stumped.

Finally, I checked the 120v breakers and fuses, I figured it was worth a shot. I have no idea how a 120v fuse could affect the 12v water pump, but it had. One of the fuse warning lights was on. When I touched it, the light turned off and the pump kicked back on. It was the strangest thing.

After she finished in the shower, I fiddled with the fuse for a bit trying to figure it out. All I learned was that I needed to push one corner in hard and it would stay connected. If I just pushed it in the middle the light would stay on. I made a short video about it and put the fuse on the ever-growing problems list.

By that time our list was around 80 items. After Cedar Creek told us they'd cover everything found before the appointment I went through the RV with a fine-tooth comb, several times, trying to find every problem I could. We knew some of it was small stuff, but we didn't want to pay to fix anything we didn't have to. I could start the DIY jobs after the warranty expired.

The next day we emptied the fridge/freezer and took everything left to my mom's. We stayed there that night as there was nothing left in the RV, we'd even packed up the bedding. The next morning, we kenneled the dogs and drove back to the RV. The last thing we did was put a plastic cover on the mattress, we didn't want it to get dirty while they were working on everything.

We didn't try to put the mattress in storage since getting it out of the RV would have been a real pain. Actually, I'm not sure if we even can remove it without taking out a slide or cutting it up. It's a king and our door isn't a standard residential size.

As we pulled away from my aunt's house, I marveled at how easy it was to tow the RV when it was empty. It was so much lighter that it felt like I was pulling a travel trailer. The wonderment was cut short as I remembered where we were going. Our hearts were filled with worry and trepidation (just because I wanted to throw a large word in here) as we turned that first corner.

I left a major event out of the timeline because it would have just been too confusing to try and weave it in. Especially since I don't have any videos or blog posts to jog my memory with.

During the entire move out process we were helping my mom renovate the bedroom we would be staying in for the summer. She'd been wanting to update it for years and had planned on doing it that summer. Unfortunately for us, the man that was helping her do most of the work was on a tight schedule. So, the work had to be completed during the week we were packing and moving.

We had planned on cleaning the entire RV before it went in and didn't have a second to touch it. We probably put 80 hours into that room between the two of us that week. By the time we turned the RV in we were running on zero sleep. We had to finish the room before we handed over the RV so that we'd have someplace to sleep. Surprise, surprise, we had our backs against a wall, as usual.

The day we dropped the RV off, we ran back to the house and worked the rest of the day, because it wasn't finished yet. That night, while Laura was in the shower, I drug the bed back in there and set it up, so we'd have someplace to sleep. It still took us another few days to finish, mostly because of complications due to the house being over 100 years old and having settled. When it was completed, my mom was so thankful that we helped her.

We were so busy working that we didn't even try to make a video about the renovations. Although, during a Camping World update video you can hear a skill saw fire up before a scene cuts out.

CHAPTER 25

We Give Our House to Camping World

———— ꝏꝏ ————

Camping World was only a 15-minute drive from my aunt's. I knew where it was since it had been there for many years. It was one of our only tow days we didn't have to use the GPS.

As we pulled into their parking lot we were in for a big surprise. I may have known where it was, but I'd never been very close to it, so I'd seen that the entire parking lot is absolutely packed with RVs awaiting repairs.

There was no place I could park the rig, so I made the executive decision to pull it alongside another one and blocked half the road.

Laura stayed with it so she could call me if someone needed it moved. I had to go inside and speak with our service advisor and figure out what we were supposed to do, and where we could park. It's not like they send you instructions prior to bringing in your aircraft carrier.

After ensuring my ringer was on, I ran inside and found our service advisor. We spoke for a minute to get him up to speed, but when he showed me the last list Cedar Creek had sent him, we encountered our first problem. The list he had was from two months prior and only around 30 items long. Since I'd just emailed our updated list to Cedar Creek after the fuse problem, I was able to forward it to him and he printed it out.

He said he needed to show the new list to his manager which was fine with me, I still needed to dump and flush the tanks. He told me to park anywhere I could fit when I was done, he agreed the parking situation was out of control. We agreed to reconvene after that.

I ran back to the truck and pulled the RV over to the dump station. They had sewer and flush hoses which was great since I didn't want to use ours and pack them away for a few months still wet. In the middle of the dirty business another RV pulled up behind us but couldn't get close enough to dump. Rather than just sitting in his RV and watching me he got out and we got to talking about….something. I don't remember. Nothing like bonding over a sewer hose. That's just part of RV life.

Little did I know but one of the funniest things I've ever experienced was about to happen.

Since I wanted that black tank crystal clean, I was flushing longer than usual. I was still talking to the guy waiting behind me, listening to crap flow through a tube at my feet, when a man wearing a blue Camping World shirt suddenly came storming around the corner holding a crumpled stack of papers in his fist. He was waving them around like a sword as he targeted the poor guy talking to me.

Pointing the fistful of papers at him Mr. Blue Shirt shouted, "Are you John Hebard?!"

My unwitting partner in crime was obviously confused. He quickly shook his head and squeezed out a weak sounding, "No...." Mr. Blue Shirt then turned his sights, and stack of papers, on me. Pointing them at me as if he could literally strike me down with them, he angrily asked, "Are you John Hebard?!" Against my better judgement, I said yes.

Mr. Blue Shirt marched right up to me, opened the papers and glanced over them, as if to reassure himself they still said the same insane things. While waving the fist-full of papers around he very angrily exclaimed, "I'M NOT TOUCHING THIS THING, I DON'T WANT ANYTHING TO DO WITH THIS LEMON, NO ONE TOLD ME THE LIST WAS 80 ITEMS LONG, THIS WILL TAKE ME ALL SUMMER TO FIX!!"

I responded the only way I could. I said that I understood and didn't blame him for not wanting to fix it. After all, they didn't build or sell it.

My response clearly put him back on his heels. He was still visibly upset, but at least he stopped yelling. He then announced himself as the service manager and proceeded to inform me that it would take months for him to even attempt to fix everything on the list. You should have seen the look of shock on his face when I just said, "OK."

I think he was expecting me to blow up and yell back at him or something. What he didn't yet know was that we'd already planned for it to take months. After my obviously unexpected answers, he began to visibly calm down.

Around that time, Laura got out of the truck and came to see what was happening. She'd heard him yelling and was very worried. When she joined me, he finished calming down. I don't know what that guy had going on in his life, but I hope he's learned how to process anger better or reduce his stressors. Thankfully, I didn't respond with anger because we may have ended up in a fight.

The manager then explained how difficult it would be for his shop to complete the mile-long list of repairs. Summer is their busy season and the shop had about 100 other RV's awaiting repairs in front of us. He decided to suggest that Cedar Creek take our unit back to their factory for repairs or buy us out of it.

Obviously, we were very excited to hear this news. We knew the factory was the best place for the repairs to be completed. Also, they would probably be much faster as they only deal with Cedar Creek's. The Camping World techs probably don't work on Cedar Creek's that often, and they certainly don't work on them exclusively.

The manager let us leave it there that night but told us we may be coming back the next day to get it. He said he'd talk to Cedar Creek and then decide what to do. His primary concern was whether Cedar Creek would pay them appropriately for their labor hours. He wouldn't even attempt to repair it unless he was guaranteed to be paid the full labor rate, not the usual 60% warranty work rate.

Just from looking at the list he estimated it would take a minimum of 100 labor hours, about $15,000 to fix it. Of course, he wouldn't really know until his techs inspected and diagnosed everything. Just that process could take a team several days. He obviously didn't want to waste that time if they wouldn't be paid back for it, and I didn't blame him. Finally on good terms, I parked the RV and we went inside together, signed some paperwork, and handed over the keys.

Emotionally and physically drained, we filmed some updates then drove away wondering if we'd ever see our home again. We went straight to Red Robin and binged on some killer burgers and bottomless steak fries. We were starving since we hadn't been eating well the previous week, we'd just been too busy.

The next day the Camping World service manager called us. He'd already been in contact with the Cedar Creek warranty manager, Mr. Oliver. Supposedly Mr. Oliver had said they would take the RV back, fix it at the factory, and pay for us to drive to Indiana to pick it up. It was the same thing we'd heard a few months prior but had yet to receive it in writing. We were skeptical after we couldn't get Cedar Creek to put it in writing earlier. Although, hearing it again gave us some hope that we desperately needed.

After fighting to get it fixed for months, driving halfway across the country, dealing with poor communication from Cedar Creek, hearing countless horror stories of people that couldn't get theirs fixed, internet trolls harassing us, and many sleepless nights worrying about our future, we sat there stunned. It was everything we could have hoped for and dreamt of.

Of course, this news was hearsay. Until we heard it directly from Mr. Oliver, and got the same in writing, we would remain skeptical. The Camping World manager said Mr. Oliver would be calling us in a day or two once he worked out the logistics. They would have to find a hauler before anything else could happen. Although, the Camping World manager said that shouldn't be hard because most haulers don't get paid to drive back to Indiana after they drop off a new unit and someone would likely jump at the chance for a paid return trip.

The next morning, I missed a call from an Indiana number, after a little phone tag, I finally spoke with Mr. Oliver and he confirmed everything we'd been told the day before. However, the good news didn't stop there. He told us it would be picked up within the week, that wear items not usually covered under warranty would be covered under good will, and that Cedar Creek would pay for our fuel and hotels to drive to Indiana.

Mr. Oliver wanted us to be able to inspect it ourselves before we took delivery. Simply to ensure it met our expectations before they gave it back to us. He also said they would cover the warranty work completed in some fashion, which they normally don't do.

Mr. Oliver explained a few things to us, so that we'd understand exactly why he made the decision to take it back. For instance, the paint on our fiberglass front cap was prematurely fading and the whole thing needed to be replaced since it was cheaper than sanding and painting. He said it would cost around $500 just to ship a new front cap, and there's still the installation cost after that. Rather than paying to ship all the parts to Washington and paying another shop to install them all it would be cheaper for Cedar Creek to just bring the RV to the parts. He felt confident that we'd have a better experience if they fixed it anyway, which we agreed to of course.

Wow, too bad we didn't spend months calling and emailing begging for them to do exactly what they'd just decided to do. Is that irony? I don't know, we were just happy to finally get some good news. It seemed the Hebard Luck was alive, well and working overtime!

However, after the good news the conversation took a hard left. He went on a little unprovoked rant about how he can't go back in time and make everything perfect, he's not a miracle worker, and he can't make everyone happy. I don't know what brought all that on, but Laura and I were genuinely confused. We didn't think that we'd been asking for a miracle time machine. We just wanted our house fixed. Changing burned out lights isn't miracle work.

Before we ended the call, he said they would send an email covering what we spoke about. When that email didn't show after repeated requests our skepticism increased. The good news started to feel too good without something in writing holding them to it.

After the call I thought about everything Mr. Oliver said for a while. Much of the conversation (the unprovoked tirade) was strange enough that I couldn't let it go. Here's what I came up with:

- He likely deals with disgruntled angry customers all day every day. You would have to be a heartless soulless monster to not let that affect you.

- He's the warranty manager, not the production manager. I doubt very much that he has any say over build or material quality. And his job is directly dealing with the aftermath of those problems. I'm sure it wore on him.

- He was likely experiencing extreme burnout from trying to do the best he could within the confines of corporate policy.

We'd been given great news that our home would be fixed. However, we had no idea when it would be finished. We were staring down the barrel of a long summer, and possibly fall, being landlocked in one location. Those thoughts were more than a little unsettling. It didn't take long before the situation became very stressful. After all, just a few weeks prior we'd been driving around the country on the road trip of a lifetime. We'd finally tasted freedom and the thought of losing it was a bitter pill to swallow.

CHAPTER 26

What Do We Do Now?

———✎———

Our greatest stressor, at that time, was losing the momentum we'd recently had on our YouTube channel. We knew that we were growing much faster than similar channels did in their first year, and we needed to maintain that growth if we wanted to survive. But how to pull it off when we couldn't travel was a hard question that we didn't have an easy answer for. Our channel was built on traveling and RV life.

During the first week without the RV we scrambled to keep our channel alive. We decided to run a shock-and-awe campaign. Every other day we went someplace unique to film and produced a video the next day. We actually produced five videos that first week. Sadly, every one of them flopped. By flopped I mean they died at 1,000 views or less, most were less.

Just as we began to wonder if we could keep the channel alive, we received a surprise reminder of why we were working so hard. Our first $100 payment from YouTube advertising revenue came in.

After seven months of working on our channel we'd finally seen our first monetary return, and we wanted it to continue. When the shock-and-awe videos went nowhere, we were forced to get creative. We quickly found that any update videos about the warranty/repair process were guaranteed winners. Of course, we couldn't just manufacture them like other videos. We had to wait for something to happen before we could make an update video.

In the meantime, we made videos about anything and everything happening in our lives. I filmed my cousins and I buying fireworks for the Fourth of July, we made another video about us all getting together on the Fourth and lighting off said fireworks, an eating challenge I failed at miserably (several pounds of biscuits, gravy, eggs, and bacon was a delicious bad idea), chainsaw wood carvers (which are REALLY cool), a sprint car dirt track race, Mt. Baker campgrounds, a local car show, and so on. If we thought the topic was even mildly interesting, we made a video about it.

So how were we keeping our sanity throughout that whole mess? Leading up to us stopping in Washington, Laura made a request. She wanted to begin lap swimming again and didn't really care what it took. She'd been a competitive swimmer for 16 years and the water was her Zen zone. Before we even arrived in Washington, I found a YMCA with a lap pool 30 minutes from my mom's.

Explaining our situation to the YMCA, we hammered out a deal that let us use their pool daily during our time there without buying a year-long membership. They were very interested in our story and more than happy to accommodate us. We find people are willing to work with us more often than not. If you're a fulltime RVer it doesn't hurt to ask. So many people dream about getting away from it all that they'll instantly latch onto our story and want to help us. The key is being respectful and not entitled. We've seen other people abuse that reaction.

All summer, every day we'd get up early, eat breakfast, and go swim for an hour or two. Ok, Laura would swim for an hour or two. I'd flounder to the other end of the pool, marvel at the fact I didn't drown, and then wait five minutes to catch my breath before risking my life again. AKA "swimming" back to the other side. All the while Laura was flying down and back like the fish out of water she is. She'd swim a whole length without taking a breath just to show off. But after a decade and a half of competitive swimming I'm not surprised she retained so much ability.

I had a stroke of luck though. (I know, I know, it's hard to believe.) There were two men usually swimming at the same time as us. We quickly learned that one was a senior Olympian and the other had swum in college and then taught for several years afterwards. Luckily, they took pity and gave me some pointers. I know I'll never be able to keep up with Laura, but I can at least not drown when swimming a lap now.

I don't care how laughable you may find that statement, it's a really big deal for me.

314

Laura loved getting back in the water and it was definitely a stress release for everything we were dealing with. A wonderful side effect of swimming every day was how fast we got back in shape. We were both dropping inches. My cardio improved so much that I was able to go running on days we couldn't swim. It had been a few years since I'd been able to run, and it felt wonderful. After the thousands of miles I ran in the Army it was like reuniting with an old friend. I just had to take care of my bad knee.

Another thing really helping our mental state was my family. They lived near the pool and we were spending time with them almost weekly. It also helped that they all love Laura. I think the hardest thing we dealt with from my family was questions about when we'd have kids. Considering how terrible some families can be I saw that as a non-issue. I'm very lucky in that my extended family is loving and accepting.

Knowing that we needed some help one of my cousins hired me to do yard work at his place and my Aunt's we parked at to move out. She had about 20 trees dropped on her property and it was cheaper to pay me than the tree company for cleanup. I sawed them all into rounds, stacked them, and found people online willing to take all the green wood. Unfortunately, it was mostly cottonwood which burns fast and ashy, so it was a bit difficult to get rid of.

After a few weeks I finished all the work my cousin and aunt needed, I'm happy to break a sweat to earn some cash. That was a perfect arrangement because we needed fuel money to keep swimming daily.

Of course, Laura wasn't just swimming and sleeping. She was editing videos, creating a channel logo, responding to comments, researching how to keep our channel running, revamping our website, setting up affiliate programs, posting on Instagram and Twitter, etc. There was no shortage of work to keep us busy.

Back to the epic RV repair saga!

It ended up taking two weeks for someone to pick up the RV after we dropped it off. The transportation company picked it up July 6th and it arrived at the factory on July 10th. Wow, they drive fast! They powered through 2,300 miles in four days. I don't how fast they were going, but that's 8-10-hour travel days. My brain would be mush driving that many hours day after day. I quickly realized I could never be an RV hauler.

It was immediately inspected upon arrival and they began working on it shortly thereafter. We were very happy with how quickly repairs began. Other Cedar Creek owners had told us it took months before work began on their units, even though they were sitting at the factory.

During the week after it arrived, we were emailed several times seeking clarification for the techs trying to diagnose problems on our list. Everything was going well until we received a line itemized full update email. While scrolling down the list, we saw that our soft storage bay floor was determined be solid with no defect found.

I wrote back telling them that it was in fact a serious problem for us. We'd repeatedly seen water in there and had been smelling mildew in there for months. There was a gap around our storage bay door which prevented it from latching (number whatever on the list) and we thought water may have been getting in through the gap when it rained, even though I'd added more weather stripping. It may have been leaking from somewhere else though, we had no idea.

> *A few months before we turned in the RV dumb luck struck me one day (I REALLY wish my luck translated to the craps table). I was poking around in the passthrough storage bay, and I noticed a drip of water on a pipe end cap. I found the cap was barely screwed on, and there was no thread tape or PVC glue of any kind. It was the shower drain pipe, and it had been leaking into our storage bay for who knows how long. Obviously, I tightened it, but the damage was already done.*

> *We later learned our hot water tank was cracked and leaking as well. But that's a story for the next book.*

Our customer service representative wrote back about a week later to say the problem was being pushed up to her boss. It seemed they were making quick work of our list. They'd fixed the outer wall adhesion separation as well as replaced the front and back caps for fading and oxidation. Most of the big-ticket items, and many of the smaller ones were already done.

We learned something throughout this process. If you're dealing with Cedar Creek customer service, don't expect them to always respond quickly. The few people working that department work hard, but unfortunately the company doesn't have enough staff to handle the workload.

The woman handling our account was out sick one week and there was no one to pick up her work while she was out. I understand it can be frustrating when your home breaks and no one returns your calls, but make sure if you call you also email. It's too easy for someone who's overloaded to forget what you said while on the phone leading to further frustration. We had much better luck with email, and it also protects you. Email will give you a record of everything that was said.

During that whole time, we'd upload a video about the repair process every chance we had. That wasn't just reserved to when we received news though. We were reporting on everything they did. Every missed deadline or email/question they didn't respond to, and any good news of course, was filmed. Those videos were the only thing keeping our channel alive.

I suppose I should explain why it was so important to us to keep it alive. We knew we'd be getting "an RV" at some point and go back to traveling. It was still possible they'd decided to replace it if they found something too expensive to fix. Staying at my mom's place for free all summer was great for our finances, but that was only temporary. If our channel was stagnant whenever we could go back to traveling it would likely take months to get it up and running again. We knew we'd need that money when we started traveling again.

Even though our channel was growing much faster than most do in their first year, it still wasn't producing the income we needed to stay on the road. This is why I tell people to never solely rely on YouTube for income. We still experience months where our revenue is cut in half from the previous month for a multitude of reasons. YouTube isn't easy to work for.

During this time, I decided to take a serious look at our finances, and it was very troubling. I tracked how fast the channel was growing and how much we could expect to make over the next year. I then looked at our burn rate, which was insane mostly due to paying for RV parks. I figured we'd be broke long before YouTube would be paying the bills, almost a year before. Unless of course something radically changed.

I kicked around the idea of getting a job while we were stopped, but it didn't seem fair to whoever hired me. I didn't want to get hired and have to leave a month later, we didn't know when Cedar Creek would finish the repairs. Every potential job I was looking at came with the side effect of sacrificing our channel by settling down. We'd worked so hard on it we couldn't just abandon it.

As far as we were concerned, our social media and YouTube channels were no different than us starting a small business. We were investing our savings and lives into making them profitable. We couldn't even take out a small business loan since there was no profit to show a bank.

Right about the time I was beginning to lose hope, something....unexpected happened. In the middle of scrambling to keep us and the channel afloat, unbeknownst to me, Laura made a friend online. They were talking most of every day because her new friend had found our channel and really liked us. I still remember asking Laura one day who she was texting so much. She told me about this girl that had found our channel and was thinking about full-time RVing.

I didn't think much of it because we were often contacted by people wanting to start RVing. Usually it would be with questions they couldn't find answers to online. Other people just needed a little reassuring they weren't stark raving mad for considering living in an RV. Of course, they don't just come out and say that, but you can tell it's what they're thinking. They want to know living in an RV won't make them a "cousin Eddie."

We've spoken with many people that are worried about the stigma surrounding RV life. It can come from all sides and be very difficult to fight. We've heard of parents, siblings, coworkers, spouses, best friends, extended family, and in-laws making life very hard for people wanting to go full-time. I have a hypothesis about the haters and why it's so important for them to try and stop us all from breaking free. It's because they're too scared or weak to do it themselves. They're jealous that we had the courage and they're angry they don't.

See, it's easy to just put your head down and power through 30-40 years of life working some job all the while gambling you can retire before you die. But what happens when someone in your life decides to abandon everything you've sacrificed your life to earn? Suddenly it makes decades of sacrifice look meaningless. That would make most people angry.

When you look at it from that point of view a lot of things begin to make sense. When Laura and I were preparing to hit the road, we were constantly talking to our coworkers about our plans. It was a huge thing in our lives, we were talking to everyone about it because we were so excited. Most of them acted interested, some more than others. However, after we left our jobs the friends disappeared. They were people we'd worked with for years and suddenly they acted like we'd simply ceased to exist.

I'm speaking in generalities of course. There were a handful of people that were excited for us, expressed interest in doing the same, and we still speak sometimes. However, they were the exception, not the rule.

Like I said, a lot of people would contact us looking for reassurance. It was usually out of desperation because they couldn't get it from the people that called themselves their friends. Sure, they were friends, but only until they rocked the boat.

I forgot about Laura's new friend shortly after I heard about her. I didn't have a lot of free time. I was switching to the Washington state VA healthcare system, trying to get my VA disability rating raised, registering the truck and trailer in Washington, and making a bunch of RV walkthrough videos trying to keep the channel going in a different way.

After a few weeks of killing ourselves, we finally scrounged up two different free days to drive down near Seattle. We spent one with my best friend I grew up with, the other with him and his parents at their house. They had all flown to Florida for our wedding when many of our blood relatives didn't, and they've always been family to me. It kills me to go through WA without seeing them. I wish we could have gone down there every weekend.

During a period of no communication from Cedar Creek we made a video talking about it. The next day someone contacted us, under a fake name, because he had information for us. It was the first time since the Lemon RV videos that someone using a fake name had called us. It almost felt like we were spies trying to take down some corrupt government.

Apparently, he was successfully winning a lawsuit over his lemon RV and had learned some behind-the-scenes information. He told us a term that's apparently the "super-secret cool guy code phrase" used when an RV is going to be replaced. Of course, don't expect dealers to confirm it's a real thing. We highly suspect it's one of the best kept secrets in the RV industry. And that phrase is…..did I ever tell you about the time I wrote a book and led the readers on and on and….

Sorry, I crack myself up sometimes.

Anyway, it's called collateral exchange. If you have a new lemon, throw that phrase out like you know what you're talking about and just see what happens. What do you have to lose? Maybe it's been changed, maybe not. Maybe he was just lying to us, I have no idea. I'm just so sick of seeing good people get screwed by bad products and lied to that I'd love nothing more than to blow the lid off their little club.

After the secret call, I went back to Camping World to have a little in-person chat with their service manager. I wanted to see his reaction when I asked for a collateral exchange. It was interesting. We chatted about RV stuff for a few minutes then I asked him if he thought I might get a collateral exchange instead of Cedar Creek fixing it. The instant surprise on his face almost made me laugh, almost. But I kept a straight face and listened to him stutter on about having never heard the phrase before.

I'm guessing it's real, and the little people aren't supposed to know about it. But who really knows?

Range Day

My cousins had been wanting to go shooting with me for a decade and we'd just never been able to make it happen. Since we were in Washington, we fixed that and booked a range day where they typically shoot.

Two of my cousins, two of their children, and their mom (my aunt we stayed with) all came. Everyone brought a pile of guns and ammo, it was a blast! All pun intended. I hadn't taught anyone how to shoot in years, but I guess it's like riding a bike. My shot groups weren't as tight as they were a few years ago, but they were still decent. I killed the crap out of those paper targets.

I ran them all through an impromptu safety, handling, stance, trigger control and grip course, and they all listened to my suggestions. Half the people at the range I used to work at would ignore my advice at first. Then they'd come off the range crying about their pistol sights needing to be adjusted because all their shots were hitting low left. I'd take them back out and shoot it to prove it was them jerking the trigger and not the sights. Then I'd show them how to shoot correctly a second time. Ammo is too expensive to shoot with an ego, check it at the door.

Once I had my family all grouping nicely on target, I ran them though some basic drills. I started off with a rapid follow up shot drill. I hung targets with multiple 6" circles so they could fire at a new target each time. At first their second shot was off paper half the time, but after showing them how to flex their wrist down they improved considerably.

Then I moved them to a drill that gets me some crazy looks. It's firing while looking over the sights with both eyes open. People are usually very skeptical about this one, but I know it works. I use it because the average self-defense engagement is around 7 yards. You don't need to perfectly line up your sights like you're competition shooting, actually you don't even really need them at that distance.

They were all pleasantly surprised to find about 60% of their first un-aimed shots were hitting in the silhouette. They were really surprised at how quickly they picked it up. No one had ever suggested they could shoot without using sights, so they'd never tried it. I recommend that drill to everyone, it's a lot cheaper than installing laser grips. Although, laser grips are a nice tool.

I rounded off the training with present and fire drills. We used a multi-target again. The drills are meant to build on each other, almost like algebra. I ran the final drill by having them start in stance with the pistol held at the sternum while pointed downrange. On their time, they would quickly extend their arms presenting the firearm to the target, fire two rounds while looking over the sights, and then reset by bringing the pistol back to their body. It only took a few rounds each for them to really get the hang of it. Suddenly they found their ability to quickly engage targets transition from basically nonexistent to fairly proficient.

We even found a new gun for my aunt that she was able to shoot comfortably and accurately. It was the Sig P238, a small .380 pistol. It's identical to the 1911, the most popular handgun in history, that's been used by the US military in every conflict since WWI. This was a miniature version, but the mechanics were the same and it was the smoothest shooting sub compact .380 I've ever fired. Usually those little .380's are very snappy.

My cousin had one and I loved how well it fired. My aunt hadn't fired a gun in about 40 years, after the drills, she was shooting confidently with it. She's a smaller woman in her 60's and was loving it. That's my new go-to suggested gun for many people.

It was so much fun watching them all gain confidence and shrink their shot groups. I hope no one ever needs to shoot someone, but if they're forced to, I want my family to walk away alive.

CHAPTER 27

I Know, Let's be in A Movie!

———❧———

Near the end of June, Laura's new friend asked her an odd question. She wanted to know if her boyfriend could call us. We'd had people ask to call us before, usually I found the time and it wasn't a big deal. However, Laura's friend was being very cryptic about what her boyfriend wanted. She wouldn't just tell us what it was all about. We agreed to the call. What's the worst that could happen?

A few days passed, and we'd forgotten about the call. While driving back from the pool one morning my phone rang. It was a Chicago number, which was odd, I never received calls from Chicago numbers. I answered and put the call on the truck's Bluetooth. We found ourselves talking with a very soft-spoken man, the friend's boyfriend had finally called. I had to pull over and turn off the truck because we couldn't hear him over the engine and road noise.

He introduced himself as Eric Odom. We'd never heard of him, nor should we have. We sat in that parking lot and spoke with him for an hour. He had an idea to make a movie about full-time RVers, and he wanted us to be in it as cast. He'd seen our Lemon RV videos and was impressed with how calm we were while dealing with such adversity. He was also impressed with the fact that we didn't use our public platform to slander anyone, we just stuck to the facts.

He further explained that the movie would be a low budget documentary, compared to Hollywood standards, and he wouldn't have money to hire actors. He was looked for people, like us, that were already used to being on camera. He also wanted people that were living the full-time RV life, because of their stories. We fit the bill perfectly.

He spoke a while about his back story and why he wanted to make the movie. He'd come from the political world and was sick of the division and hatred. One day, when traveling across country for work, he met a full-time family that was Waldocking. During a short conversation with them, he had his AH-HA moment and realized that full-timing was a viable life option.

Much like us, he was instantly enthralled and immediately tried to learn as much about full-timing as possible. The first thing he did was search for a movie about it, but he couldn't find one because there wasn't a movie about the full-time RV movement yet. To Eric that just meant he needed to make one. Isn't that what everyone does when they want something, but it doesn't exist yet?

The conversation went well, but something was off about it. Neither of us could hardly get a word in. Thinking back on that initial conversation it felt like he was selling the job to us. It was very reminiscent of the time I applied for a job with State Farm as an insurance salesman. The manager spoke non-stop for an hour trying to sell me on the job.

Eric and that State Farm manager both did the same thing and it took me a long time to realize it. They never asked any questions to see if I was right for the job. Isn't the point of interviews to judge the candidate on their ability to do the job? Laura helped me catch that with State Farm and I turned it down.

After Eric spoke to us for an hour we were totally blown away. Seriously, how would you respond to someone calling you out of the blue to ask if you'd be in a movie? We told him we would need a few days to think about it, which he completely understood. He said in the meantime he'd send us the movie contracts. The next day we received our contracts as promised.

There were several things in the contract we had concerns with. We mulled it over for a day or two before I decided to just write Eric a very direct email stating our concerns. I decided that how he responded would likely tell us everything we needed to know about working with him. His response to my email was to completely restructure the way we'd be paid for our part in the movie. He willingly handed over a percentage of the movie profits with no negotiation. He was also willing to accommodate my other requests. He even apologized afterwards saying the contract should have already included the things we requested.

Have you ever worked for someone that was willing to give up a portion of their profit so you could be paid better? Yeah, neither had we. That single interaction told us pretty much everything we needed to know about him. He's the 1% of the 1% that believes a rising tide raises all ships. In other words, if we all threw 100% behind the movie, we'd all make money. Well, as long as the movie was sold, we'd be paid. But why wouldn't it be sold? Of course, it would be sold so we could all be paid. Anything else would be crazy.

He believed that if everyone has skin in the game they'll work harder, and everyone will make more money in the end. That was such an alien concept to us, even though we fully agreed with it. We'd never even heard of anyone that would operate like that and we were only two signatures away from working for him. We couldn't fax those contracts back fast enough. It sounded too good to be true.

After all the crummy jobs we'd worked, barely making ends meet while someone up top got rich, this sounded like a dream come true. It wasn't a socialism "everyone is equal" commune thing though. It was a very capitalistic thought process.

> *When I'm given the opportunity to make more money by working harder, I'll run myself into the ground. Several of my previous jobs had a commission system and I always blew away my peers. I have this thing where I want to be financially rewarded for working harder. If I'm not paid for my work, then what's the point of continuing or working harder?*

Eric was offering the perfect job for us and our lifestyle. We'd still be traveling, so we could keep making YouTube videos and not lose all our hard work. But at the same time, he was offering us the chance to learn more about filmmaking and video editing, and to get paid for it. We realized that even if the project was a total failure at the very least, we'd learn how to make better videos, and probably grow our channel more. Eric said he even wanted to cover fuel and other travel expenses during production, we didn't have anything to lose!

We sent him the contracts around July 1st and our reality was forever altered. He was calling and texting almost daily to bounce ideas off us. Eric and his girlfriend, Jenna, were also RV shopping. They'd set a tentative date to go full-time for January 1st, 2018, we told them it would be a lot closer to November 1^{st,} 2017. In actuality, they hit the road just before Halloween. Once the bug bites, it bites HARD.

We got to watch them go through the entire downsizing process. At the same time, we'd wake up to a text from Eric with a URL and a message saying he couldn't sleep the night before. One day the URL took us to epicnomadtradingpost.com. He'd built an online store for the company. Now I don't mean he hired a company to build the website and create the clothing designs. He and Jenna had knocked it all out in a night.

For only being the first version of the store, it still had a bunch of items for sale. They had even designed many of the catchy phrases and designs. But that wasn't all, he made the website in a night, and it was nearly flawless. It looked better than most small business sites I've seen that people paid a lot of money for.

He called us one afternoon to tell us about a conversation he'd just had with the CEO of a company he was trying to get a sponsorship from. The CEO told him the movie sounded like a great idea, but the real money would be in episodic content. Think of a Netflix series. Eric left that meeting with a whole new idea for his fledgling company. He asked us what we thought about episodic content, and of course we loved it and said we'd support him in that venture as well.

> *As I write this, one entire show has already been filmed and there are multiple others planned. ENTV could be the Netflix of nomads. As long as it can film and produce a few more shows for a strong launch. We're still waiting to see what happens.*

We watched as every idea he had came to fruition. It was like being in the garage with Steve Jobs as he built the first Apple computer. We'd never met anyone before with the intelligence to even have the grandiose dreams Eric had. It went a step further, though. He wasn't just a dreamer, he made his dreams come true. If he didn't already know how to do something he would just learn how, and then he'd do it.

If someone told us he had a genie in a bottle granting wishes we'd believe it. For crying out loud, he made a trailer for a movie that was only a concept, before we ever filmed a scene. He put out a casting call to full-timers and was inundated with hundreds of responses in a matter of days. HUNDREDS of people wanted to sign onto a project that only existed on paper. We didn't even have the money to make it yet.

The fact that he was six figures short of his projected budget didn't even phase him. Rather than crying about it, he figured out how to make it happen. He knew we'd get sponsors to finish it. I don't think there was ever a doubt in his mind that we wouldn't be able to make the movie. There were some doubts about whether people would like it or not, although I think that's a natural fear to have when you've never made a movie before.

As far as we know he never slowed down for a second. He told us that he was working 16-hour days. He quickly found other RVing YouTubers that wanted to be part of the movie and put together a cast of about 15 people within a month that signed contracts. He pulled in some pretty big names from the RVing YouTube arena. We were definitely the small fish in the pond. We only had around 1,500 subscribers and he signed a monster channel when they had around 65,000.

We quickly realized that we had to find a way to make ourselves indispensable. Yes, we may have come in on the ground floor, but that didn't make us special. We knew we would have to work harder than anyone else at whatever task we could find. It was too good of an opportunity to squander by sitting back, watching him work and waiting for filming to begin. If we wanted the movie to succeed and get paid for our work, we had to do anything and everything to make it as big as possible.

Of course, at that time we had no idea how we could help him or the company at all. We could provide a sounding board for him to bounce his ideas off, and we could offer advice on buying an RV and everything involved with going full-time, which we gladly did. Although, 1,000 other people could do the same, so we continued to look for ways to stay relevant.

What struck us as odd was why they would choose us as the first people to sign on. We had a small channel and no RV. We were very transparent about the fact we didn't know when or even if we'd be able to travel again but he didn't seem to be bothered by it. We didn't even know how to help make a movie. But he said we were the first people to believe in him and that made us feel pretty special. So, we pushed the doubts from our minds and just worked on helping him.

I wish we'd made videos about what was happening. Even if we never published them, a record of everything would have been invaluable. No matter how much, or how eloquently, I write about those events I can never do them justice. Laura and I used to joke that one day we'd wake up and he would have taken over a country. He doesn't know a speed less than super human.

One day I got a hell of a surprise. Eric sent us an email asking us to write a short story about how we'd found full-timing and why we decided to make the change. He was writing a book about his past that would explain a little about who he was and why he wanted to make the movie. A few weeks after I sent in our portion, he sent back an email with a link to a google document. He'd written the rough draft. Somehow, he'd found the time to write a book around the whole planning-a-movie-and-building-a-company thing.

I started reading through it and realized there were a few grammatical and punctuation errors. Also, his style of writing used very long sentences that didn't always flow well. Since Google Docs allows suggested edits, I went through the first chapter suggesting any edits I thought would help. I sent it back to him and suggested that if he liked my edits, I could go through the rest of it. And that's how I found myself listed as the editor of the book RV Nomads. But what qualified me to edit his book?

My Writing History

I've dabbled in writing a few times throughout my life. I wrote some interesting things in Iraq, when we had down time. However, I'd never written anything longer than a 3,000-word short story. Even though I'd never written anything long, I had written a lot. I was 15 when I tried writing my first book. I've kicked around the idea several times since then, but just never had the time.

Throughout college I received A's on every paper I wrote, except for one professor and I won't get into that. During my first college semester there was a writing competition and I submitted a piece for each of the three categories. I'm proud to say I won the essay portion.

Funny thing, I was already writing about something traumatic in my past when my English Composition 101 professor gave us a personal essay assignment. I finished the essay I was already writing about my dad and received something like a 98%. A few weeks later I learned about the writing competition and went back to the essay to clean it up for submission. There was a $1,000 prize after all. Rather than leaving the prize up to chance, I decided to write for the poem and short story categories as well.

I spent the entire nine days of spring break writing. I finished the poem quickly then spent the rest of the time writing the short story. I really enjoyed creating a story purely from my imagination. My ex-girlfriend was not happy about me sitting in front of that computer for 12 hours a day though. The bug bit and I remembered that I loved writing.

Sadly, my writing days were shelved when I had to find a job. I'd been medically retired from the army for a few months and I realized it wasn't enough money to live on. I had the pleasure of finding a job, for which I had no qualifications, in 2010 during the recession. Once I started working, I no longer had the time needed to write.

> *That was about nine years ago. I'm having a hard time sleeping while writing this, I'm so excited to finish it. I've read hundreds (or thousands?) of novels and books, but never wrote one myself. If you're interested in reading the winning essay, I've included it at the end of this book. It's not exactly the same though. I've changed it a few times over the years as I remember different things.*

I knew that everything Laura and I were going through was an incredible story and I'd been kicking around the idea of writing about it. After I wrote the piece for Eric's book, I think the bug bit again, though I didn't realize it at first.

One sleepless night (thanks PTSD) I found myself lying in bed watching Laura sleeping and decided to get up. I was going to watch Netflix or something on my computer in the living room but changed my mind when I turned it on. I don't know why, but I opened a Word document instead.

There's something interesting about staring at that blank white page and flashing cursor. I look at it like a blank canvas, I can make it whatever I want it to be. I can choose to write in first or third person. I can pour my overactive imagination out and make it come to life, or I can sift through my memories and write about those. I'm glad I chose the latter because here we are.

I stayed up for hours that night with our story pouring out of my fingertips as fast as they could type, which wasn't very fast then. I'd never written about my past in book form before and found it very enjoyable. There were no restrictions or rules, I could choose to tell our story however I wanted. Of course, I wondered if anyone would like it or not. But I couldn't focus on that while I was riding the high of finally starting my first book. I'd dreamed of doing it for decades.

Over the next few days I lost myself chasing that cursor. I'd put on my headphones, fire up Metallica or Lindsey Stirling (I know they're polar opposites, but they're both incredible) and flip through my memories as if they're all filed on a Rolodex. I'd find the memory I wanted, mull it over for a minute, figure out how I wanted it to flow and write it out. It was even easier than writing from my imagination.

I had to be careful though, it's easy to get lost in those memories while staring out a window watching a grey squirrel jump from branch to branch in a walnut tree and then run across a power line and

I'd start to wonder how can they run on power lines without being cooked well done and then I remembered how good squirrel tastes from that time I shot two because I'd been out duck hunting with a friend from my squad during the Iraq invasion, duck hunting had been a bust that morning, but red squirrel was in season, so I didn't go home empty handed, oh man are they a pain to skin but they tasted good in that old black frying pan I don't have any more with some olive oil and Lawry's seasoning salt, I miss hunting with him, we'd sit out there and reminisce about our time in Iraq and the Rakkasans back when we were young and indestructible running around the world always wondering if we'd wake up the next morning, I wish I'd taken more pictures in Iraq…..

That can continue on forever if I don't recognize it's happening and drag myself back to reality. I like to call it a run-on memory, that's just the way my brain works. But knowing that's what it wants to do helps me combat it. Laura often wonders how I can jump from one topic to the next when they have no clear relation to her. Then I have to explain the totally obvious relation between eating squirrel and the Baghdad invasion. It gets exhausting having to constantly explain the obvious. Of course, I'm being facetious, but that really is the way my thought process works.

Just as I was finding my writing groove again, life threw a curve ball in the form of an update email about our trailer.

CHAPTER 28

Out of Time

———≈≈≈———

W e'd been receiving sporadic updates on the warranty repair process over the summer. A month after we dropped it off, Cedar Creek finally told us they would reimburse us for the storage costs, which was great news. We couldn't get a straight answer out of them on the overall progress of the RV, however.

A week later, Cedar Creek sent a short email stating that it was 98% complete. But that's all it said, there wasn't a list showing what was fixed. More importantly, there wasn't a list of what they may not have fixed. We'd been worried about that particular list for some time. We knew they could just decide not to fix something and there wouldn't be a thing we could do but plead our case, and it would be a whole lot easier to do so while they were still working on it. We thought that once they moved on to the next unit it would be highly unlikely to see any more work completed on ours.

Seeing that 98% on my phone lit a fire under my ass, we still had so many projects left to do. I'd told my mom that I would do a lot of work around the house and on her car, and I meant to do it before we left. Over the following days I was mowing, weed eating, trimming, setting mole traps, watering the flowers and making dump runs trying to complete the list while we still had time.

I also changed the oil and spark plugs in my mom's car. It's amazing how much better a car runs when its original plugs with 120,000 miles are replaced and you switch to full synthetic oil. I was just going to drive it up on leveling blocks in the driveway but our neighbor two doors down offered to let me use his garage. His garage with a smooth concrete floor, floor jacks jack stands, air compressor and oil barrel. That was WAY better than crawling under a Volvo sedan on my back in gravel with it an inch higher than my face. A few weeks earlier I'd tried to help him fix something and I guess he wanted to repay me.

We were getting all our ducks in a row and preparing to leave, but there was still a serious problem. We couldn't get any more information from Cedar Creek. Had they finished the final 2%? If not, did they have an estimated ETA? Were there any items not covered? Would we have to pick it up or would they ship it back to us? They had previously stated we would pick it up and be reimbursed for the travel costs, but we'd never received that in writing.

Several people in our Cedar Creek Facebook group were also stumped over the complete and sudden cessation of all communication with Cedar Creek customer service. After multiple people wrote in wondering what happened, someone mentioned the annual Forest River Owners Group (FROG) rally had just begun. It's a weeklong gathering of Forest River RV owners. Forest River offers free repairs, there's conferences on maintenance, and social gatherings and potlucks where you can meet people.

Someone else in the Facebook group informed everyone that the factory shuts down during that week. Apparently, they send all their staff and techs to the rally. Maybe a warning would have been nice?

I was talking to Laura about the FROG rally when we realized they had sent the 98% email a day before everyone left for the rally. It felt as if they sent us the email simply to placate us during their absence.

The FROG rally happens every year and it would have been unrealistic for us to expect them to continue working on our rig during that event, so we decided to contact them after the event finished. The next Monday we expected them to be back at work after the rally. We were all in for a big surprise though.

Suddenly our Facebook group exploded with questions asking why customer service still wasn't answering the phones. Normally Cedar Creek wasn't very responsive, we were all used to that. But something had changed, and no one knew what. We called as well, hoping we'd have better luck and our call went straight to voicemail, and the voicemail was full. That made it in a video.

Eventually someone in the group told us all that the factory takes a one-week vacation after the rally ends. Customer service failed to inform us, and the rest of the Cedar Creek owners in the world, that they take a week-long vacation after the rally. Everyone needs vacation time, we don't have a problem with that, just tell people first.

As a customer, a total failure in communication is just unacceptable. How hard would it have been to send a mass email to their mailing list explaining the two-week break? Or leave a message on their voice mail explaining the FROG rally? Or at least notify the customers whose RV's they had for warranty work? Anything other than abject silence would have been preferable.

Around that point is was time for my mom to leave and go back to Taiwan. I was sad to see her go since we don't see each other often. One week a year is about common now. Those two months were the most time we'd spent together since I was 19, before I joined the army. It was nice, however, to have some time with just Laura again. After two months of living with my mom we sorely needed some couples time.

A day or two after she left Cedar Creek suddenly broke radio silence and emailed us. We woke up to an email saying that it was finished.

FINISHED!!!

Let that sink in for a second. On one hand we were elated. On the other we were panicking because we hadn't sorted our stuff in storage yet. We went straight to the storage unit, pulled everything out, went through each container and sorted everything. After a few hours of work, we had a truck bed full of items that didn't need to go back in the RV. I was hoping to drop enough weight to carry a full tank of water if we wanted to.

We had just helped my mom with a garage sale and decluttering of her house a few weeks before, so we just kept on doing the same with ours. One of my cousins in the city said we could set up in his driveway over the weekend, the weather was going to be nice and it was still August, still garage sale season. Everything was working out perfectly, or so we thought.

After sorting through storage, we got to work figuring out how we would get our home back. Cedar Creek still hadn't given us a clear answer on whether they'd deliver it back to us, or if we had to pick it up. We decided it would be cheaper for us if I flew out there, inspected it, and had them deliver it back to us. We researched it all, figured out the exact costs, and emailed a trip itinerary to Cedar Creek. With it finally being done we wanted to get the ball rolling immediately.

However, we weren't going to spend a dime on any plan until we had it in writing that they would cover the exact costs I'd sent them. We couldn't just sit around and wait for them to respond though, there was still so much work to be done before we could leave.

Hoping to pull in some extra cash, I went through my old childhood things stored in the attic and added some to the sale pile. I'd rather have money for fuel than 30-year-old GI Joes and Legos. We priced everything and posted the sale on all the local online sale pages four days before Saturday, when the sale was scheduled to kick off.

Two days later Cedar Creek responded to my proposed trip itinerary. They had a different idea, and FINALLY (man I'm sick of having to use that word) answered our questions. Instead of me flying, getting a rental car and hotel, they still wanted us to drive out. They put it in writing that they would reimburse the costs of fuel, the U-Haul trailer, food and hotels. Their only stipulation, we keep our receipts. They also agreed to a private inspection prior to us taking delivery.

SOLD!

We pulled some money from my IRA to ensure we could make the trip. I found the only double axel U-Haul trailer in the surrounding 75 miles and reserved it. We also planned out our trip and booked a La Quinta at each stop because they allow pets. They don't even have size restrictions which was good for us and Bullet, he's 110 lbs. One location did have a two-pet limit, but I was able to get an exception since our third was a cat in a carrier.

We also found an RV park near the factory where we could load all or stuff back into the trailer. It was a logistical nightmare, though. There wasn't another park with availability within an hour, and they would only let us book three nights. That wasn't much time to clean the RV if needed, unpack the U-Haul, get everything inside the RV and put it all away enough to bring the slides in to leave.

We were even gambling that it would be ready and not need more work. If we couldn't pick it up in time for the RV park reservation, we didn't have a backup plan. The hardest part about the plan was that I wouldn't be able to tow both trailers at the same time. We needed someplace we could safely leave the U-Haul, with all our stuff, then go get the RV and bring it back. Cedar Creek had said we couldn't stay on their property overnight, so that wasn't an option.

Lastly, we finalized plans with an NRVIA (National Recreational Vehicle Inspectors Association) certified RV inspector named Robert Wilhelm. Cedar Creek had given us the green light to hire a private inspector to double check their work. However, they refused to pay for him. We expected that, but it didn't hurt to ask. Once we knew it was finished, we emailed Rob to find out when he'd be available and then figured out our departure date.

We hired Mr. Wilhelm because he's one of the closest NRVIA certified inspectors to Elkhart and Topeka Indiana, where most RV's are built. He owns a company named Professional RV Inspections, LLC. After reading over his website at www.prorvi.com and speaking with him we learned that he was experienced in RV inspections and repair verifications.

We wanted a private inspection because we were more than a little afraid that we'd get our home back with a whole new list of problems. That's an all too common story among RV owners. With all the trouble we'd previously gone through, there was no way we were leaving anything up to chance. Mr. Wilhelm was exactly who we needed.

Because we only wanted Mr. Wilhelm to check the items on our list, he said he could finish in one day. Normally, if he was to conduct a full inspection on a 41' fifth wheel it would take him two full days. Also, he did have to drive almost two hours each way. Which added a fuel charge to the bill, but that was to be expected. We just viewed his fee the same as buying insurance.

We'd gone back and forth with Cedar Creek about the inspection all summer. It was great news to hear they would allow him on their property. It was even better news when they said they would heed his report. What's the point of paying a bunch of money for an inspection if they won't fix any potential problems found? We needed to have that agreed to before we finalized the inspection reservation.

In one day, we learned that we'd be fully reimbursed for travel and storage expenses, the inspector would be allowed, and Cedar Creek would fix anything they missed if he found something. That news gave us a peace of mind we'd been missing for a very long time. Even with the unknowns of driving to Indiana and dealing with the factory we slept well, for the first time in months.

The stress I was under wasn't nearly as bad as combat, but it was still bad. There was a new element I had to deal with though. In combat we knew it would only last for a set period of time, then we could go home, and it would end. Before the golden email, we had no idea if it would ever end, or if it would truly be over when we got our home back. Of course, that's why we hired an inspector, to ensure everything they said they fixed was really fixed.

The morning of the yard sale we got up at the crack of dark to start the 30-minute drive, the sun hadn't even thought about coming up yet. We wanted to be set up by 7am since most people that go to yard sales usually go early, during the estate sale I had people coming in before 7am. We only had enough time for one sale and wanted it to go well.

A few of my cousin's kids joined in to sell their extra stuff and we had a fun day. We brought the dogs with us and all the kids had so much fun playing with them. However, as noon began to creep up on us, I started to worry. Only a handful of people had even stopped by, even less had bought anything. But I worked as a salesman for four years and I knew you can have your best sale of the day five minutes before you close, so I stayed positive.

When the kids realized the sale wasn't going well, they changed up tactics and opened a lemonade stand. With that kind of entrepreneurial ingenuity and work ethic, I'm sure they'll do just fine in life. The lemonade stand had more visitors than the yard sale, but not for a lack of trying. The kids were pitching the sale to everyone that stopped by.

As 4 pm approached I knew the sale was done and began to pack up, no one had stopped to look in over an hour. I was feeling down due to the fact we hadn't even made $100, and we still had most of the stuff we'd brought. In the middle of packing up, my oldest cousin's daughter walked over and gave me a handful of cash. The kids had opened the lemonade stand to help us because they saw we weren't making any money.

Somehow, I didn't break down and cry when she handed me those thirty odd dollars. It was such a loving and selfless act. I remember how much $30 meant when I was 12, I would have mowed lawns all day for that much money. Someday, when I'm not dead broke, I'm going to find an amazing way to repay them for their kindness.

All the items that hadn't been sold went in the attic, and we figured we'd deal with it later when we came back to Washington. But our backs were up against a wall, AGAIN! Man were we getting sick of that feeling. Sick or not we couldn't cry about it, we just had to keep working.

Of course, nothing said we had to pick up the RV right away. Why would we wait though? It had been almost exactly two months since we'd dropped it off at Camping World and we were homesick. We were also itching to get out of that bedroom and back on the road.

Two days before we could pick up the U-Haul trailer, I got some maintenance done on the truck which it sorely needed before we drove a few thousand miles. It was time to drain and fill both differentials, transfer case and transmission. I'd never done them on that truck before, but I'd performed drain and fills before. I switched everything to full synthetic and immediately saw an increase of 1-2 mpg.

I asked the neighbor if I could use his garage again, which he kindly allowed me to do. He even sat out there and gave me some good conversation while I worked. He and his family were good people.

The hardest part of the maintenance was pumping the new oil into the front differential and transfer case. A $10 hand pump that screwed onto the oil bottles fixed that. Well kind of, it leaked a lot. I must have used half a roll of shop towels cleaning up after it. Fun tip of the day kids. I learned the hard way to ensure the fill hose is actually IN the differential before you push the pump down. It had slipped out, which I obviously hadn't noticed, and proceeded to spray me in the face and open mouth with 75w90 full synthetic gear oil. Fun times. Thankfully I had safety glasses on because I don't think my neighbor had an eye wash station in his garage. I couldn't get the taste out of my mouth for days.

On the final day before we could pick up the U-Haul trailer, we received an email saying that it wouldn't be available at the scheduled pick-up location, which was only 30 minutes away. Instead it would be at some other location 1 ½ hours away. We quickly checked for another available trailer online and called both U-Haul locations, but it was still the closest one. Whoever had been using it dropped it off at the other U-Haul store. Apparently, that's fairly common, we learned afterwards.

We knew that would really hurt the next day's timeline, so we prepped everything we possibly could that day. We washed the final load of laundry, cleaned the house the best we could with the time left and washed the trash cans out. We didn't want my mom to come back to a stinky house.

We'd already packed up all our items in the house, but we went one step further and staged it by moving everything to the front porch and living room. At first, I didn't think it would save much time, but when I finished staging it all an hour later, I was glad I thought of it.

We woke up early for our last full day in Washington. Not only did we have to drive three hours to get the U-Haul, but we had to ensure we'd have enough time left to also pack it. Even though it was a much longer drive than expected we had perfect weather and got to enjoy the beautiful scenery of Washington's coast.

Everything was going just fine until we hooked up to the trailer, and the truck's trailer brake system didn't register there was a trailer hooked up. I even drove it a short distance and squeezed the brake control with no response. It was the only large trailer they had, and we were out of time. I had them notate the brake problem on the paperwork and took it anyway. I was used to hauling so much more weight that I wasn't too worried about it. I figured I'd just rely on the exhaust brake a lot more.

What I didn't know, and what the employees running the store apparently didn't know either, is those trailers have a different kind of braking system. It's called hydraulic surge brakes. They work by registering the pressure change between the truck and trailer when the truck brakes. So, when I hit the brakes, the trailer would push against the hitch, which would activate the trailer brakes. It's a clever system that doesn't require an electronic brake control, but it would have been nice if we'd been told about it.

We were making videos every step of the way, because it's not like we'd ever get the chance to experience that and document it again. After we posted a video talking about the brakes a viewer wrote in and educated us. Thankfully, we posted it during the trip, so I didn't have to drive the whole way thinking we didn't have trailer brakes.

I'd bought a 7-5 pin adaptor and the trailer only had a 4-pin plug. Naturally I thought the wrong adaptor was the problem. So, we wasted some precious time on the way home finding a Home Depot where I could exchange them. Of course, the new adaptor didn't change anything, and we decided to just get on with our day.

We went to the storage shed, cleared it, packed the trailer, got the receipts and kept going. When we arrived at the house with the trailer, I had the opportunity to practice backing it in, it reacted very differently than a fifth wheel.

We immediately went to work packing the trailer until we had a sick realization. Not only could we not fit everything in with how we'd packed the storage shed, but we had too much weight in the rear of the trailer. I knew we'd packed it wrong because I could lift the tongue by hand. There were no anti-sway bars and I didn't want to fight an uncontrollable trailer for 2,300 miles.

Since we had a whole entire spare second, we decided to download the trailer, sort and consolidate the bins, and reload it. I couldn't have been happier that we staged what we could the night before! It really did make a difference and gave us a few more precious minutes of sleep. But before I could get that precious sleep, I checked all ten tires, and found the four trailer tires were low. They'd been set at the mounting pressure of 35 psi, not the running pressure of 65 psi. It took my little tire inflator over an hour to get them all up to pressure. Wish I'd thought to stop at a gas station after we picked it up and check there or ask the neighbor with the garage to use his compressor. Sleep deprivation is fun.

On the way home with the U-Haul, I had bought 30 lbs. of dry ice for a large cooler I'd bought for the trip. We still had a few hundred dollars' worth of condiments and refrigerated/frozen food at the house. I didn't buy the cooler just for condiments, even though they're expensive. There's a deep freeze in the back room of my mom's place packed full of elk, deer, salmon, cod, etc.

I intended on bringing as much with us as I could possibly fit. I figured 30 lbs. of dry ice would last a few days and if we added more on the road, we could keep it all below freezing the whole trip, especially since most of the stuff going in was already frozen.

With my mom having already returned to Taiwan we couldn't leave anything perishable in the house. I packed what I could in the cooler that night and gave the rest to our neighbors that let me use their garage. I was knocking on their door around 10pm to give them the food. I hated to do it so late, but I didn't have a spare second to get over there any earlier. I don't think they really cared after I made three trips giving them every perishable food item I could find. It would be silly to hang onto cereal that would just go stale.

By that point, I think we had more Aleve than red blood cells keeping us going. We were running on fumes, caffeine, and adrenaline, but we had a deadline and couldn't slow down. After we finished packing the trailer, except for what we were using that night, we crashed.

CHAPTER 29

On the Road Again!

———— ∿ ————

Our last morning in Washington is a blur. I wish I could tell you everything we did, but sleep deprivation really messes with long term memory. I know we threw the last of our stuff in the trailer, grabbed all the trash in the house, locked the door, and hit the road. We pitched the trash on the way out of town of course. I just want to make sure no one thought we hauled it across the country. Because that would just be weird, and smelly.

With a partly cloudy day, we pulled out onto the North Cascade Highway (Also known as SR 20) heading east and began the next leg of our epic journey. The first two hours of the day were so beautiful. The route follows the Skagit river as it winds its way down from the mountains and flows through several dams. We passed through the dense green forests of the North Cascades National Park again and saw the emerald green of Diablo Lake one last time.

After Washington and Rainy passes is a town named Winthrop. It's a neat tourist town that's built to look like it's the 1800's. We'd been there several years before and wanted to stop for lunch again.

When I finally found someplace I could pull over with the trailer we encountered our first problem on the trip. Oh goody, we got that out of the way quick! The trailer had a flat tire. Not only did we have a flat, but the trailer didn't have a spare.

Oh man I wish this was fiction.

We pulled out the rental paperwork and called the roadside assistance number, because that's what they told me to do when I rented it. Cool, I can handle that. I called them, went through the automated menu, listened to a very long message about how I can use their website instead of calling them, and then it hung up on me.

Thinking it must have been a mistake I called back. Because an automated system that hangs up on customers is insane, isn't it? I put the call on speaker and had Laura film the second time. They didn't disappoint, the same thing happened, and we got it on film. But however cool that would be in the upcoming video it didn't fix our problem.

I'm sure you're asking yourself right now why we didn't just go online like it told us to, right before it hung up on us. Well, T-Mobile didn't exactly have stellar service there. When I finally found the right direction and angle to point my phone, I was able to load their site. I filled everything out, submitted it, and we sat back to wait for a call. Of course, we didn't really just sit back and wait. I walked the dogs, let Sox use her litter box, and went into the nearby gas station where I found coffee for me and food for both of us.

Soon after we finished eating my phone rang. It was a representative from U-Haul who informed us they would find someone to come change our tire. A short time later the nearest U-Haul vender called us. They regretted to inform me they didn't have any spare tires and weren't even supposed to be providing roadside assistance. Thanks to years of sales I can be fairly convincing when needed. I pled my case and they decided to pull a tire from a trailer on their lot and come swap it with our flat tire.

Nothing required them to help us, but they still chose to anyway. I was so thankful that I stopped there after we got back on the road. I went in to personally thank the manager for allowing his employees to help us, and to tip the guy that came out. Sometimes my brain just misfires and tipping him didn't cross my mind until after he left. Good deeds are rarely rewarded anymore in today's society so when someone goes above and beyond, I do what I can to thank them.

We made it to Coeur d'Alene that night and stopped after only driving for six hours. We had to find a new hotel due to the hour and a half tire debacle. We also had to scrap our original travel plan and find all new hotels for the entire trip. After moving the pets and our clothes in the hotel room I left to find dinner. After dinner I threw together a quick video about the day and uploaded it.

While at the hotel, we were paranoid someone would try to steal or break into the trailer that held all our worldly possessions. Before the trip I bought a tire boot and I booted the U-Haul every night on the trip. If I had the chance, I would also back it up against something so no one could get into it if they cut the lock.

Day two was wonderfully uneventful. Well except for us making a big fat giant two-part mistake. Since we weren't towing a fifth wheel, we felt safe using Google maps. That was fine, except that Google maps uses the posted speed limit to calculate time. The speed limit was 75-80 depending on the state and we were going 55-60 thanks to the trailer only being rated for that.

The other half of the mistake was that we didn't leave early enough because we thought it would only be an eight-hour day. To top it all off we didn't realize we'd even messed up until we were seven hours into driving that day and started wondering why we were still so far away from the next destination.

It's a good thing we didn't try to push it the night before, because the second day ended up being a 10-hour day. We stopped in Billings, Montana and went through the same routine as the night before except for making a video. We were far too exhausted to edit video that night. Besides, there wasn't enough footage to make a video with anyway.

Our third travel day went well except for the "short cut" our GPS took us on. Cell service was spotty, so we used the Garmin in the truck dash instead. At one point it decided to take us off I-90 and reroute to some other road. That put us on a road under construction. Construction is kind of loose term here though. You know how when a DOT decides to repave a road, they normally work on one side at a time? Well, these guys were some overachievers. They just ripped up the entire road, didn't close it, and let us drive on 15 miles of washboard dirt.

If you've never driven a 1-ton truck on washboard let me explain something. That heavy-duty suspension is designed to tow a lot of weight, not to be comfortable. If we wanted to keep our fillings in our teeth, we could only go 5-15 mph, depending on how smooth it was. After we cleared the "construction" zone the rest of the drive went wonderfully.

Day three had us planning on stopping in Rapid City, South Dakota. We encountered another problem when we arrived (big surprise, I know). Rapid City is right outside of Sturgis, and even though the annual Sturgis biker rally had been over for several weeks, the hotel was still using its high event pricing. To make matters worse, it was Labor Day weekend and I guess Rapid City is where a lot of people go for vacation since there isn't much else to do in South Dakota.

So, while all the other La Quinta's we booked were $100-150 a night, this one was $430 a night, and due to the nature of South Dakota being mostly void of large cities, there wasn't another La Quinta within several hours. Of course, we would be reimbursed for it, but it left us dangerously close to running out of money before arriving in Indiana. We definitely didn't budget for that.

Laura was exhausted and fell asleep right after dinner. I was putting together the day 2-3 video when I realized we forgot to shoot a closer. I decided to talk about something a lot of our viewers had been warning us about. Many people were writing us during the trip with comments and advice, and one topic kept coming up. Non-disclosure agreements (NDA).

Over and over we heard the same story. Someone's RV went back to the factory for repairs, they went to pick it up, people at the factory told them they wouldn't be reimbursed for travel expenses unless they signed a non-disclosure agreement, AKA a gag order. Apparently, they didn't even want people talking about how the factories were fixing RVs.

Naturally I turned on our camera and talked all about it. I ended the video by reminding our viewers how we'd been open and honest throughout the entire process and that if we suddenly clammed up, then everyone would know what happened.

The trip and storage were costing us a few thousand dollars and we couldn't afford to not be reimbursed. I was really hoping it wouldn't end with an NDA, but we had no way of knowing. Just in case it did, I wanted to get out ahead of it.

Day four began with me buying more dry ice as Laura got everything packed up. I hadn't added more yet because I was checking the cooler each night, and everything still felt frozen solid. It was a good thing I added more, because it was over 90 degrees most of the day. The plan for day four was driving across South Dakota, that was all. We were only driving from one side to the other, but that was still a full travel day.

Of course, we had to stop at Wall Drug. I'd never been before, but I'd heard about it obviously. If you've never been there it's worth stopping. They have a lot of RV friendly parking which made parking the trailer easy. I grabbed some food for us and coffee for myself before we got back on the road. I was starting to wear down badly. I hadn't slept well one night of the trip and I was staying conscious with an IV drip of coffee. That's what I wish I'd had at least.

That evening I went out to find dry ice again but could only find a few small pieces as the store was sold out. I checked the cooler and everything still felt frozen after that mornings dry ice, so I figured it was good. After dealing with my insomnia for so many nights in a row I wasn't up for any more driving around. I grabbed us dinner and went back to the hotel.

Day five was our last long travel day, nine hours, with plans to stop in Kenosha, Wisconsin. We hit the road excited to see our home the next day but exhausted from driving for so long. Halfway through, I told Laura that we had to find something other than music to listen to. My brain was starting to shut down and caffeine wasn't even making a dent any longer.

Let me explain what I mean by "shutting down." When I reach a certain point of exhaustion my brain will turn off like someone flipped a switch, and there's not much I can do about it other than to get on my feet and keep moving. Caffeine only works for short periods. This is largely why I couldn't pass the Green Beret training. I couldn't be trusted to stay awake. It worries Laura, but I've found a few things that help such as books on tape. Something that keeps my mind engaged really helps.

Laura found a podcast about true crime. It was read by a detective that left out names and dates, but still discussed the evidence and investigatory process in detail. After my criminal justice classes I found it very interesting. It was engaging enough that I was able to stay awake and we made it to Kenosha without a fiery crash, just as the sun was setting. It would have been earlier if not for the evening rush hour we caught in the last hour. We forgot to plan for that.

I have this funny story about how after a few months of not towing the fifth wheel, I stopped thinking about bridge and awning height. It probably didn't help that I was only awake because I'd glued my eyelids open (not really, but I may as well have).

We pulled into the hotel parking lot and I circled around to park at the doors and offload everything. There was a concrete awning for people to park under in front of the doors with a posted height of 9'. We learned that evening that we need about 9' 2-3" with the bikes on the roof.

After Laura's bike had fallen out of its rack, I switched hers to the wheel on rack, so it was slightly taller than mine in the wheel off rack. Her handlebars hit the edge of the awning and the impact broke both tire straps while also knocking her bike out of the rack.

Thankfully the bike lock around the rack kept hers from falling to the ground for the second time. My bike seat was a half inch too high and scraped along the ceiling, scuffing it up badly. At least I was able to keep my bike on the roof afterwards, Laura's had to go in the truck bed for the rest of the trip since her rack was damaged.

I was extremely angry at the situation, and it took a while for me to calm down. Poor Laura tried and tried to calm me down saying she didn't blame me and that everything would be alright. I guess I wasn't done beating myself up because I stayed angry for hours. Though I am working on it, sometimes my PTSD makes a situation harder to deal with than necessary.

It just so happened that Eric's girlfriend lived a short distance from where we were staying. After the awning incident, Laura called her, and she came over to try and cheer us up. She even let me use her car to grab dinner and more dry ice so that I wouldn't have to deal with towing the trailer any more that night. It was nice finally meeting her, but unfortunately, we couldn't spend much time together since I needed sleep badly. We said goodnight and goodbye with plans to meet up in a few months when they finally hit the road.

CHAPTER 30

The Factory

—⁓—

W e woke up the last morning of the trip excited to drive the remaining 3.5 hours to Topeka, Indiana. Although, we quickly learned that we shouldn't have stopped in Kenosha. If we'd stopped earlier, we could have driven south and gone around Chicago. Instead, we found ourselves driving through Chicago during Tuesday morning rush hour. It was less than ideal, but surprisingly not as bad as Seattle rush hour. Of course, our GPS and the road signs not saying the same things made the drive a bit more interesting. I missed our exit to I-90 and had to reroute through downtown Chicago. At least we didn't have the fifth wheel.

Once I extracted us from the downtown traffic nightmare, we only had five (that's right, 5) toll booths to go through to finally escape Illinois. I'll never drive through there again, I don't care how many hours it adds to a trip.

Before long we began to see farmland and Amish buggies, we were almost done. The closer we got to Topeka the more RV related companies we saw. It really is the birthplace of modern RVs. For every RV plant we passed there were two making components such as frames or axles. I imagine there's a few job openings around there. We'd never seen so much industry in one area before. While driving through there, it suddenly made sense how they can build an RV in day. Everything they need to construct it is made within a few miles of the plants.

We were both shocked when we pulled into Topeka. It's a very small town, surrounded by mostly Amish farms. Yet in the middle of the town sits the Cedar Creek factory, which was also quite surprising. We were expecting some sort of giant Costco looking building, but instead it was the size of a neighborhood grocery store. We pulled through the gates and into a sea of brand-new Cedar Creeks awaiting haulers.

There must have been over 100 new RVs parked there. Considering we rarely see other Cedar Creek's it was a little hard to wrap our heads around. On top of all the RVs, half the parking lot was full of parts. There was a pile of frames in one corner, a mountain of axles sat next them, and the racks of front and end caps were in another section. Pallet after pallet were stacked high with boxes of parts sitting everywhere, with forklifts zipping all around them. It was clearly a very large and complicated operation.

We had no idea where we were supposed to go, and there wasn't a phone number to call other than the general customer service number that's never answered. I found a place to park with the U-Haul and walked through a side door to find someone to speak with.

I happened to walk into the woodworking section, and it was like nothing I'd ever seen before. There were Amish guys running all over. I'd never seen so many beards and suspenders in one place. Imagine Santa's workshop, but staffed with Amish men instead of elves. They were slapping together cabinets and drawers so fast it was like they'd started in the womb.

I grabbed someone when they came up for air and asked where I could park and find Mr. Oliver. He ran off and found someone that could answer my questions. I told him who I was, and he left to find Mr. Oliver. As we pulled around the end of the building, we saw our house parked against the side of it with Robert, our inspector, already waiting to meet us. The morning rush hour had pushed us back so much he'd already finished. Laura stayed in the truck with the dogs and I went to meet him.

Mr. Wilhelm introduced himself since we'd never met in person and we walked through the RV together, going over his inspection list item by item. It was such a strange feeling walking through our house after having not seen it for almost three months. Stranger still, it was completely void of everything we usually had in there to make it our home.

While going through it, Mr. Oliver came out to introduce himself and the woman from customer service we'd been working with, Denise. We all spoke for a minute and they went back inside so I could finish up with Robert.

Even though there were a few things he couldn't fully inspect he did find some problems. None of them were terrible, but they would have cost us time and money to fix on our own. Otherwise he said it looked pretty good overall. I'm pretty sure the problems he found would have cost more to fix than his fee. And they were still there after the factory had it for two months. Laura and I were both very happy we hired an independent, unbiased, NRVIA certified inspector.

After Mr. Oliver came back, I spoke with him about the problems found, and he agreed to get them all fixed, which was incredibly nice because they weren't small things. For instance, several of the bulb seals around the slides were beginning to rip, and they aren't cheap.

However, it was noon which was quitting time at the factory and all the Amish workers were jumping in horse drawn buggies to go home. Mr. Oliver explained how they start at 5:30 am so they can work a full day at the factory and then go home with time left to still work on their farms in the afternoon.

If not for the flat tire, we would have been there in the morning and could have had it all fixed while we went over paperwork. Instead we would have to stay in a hotel again that night. They said they'd reimburse for another night, so it wasn't too bad.

With the factory shutting down Mr. Oliver was able to give us some time and was nice enough to walk through our list personally instead of passing it off to someone else. It took over an hour. He had a stack of paperwork and work orders with him. He laid them out of the kitchen island, and we went through them item by item.

Sure, that took a while, but we wanted it to be thorough. It's not like we'd get the chance to do that ever again. Nothing on our original list had been denied, they'd even fixed extra problems they didn't have to. For instance, several of our roller shades had broken. Instead of just replacing the broken ones, they replaced all of them.

Mr. Oliver was very pleasant to work with and listened to everything I had to say. At one point he was explaining how they couldn't figure out what was wrong with our kitchen faucet, so I showed him what I was talking about. He immediately had someone grab us a whole new faucet assembly that we could put in later. Then he changed his mind and said he'd have his men do it since it was staying overnight for the problems Robert had found.

Because we couldn't take delivery that day, we had some free time and Mr. Oliver took us on a factory tour. I'm sure it would have been more interesting during work hours, but it was still very eye opening. We got to see the multiple stages Cedar Creek's go through during construction, because there were RV's sitting partially built in each stage.

If an RV isn't finished before everyone goes home, they just pick up where they'd left off the next day. I wonder if that could have something to do with the problem's owners have been having? I imagine it's tough to remember exactly what you did and didn't do each day. I doubt they leave off at the same point each time.

He showed and explained a lot of things about their construction that sets them apart from their competition. I tried to pay attention to what everything looked like inside the walls, floor and ceiling since I knew I'd be doing most of our future repairs. We learned a lot about our home that day. There are things they do better than their competitors, but there's still a lot of room for improvement.

We finished the tour and found another La Quinta hotel an hour away for our last night. On the way to the hotel we called the RV park to tell them we wouldn't be checking in that night and why. They were very kind and didn't charge us for that night. I wonder how often they hear the same story? We also asked how early we could drop of the U-Haul trailer. Amazingly they didn't make us wait for check in time and said we could in the morning.

That night I bought more dry ice for the cooler and we planned out the next day. We figured out how early we'd have to get up to drop off the U-Haul at the campground and get back to the factory to finally pick up our house. Luckily, the campground was just outside of Indiana.

The next morning, even though we arrived around 9 am, all the extra repairs had already been completed. I swear they have elves working a third shift overnight.

Mr. Oliver walked me through the new repairs immediately after we arrived. The goodwill repairs continued. Instead of only replacing the two ripped bulb seals, they replaced them all. While we were talking, I realized I'd forgotten to tell them our driver's side outdoor light had burned out. He had someone run and grab us a replacement, just like that. Although when she came back, she regretted to tell us they weren't using the same model anymore. They had switched to an LED model that was slightly larger, which she apologized for.

I couldn't believe they were apologizing while literally handing me an upgrade to the original incandescent. All I had to do was install it, oh shucks. But it didn't stop there. Since I'd have to install it, he grabbed me a tube of Dicor, a tube of exterior clear sealant, and several feet of butyl tape so I wouldn't have to buy anything for the install.

After we finished with the RV, we went inside to run copies of all our travel and storage receipts to give Denise. Walking into her office I was blown away by the stacks of customer files on her desk. There must have been 2' (that's two feet) of files if she'd put them all in one stack.

We were told during the tour that 91% of their workforce is Amish. Apparently because the local population is almost completely Amish, it's very difficult to find computer literate employees, which is why they only had three customer service reps for such a large company. Suddenly the slow response time, the phone never being answered, and calls not being returned, it all made sense.

On one hand we felt bad for them. They seemed to genuinely care but were too overloaded to give any one customer enough time. And they only had two days to complete repairs. Clearly it didn't matter how much they wanted to help customers, their hands were tied by their capabilities, although Denise was very clear that she wanted to mail parts to owners to help them. Obviously, she can't send just anything, and she can't send as much as she wants due to cost, but she does the best she can when people ask for parts.

On the other hand, I was angry at the people running the company. I know if they offered enough pay for customer service reps, there wouldn't have been a shortage. If they would offer enough pay, people would move or commute hours for the job. Sure, the town being all Amish was a problem for them, but it was a fixable problem, if the people in charge actually wanted to do something about it.

Our displeasure with Cedar Creek's customer service shifted from the people at the factory to whoever's at the top making the decisions. Those are probably the same people that don't allow them to build the quality RVs Cedar Creek used to be known for. We learned the factory-floor quality assurance position was eliminated a few years prior. I'll bet it was the people up top trying to save a buck.

Going to the factory was eye opening and heart breaking all at the same time. We were so incredibly happy that we'd just stuck to the facts in all our lemon RV videos. If I had gone on camera and insulted or slandered the customer service reps for being slow, that would have been horrible. I can only imagine how much that would have hurt them. I know the feeling of wanting to do a good job while having your hands tied at the same time.

Don't get me wrong though, I'm still angry at the people up top for choosing not to fix obvious problems. They're making everyone's lives harder by trying to save a buck. I don't know exactly who's responsible, but I hope they realize what their greed is doing to their customers and employees.

Think this through for a second. If they'd allotted a larger budget for personnel, higher quality materials and allowed the build time to slow down for quality assurance, you wouldn't even be reading this. The hundreds of people that have contacted us saying they'll never buy a Cedar Creek, or any other Forest River product, wouldn't have bought something else.

I added up the lost sales just from the people that told us what RV they weren't going to buy, and it was over $1,000,000. And I must assume the people who told us are only a fraction of everyone who decided to buy something else due to our videos.

A non-disclosure agreement was never mentioned, we didn't partner with Cedar Creek, nor did they sponsor us or pay us off, and there were no strings attached to picking up our rig or for getting reimbursed. Other than showing receipts of course.

We still don't know if all those people that contacted us with their horror stories were telling the truth or not. It's possible we didn't receive the same treatment from Cedar Creek because they wanted us to make a positive resolution video, we'll never know. We do know they took care of us in many ways they didn't have to and made us happy customers. Mr. Oliver stayed two hours late both days just to help us. After that, we understood why he always works 12-hour days.

Mr. Oliver and Denise hugged us both before we left. They were incredibly nice people. I'm glad we had the chance to meet them and gain some much-needed perspective.

A lot of people have asked us if we'd ever buy another Cedar Creek and I don't think we would. I still have an issue with the people up top not allowing their employees to build better quality RV's or hiring enough customer service staff. I don't like supporting companies that treat their employees and/or customers badly.

CHAPTER 31

We're Home

———∿———

We were both elated as we drove away from the factory with our home in tow once again. It had been so long since I'd pulled our aircraft carrier that the narrow Amish roads were a bit of a challenge, but we made it to the campground without incident. After I remembered how to back it up, we jumped right into work. We had the rest of that day, all the next, and a morning before checkout to repack the RV and return the U-Haul.

I cracked open the back of the U-Haul and got to work....trying to find our power, water and sewer items. Clearly, I wasn't thinking when we repacked it because I hadn't left them near the door, I couldn't hook up for the first hour we were there.

It all had to come out anyway, so I just started hauling it all to the front door and made a pile there. I would move a new tote inside for Laura to put away as soon as she emptied the previous one. I was also loading the basement and garage storage bays while Laura was working inside.

We had a good system, and all was going well until I opened the cooler to load the fridge and freezer. Somewhere along the way the dry ice hadn't kept up, even though I'd thrown another few pounds in the night before. Except for a small portion directly under the previous night's dry ice, everything had thawed. Remember when I said I packed the cooler full of elk and deer? Well, it thawed and bled all over everything.

I stood there, my hands sticky with slightly chilled blood, staring in disbelief at our next few months' worth of food covered in blood. We had no idea what temperatures the food had reached, or if the blood would have warmed up enough to start forming bacteria, so it all had to go. I was able to save a handful of condiments that were still sealed and soaked them in bleach water, but the rest had to be thrown out.

While that was a crushing blow to moral, we didn't have time to dwell on it. Rain was forecast for the next day and we didn't want to still be moving in during a thunderstorm. We unpacked, organized and arranged until we were ready to drop that night. I went down the street to a restaurant and brought dinner back before we passed out.

The next day was more of the same rhythm. I staged everything I could near the front door to expedite the process. It's a good thing we were working fast because a heavy rain storm rolled through. I was able to move everything still outside under the awning and we didn't have to bring a bunch of rain and mud inside while we continued to work.

The instant the U-Haul was empty I hooked it up for the last time to return it. Before I left the RV park, I thought it sure was bouncing a lot, so I stopped to check. Thanks to my recent lack of sleep I'd completely forgotten about the tire boot. It was still clamped onto the wheel, but it was destroyed. The lock was mangled, and the handle had been sheared off. I was only able to remove it by getting a pry bar under it and ripping it apart until it finally released. At least it hadn't damaged the U-Haul.

Unfortunately for Laura, the return location was over an hour drive each way, so she had to work on her own for a few hours. We worked until we couldn't move again that night.

We woke up early for our last day at the campground. Somehow, we managed to put everything away and arranged it enough to bring the slides in to leave on time. There may or may not have been a mountain of stuff in the living room between the slides that we dealt with later. The only casualty of working so fast was our brass Y-hose splitter that was left behind. Not bad.

We proceeded to haul our butts down to Kansas City as fast as possible. It had been a year since Laura had seen her parents, she didn't want to wait another minute. We made a week-long reservation at the same RV park we stayed in for five months before we hit the road. I'm happy to say I made the corner much better that time, and I didn't need their help to back into our spot. It was nice talking to the people running the park almost a year later and telling them what happened since we'd left. The big news obviously being the upcoming RV Nomads movie we were cast in.

The joyous return was promptly cut short when our fridge stopped working again. Sigh….we hadn't even had it back a week yet. The fridge not working was one of the biggest reasons we wanted it to go back to the factory. We KNEW something was wrong with the electrical system. The factory had sworn up and down they checked everything, even the inspector had looked it over. Clearly something was still wrong. After troubleshooting it for a few hours, I decided we needed to put four batteries back in the RV.

If you remember, our first day on the road all four batteries were dead, and we replaced them with a pair of 12v marine/RV batteries because we couldn't afford to buy four at that time. From what I could tell, everything checked out, except the batteries.

The final test was to plug the fridge into another outlet to see what would happen. It immediately kicked on and ran perfectly. The only difference was that I'd bypassed the batteries and inverter. We had to live with it plugged into an extension cord run to another outlet for a month before we could afford the four batteries.

> *The fridge saga ran on for another six months, well past the point I'm ending this book. It wasn't fully resolved until we installed solar and bypassed all the WFCO components that came with our trailer. I figured you'd want to know how it turned out since it's been mentioned a few times before.*

Later we learned the fridge outlet was only powered through the inverter and batteries. There were multiple problems this setup was causing us.

1. If we plugged into a power source less than 30 amps, the fridge wouldn't receive power because the inverter had an internal 30-amp transfer switch. We had a 2k generator, hence the confusion.

2. If the batteries didn't have sufficient power for the inverter, the fridge light would turn on, but the compressor wouldn't run.

3. The inverter wasn't smart enough to know if the batteries were too low and it would still try to draw from them. That's how the fridge light could be on without it actually cooling. Which made us think something was wrong with the fridge.

4. The fridge needed a larger inverter, 1000w was cutting it too close. Because the compressor draws such a large amount of power at startup, a larger inverter was needed to handle the load. It eventually died and had to be replaced, probably from being forced to work too hard.

5. If the batteries didn't have enough power, we could be plugged into shore power and the fridge still wouldn't run. Because the inverter was wired directly into the batteries.

Now I'm sure there's an electrician reading this saying I've got it all wrong, and that may be the case. But it was wired so backwards that it took multiple RV techs (our friend Kevin Barone helped again), an electrical engineer/fellow full-time RVer/YouTuber (Tom Morton) and a full-time RVer/solar installer (Brian Boone) to figure it out.

The worst part was the batteries were wired wrong from the factory. We finally figured that out later when we put four batteries back in and continued to have problems. No one could figure it out because the wrong battery wiring diagram sticker had been placed in the battery bay. The incorrect diagram, and only having two batteries at the time, also explains why our inspector didn't find a problem. I can't blame him for that one.

A few years before, Cedar Creek had switched from propane fridges to residential. That's all well and good, except no one thought to change the wiring diagram when they added the inverter. The inverter had a positive and negative cable running into the battery bay to power it, and there was another positive and negative from the RV for the 12v systems. The inverter didn't combine the two pairs of batteries. Thousands of CC owners were having this same problem.

After spending a few days on the phone with Tom Morton, Kevin Barone and Brian Boone, they figured out the batteries weren't wired in series and parallel, although it looked like they were because four wires were running into the battery bay. They determined I needed to add two more wires to connect them properly. When we emailed Denise to tell her what we'd learned she apologized and said it was a known problem. Cedar Creek had issued a new diagram around the time we bought the RV.

> *Gee, it sure would have been nice if Camping World had put it in there before they sold it. That would have saved us a lot of money and headache.*

After we had the fridge running on the extension cord, we got back to life. We had a lot to do in Kansas City before we could leave to meet Eric and Jenna in Oklahoma. We spent time with Laura's family, stocked up on good KC BBQ, pulled some items out of storage we'd been wanting, put some other things in storage we didn't want, finished organizing the RV after moving back in, got some work done on the truck and did a bunch of random maintenance on a lot of RV gear we hadn't used all summer.

We had a nice surprise while we were back in our first RV park. We ran into the man that helped us unhook the night we'd bought the RV! A few days after we arrived, a super C with a lifted black Jeep Wrangler pulled in and we instantly looked at each other wondering the same thing. Was it really our first RV friend? I think he was just as happy as we were. We all ran outside, hugged and swapped stories about what we'd all been doing over the previous year.

Our time in Kansas City was very busy. We only had a few days before we had to leave to meet Eric and Jenna. They'd bought an older Class A several few months prior and were stretching their legs with a small trip before they'd be able to go full-time.

Of course, it wasn't just a vacation, this is Eric we're talking about. Yes, he was getting out of Chicago for a few days, but he was still working. He was on a tight deadline because he had a meeting scheduled with a city manager in Texas. Although, due to all the work with getting the RV back we hadn't been in close contact with them and were a little out of the loop. We were more interested to meet them than whatever he had going on in Texas.

We said goodbye to Laura's family and got back on the road headed to Oklahoma. It was only a one-day trip and we were excited to finally meet this guy who wanted to make a movie with us. On the way down, we ran into a new problem. I've mentioned before that we use an RV GPS while towing. The main reason is to protect us from low bridges. Our fifth wheel is 13'6" tall and we'd love to keep it that way.

Something most people don't think of when they see bridge height signs is, was the road repaved and the sign not updated? We'd never before seen a bridge low enough that required us to ask the question, "Is it really that tall?" That is until I drove around a corner and we found ourselves staring at a 13'8" railway bridge.

There wasn't anywhere to turn around and there'd been no prior warning. Before I tried to back up for a ½ mile I wanted to at least try it. We were both nervous, so Laura got out with a radio and watched from the side to ensure the front air conditioner would clear. Luckily, the posted height was correct, and we didn't have to find a new route, or a new air conditioner.

Just as we were unwinding from the 13'8" bridge it was time to get off the back roads and onto the turnpike. As we approached the turnpike entrance, to our dismay, we saw a posted height of 13'6". There was no way we would consider risking that, so I turned down a parallel road. The strange thing was the GPS kept trying over and over to route us onto the turnpike. Laura even went and changed our height settings to 13'8" to see what it would do, and it still had us using the turnpike.

We drove alongside the turnpike perplexed for several miles. Every entry point had a 13'6" sign, but they were all clearly several feet taller than that. Laura even went online trying to find an answer with no luck.

After watching semis and other fifth wheels flying past us on the turnpike for 20 minutes, we decided to give it a shot. If we'd stayed on the side roads it would have added hours to the trip. When we pulled up to the toll booth, I asked the lady running it why they had 13'6" signs posted everywhere? She said there was a bridge that low, SOMEWHERE on the turnpike, and she didn't even know where!

I now have a new philosophy, follow the semis. If there are ten semis all going one direction, it's probably a safe bet there's no low bridges that way. Trucking routes are well established, and I highly doubt a bunch of different drivers from different companies would all make the same mistake at the same time and drive into a low bridge. We got on the turnpike and I can happily say, we didn't encounter any more low bridges.

Eric had picked the campground where we were going to stay. Eric, who had never been RVing before. Normally we do a lot of research on the campgrounds we pick to ensure we can make it there and fit in the it. We found out later the only research he did was;

1. Is there cell signal?

2. Is it in the middle of nowhere?

The campground he picked fit the bill nicely, for those questions. Having not towed all summer and having towed very little on small backroads at all, getting there was a little nerve wracking for me.

There were miles of country road with no lane lines, because it wasn't wide enough for two vehicles in many spots. I was swerving to dodge low branches and pot holes left and right. By the time we arrived at the RV park, I wasn't in a good mood.

I'm using the term RV park loosely here. It was someone's personal property, with their home on it, and they had installed a few RV and tent sites. I pulled in next to the house and saw no signs of movement. I got out and began to walk around looking for an office sign, which I couldn't find because there wasn't an office. My mood was becoming progressively worse.

Suddenly, a man around my height, with a pale complexion came around a corner. He was wearing blue jeans, a white Chicago Cubs jersey, and a ball cap. He walked up to me, and with a soft-spoken voice, introduced himself as Eric.

CHAPTER 32

Welcome to Your New Future

———— ∿ ————

I remember standing there talking to Eric in person for the first time, just seething with anger from everything that happened that day. I tried to ignore my bad mood and we spoke for a minute about where I could park since the sites were short and tight. He showed me the one option we had then went back in his rig to work while we parked and got set up. Or maybe it was to give me space so I could cool off, I don't know.

I only had the one site I could potentially fit in, designed for a motorhome to pull straight in. It wasn't going to be easy for me. I would have to back around a 90-degree corner next to a building and squeeze in between a tree and the building to get into the site. The road was about 5' too narrow for me to swing wide enough to pull in and drive across the grass behind the site.

Since it was my only good option, I tried to back in. I got close, until my truck gave me a trailer wiring warning I'd never seen before. I stopped and got out to check. The trailer wiring was stretched taut from trying to take such a tight corner, I couldn't even unplug it. I was forced to abort the backing in plan and change tactics.

My last choice was to drive across the grass with the RV and pull in through the back of the site. That doesn't sound so bad, except there was a decent hill I had to go up, the grass was wet, and I had no idea if I'd destroy their nice lawn in the process.

We briefly considered backing in across the lawn, which would have made hooking up much easier. However, with my obviously rusty towing and backing skills we scratched that idea. I didn't want to destroy their lawn by trying to back in five times.

I was so fed up by that point that I put the truck in 4x4 and just went for it. I was able to get the trailer into the site, but the hookups were next to the passenger side of the front cap since it was designed for a class A. To hook up the sewer, I had to use all three of our hoses and crawl under the RV on my back with our sidewinder hose supporter to make them reach. Even then they were stretched to their limit. I just needed a few more inches, but it was as far forward as I could pull the RV with room left to unhook the truck.

To add to my bad mood, I was running the hoses uphill and there was nothing I could do to make it level. I used all three packs of our yellow leveling blocks under the sidewinder and it still wasn't enough to counter the slope. On a positive note, the power and water reached, that was good enough for me. After we got set up and walked the dogs, we went over to Eric's rig to have a proper introduction.

Within a few minutes we learned that the four of us had a lot in common. We were all sick of the societal rat race and wanted nothing more to do with it. You'll find a lot of full-timers feel the same way.

That evening we had a campfire and Eric set up a tripod fire grill to cook burgers. He was so excited to be away from the city, in the woods, and able to finally relax for a minute. The four of us sat around that fire talking for half the night, until we ran out of wood.

During the week we spent there, we had multiple conversations about the future of Epic Nomad TV (ENTV) and RV Nomads. Eric had so many ideas that we could barely keep up. Our heads were spinning with the possibilities and money he said we could make, we never even considered that it could fail. I wish I could have filmed those conversations. If ENTV becomes a billion-dollar company someday it would have been really neat to see those initial conversations about his vision.

We didn't stay there long because Eric had a meeting planned and needed to drive across all of Oklahoma to some small town in the panhandle of Texas. Obviously, we were going with them. Our last morning in the middle of nowhere arrived and we were all packing up to leave. Eric was standing on his roof with a broom sweeping leaves off a slide topper that needed to be replaced when I began to pack up our outside gear.

I have a system for packing up that expedites the process and lets me do a few different things at once. For instance, while the black tank is dumping and flushing, I'll put the bikes on the truck and change the tuner. I pulled the T handle for the black tank and saw all the "stuff" start flowing through our clear swivel adaptor. Everything was flowing just fine, until it suddenly wasn't. It had stopped flowing and was just sitting there.

Great…

I walked around the RV and checked the hose, only to find the "stuff" had ran out of momentum with about 10' to go. The hose was full of stagnant crap, literally. My only option was to "walk" it to the drain by picking up the hose and going hand under hand to force it to drain. I had no idea how heavy a hose full of that stuff is, it's got some weight. It was going so well before I reached the bad hose junction.

As I approached the bad hose junction, I lifted it off the ground and was just about to grab past the junction when the weight caused the hoses to detach. The bad hose, full of crap, fell to the ground and black water poured freely from both hoses all over my legs, hands and feet. As I loudly expressed my displeasure at the situation in an R-rated fashion, Eric was still on his roof across the road loudly expressing his displeasure at not having a camera.

The fun's not over yet kids!

Eric had his windows open and ceiling vent fan on, which sucked all that black tank smell straight into his rig. Meanwhile, I still had a bunch of crap in the hose that hadn't dumped all over me. My only choice was to reconnect the hoses and do it again. Sigh….

As I was reconnecting the junction our oldest, and most used, hose ripped. It didn't rip all the way through, thank God, but it was large enough to cause an 8" high poop geyser. There was nothing I could do about it but empty the hoses as fast as possible. I immediately began to walk the hose again, only to have the exact same outcome, and just as my legs were starting to dry off.

Oh, goody.

While loudly expressing my displeasure for the second time I began to wonder why Laura hadn't come out to see what was going on yet. I found out later she knew exactly what was going on and wanted nothing to do with my bad mood. She waited inside until I called for her. I couldn't go inside, obviously, but I knew the situation needed to be filmed. When she opened the door, she asked if I needed any help, to which I replied, "NO, GET THE CAMERA!"

When she came back the situation had improved slightly, and the poop geyser had mostly subsided. After she filmed me for a minute, she went back inside to get me everything I needed to shower and change. After I finished dumping the tanks, we sanitized the fresh water hoses and power cord since sewage spilled on them as well.

Once everything was cleaned up and put away, I used the campground showers to clean up. My clothes went into one trash bag and the sandals had their own, since they were much worse than my shorts.

The rest of the day I tried to ignore my bad mood and count my blessings that no blackwater got into my eyes or an open wound. Eric learned how to drive a Class A with a 40-mph crosswind that day, ALL DAY. We could tell the wind was normally bad there because of all the trees growing sideways. Later Eric said that his arms were sore from fighting the wind all day. It was easier for me to handle the wind in the truck, however it sucked the trash bag with my sandals out of the truck bed, and Eric almost hit them. I really liked those sandals.

On top of the wind, I was fighting the truck. I have the tuner installed to help it tow better, and it does help a lot. However, it can mess with the truck's computer system sometimes. On that day the truck wasn't able to complete a regeneration (regen) cycle after five attempts and it went into limp mode again while on the highway. I was reduced to 42mph until we got to the next exit. We pulled over and I was considering dropping the trailer so that I could drive off and let it complete the regen then get back to driving.

The tuner had a software update since then and no longer does this.

I didn't like that plan but couldn't think of anything else. That is until I remembered the tuner was also a code scanner. I cleared the check engine light which turned off limp mode and we got back on the highway. But a short time later it went into limp mode again. However, I was ready for it that time. I already had the tuner on the code clear screen and pushed enter, it cleared the check engine light again. I only had to do that three more times before it finished the regen.

Now if you don't know what this regen thing is I'm talking about, I'll explain it. Thanks to the EPA's insane diesel emissions regulations, auto manufacturers had to design a system that would reduce the hydrocarbons normally produced by burning diesel. That's why you don't see them blowing black smoke like you did 20 years ago.

This system involves a large chamber in the exhaust system the exhaust runs through with diesel exhaust fluid (DEF) to clean the exhaust. But the DEF isn't quite good enough, so another chamber captures leftover soot. When it fills with soot a fuel injector in the chamber sprays fuel into it, and the soot is then burnt off. That's regen, unless I made a mistake. Whatever, you get the idea, it's ridiculous.

The system robs modern trucks of their power and kills their mileage, effectively making them burn a much higher amount of fuel. And I can't wait to rip the whole thing out of the truck and fix it. But that's a project for another day. Ever wonder why so many people are driving 2008 or older diesel trucks? It's because that's the last year of modern trucks before the witchcraft was mandated.

There was still one more obstacle to overcome that travel day, toll booths. We went through four of them. None were manned, they only accepted loose change, the bill changers were out of order, and I had to get out of the truck each time to reach them. Luckily Jenna had a spare roll of quarters I was able to buy from them. Otherwise we would have had to pull off somewhere to get change. I think it only cost us $20 to drive across Oklahoma. We won't ever do that again.

We made it to our destination that night in Elk City, Oklahoma without further incident. We enjoyed two nights there and crammed in a lot of fun. We visited a Route 66 museum, ate some fantastic Mexican food, and met up with some of the friends we made in Florida the year before. We also had a few more conversations with Eric about his vision and dreams of the future. I'd be lying if I said half of it didn't go over my head.

We left from there and stopped in a small town on the border named Texola. It's a ghost town that Eric was very interested in. He had an idea for an ENTV show called Ghost Town Nomads. He wanted to take a look around the town and get a feel for what filming an episode might look like. We stopped there for a few hours and walked through abandoned, burned and collapsing buildings.

That was the first time we'd ever scouted to film something more than a YouTube video. Suddenly we felt out of place. We were used to just turning on the GoPro and talking to it for most of our filming. We'd never thought about lining up shots, sun angle, the background or B-roll. It was my first taste of filming something big, and we didn't even make an episode about it.

When we left Texola, we continued on to a small RV park outside the town Eric was so interested in and parked there for the night. The place was pretty, but Eric had to catch up on work that night after driving so much that week. A nasty Midwest thunderstorm rolled through, so Laura and I had a MASH marathon from our hard drive and called it a night. The next day life got a little more interesting.

Eric had an appointment to meet a woman in town for a theater tour and another meeting with the city manager afterwards. We woke up the next morning to a torrential downpour. The RV park was beginning to flood from the heavy rains, and we were worried about getting the RVs out later if the water rose more while we were in town.

So, we packed it up and drove the RVs into town for the meetings. On the way there we passed field after field of cotton that had just been harvested. Right before entering the town, we passed a sign reading Wellington, City Limit, pop 2,275.

We parked the RV's on a red brick road in the middle of town near a theater named The Ritz. When the woman arrived to show us the theater she was in a hurry. I can't remember why, but she didn't have much time to give us. She unlocked the doors and we walked into a theater that had first opened its doors in 1928. She explained the history of how it had closed in the 1980's but had been bought and refurbished for several million dollars a few years ago.

The place was beautiful. They had kept many of the original elements such as the metal seats, which had been reupholstered. Even though they had added some modern things, like a digital cinema projector, it still felt very much like an early American theater. It was set up for stage and screen, and she walked us through the dressing rooms and backstage area while giving us a history lesson. Even after hours of talking to Eric about his vision for the movie and NomadFEST, it was still tough to envision what that would look like as we stood on stage looking out over the empty theater.

As we walked out of the theater, and back into the rain, I wondered if all his plans would actually come to fruition. I wondered if we'd ever come back to Wellington, Texas and I wondered if this NomadFEST thing would ever happen. I knew he had a way of just making things happen when he wanted to, but a movie premiere in that sleepy little farming town 13 months later seemed like a pretty tall order. Especially considering we hadn't even filmed a single shot for the movie. I wouldn't say I was skeptical, it was more curiosity. I just couldn't see how we'd get to that point in such a short time.

We left the Ritz and drove two blocks over to City Hall where Eric met with the City Manager. We sat in the truck and waited since it was a business meeting between the two of them. While we waited in the pouring rain, I remember having a conversation about the cobblestone streets and how I loved that they hadn't ripped them up and replaced them with pavement. The red brick roads really gave the town personality.

Eric finished his meeting and we left to tour the venue where the VIP dinner would likely be held. Afterwards, he told us his meeting with the City Manager went very well. Apparently, the Manager and the rest of the City Council were all very excited about the prospect of NomadFEST being held in their town and wanted to help us make it happen.

We drove out of Wellington with no real idea of what our futures held. There was a lot of talk, projections, plans, promises and dreams that all centered around one man's vision. We hadn't even been on the road for a year and already were planning on being in a movie and having a first-of-its-kind film festival to premiere it. At that time, no one could have fully predicted what would happen there 13 months later.

NomadFEST 2018.

What's the moral of today's story kids?
RV life isn't always easy or fun, but neither is "normal" life. Which way would you rather live?

Epilogue

Want to know what happened the second year and after? Follow us at Hebard's Travels on YouTube. All the videos filmed during the time period this book covers can be found there, if you would also like to watch this story. I have to warn you though; those early videos were rough. We've stepped up our filming and editing game a bit since then.

We also have a blog and merchandise store on our website www.hebardstravels.com. Currently the store needs a bit of work, but we hope to have it running by the time you read this. I'll admit we haven't given our blog the time and attention we should have. We've been a bit busy making a movie and writing a book haha. After I'm done writing this, we'll get back to writing blog posts and finish building out our store.

If you wish to support us and our travels, please visit Hebards Travels on Patreon. There we post videos that show a more personal side of us and our monthly lives. We're also able to interact with our viewers easier and give them more time there. The lowest tier is $3.

It's my book, of course there's a shameless plug for us haha!

In all seriousness though, I sincerely hope you enjoyed reading our story, thank you so much for buying my book. If you loved it, please take a picture with it, or of it, and post it on your social media platform of choice (or all of them) with the hashtag #RVLife and let me know what you thought. I'll try to respond to everyone. It's my first book and I really look forward to hearing what you think about it.

Will there be a sequel? I sincerely hope so. I already have the outline and basic plot in my head. Whenever I start writing the sequel, I'll announce it online, but our YouTube channel needs some work before I take on a giant project again.

Safe travels. Maybe we'll see you down the road?

Dad

Here's the current version of the essay
I won the competition with.

Standing next to a pile of firewood on the front porch, I grasped the rusted door knob and pushed the faded front door open. Walking into the living room, I immediately noticed something very odd. It appeared someone had spilled a can of black paint. It looked as if this person had set the can on the recliner and it tipped over. Then they dipped their brush in the spilled paint and walked across the room several times. For some reason, they had then flung it all over the Franklin stove and the tall grandfather clock in long spattered streams. Although it may have looked like paint, I knew it wasn't. After years in combat I knew after a few days blood looks an awful lot like black paint.

Besides the strange paint scene, the tiny house looked undisturbed. It was as normal as a home could be for a man of fifty-nine, a year after his third divorce. The kitchen wasn't a disaster; but the sink was full of dishes. The aging fridge held more condiments than food, and the trash can was overflowing. A mountain of dirty laundry sat on the floor piled next to the washer. Every corner of the house was dominated by cobwebs. There were random items everywhere, crammed into every corner and sitting on top of every surface. I didn't see an open spot anywhere except on the floor; he had become quite the pack rat.

Walking through the house in a trance, I randomly opened drawers or closets and dug through the mess. It had been so long since I'd lived with him, I was looking for anything I remembered. Turning a corner, I saw an old cobweb-covered cuckoo clock on the wall. It wasn't running as its weights needed to be reset, but I could still hear the "cuckoo, cuckoo, cuckoo" of it marking an hour. My dad had owned that Cuckoo clock for as long as I could remember. I grew up hearing it every hour of every day in that past life, until we left.

The cuckoo clock hung on the wall. It was over a desk with small tools scattered all over it. This must have been where he repaired his pocket watches and clocks, a hobby for most of his life. He had the grandfather clock and five other mantel clocks scattered around the house. Each one of them was older than I was, but each one still worked perfectly. Growing with all those clocks in the house reminded me of the scene in "Back to the Future" when all the clocks chimed at the same time. The silence was eerily disturbing as none of them were ticking. My dad usually wound them every day.

I had never been to this house before, but it was strangely familiar. It felt as if I was walking through a stranger's home who had bought some of my dad's stuff. Nothing appeared out of place, and there weren't any signs of a struggle. It seemed as though he had just stepped out to get the mail or was out in his shop working. I felt he could walk through the door any minute. At that moment I would have given anything to hear him say "Hello, son" one more time. Though in my heart I knew it wasn't possible.

I was used to going a year or two without seeing him, eight years in the army had made that possible. I stood there and tried to remember when we had last spoke. The past fifteen months in Iraq seemed to blur into an indefinable eternity, but a few months ago felt about right. It had been a year and a half since I'd seen him, and we'd talked maybe six times since then. Why hadn't I called more often? I felt like a fool! I stopped to relax. Getting angry wouldn't help anything, and I had too much work to do. This was rented property, and I only had two weeks to clear it out, plan his funeral, store what I was keeping, and sell what I wasn't.

From my years in Iraq and Afghanistan, I had learned how to work now and grieve later. War was a harsh master. My dad didn't want me to join the infantry. I was his only kid and he was afraid of losing me. Though it was different back then; before 9/11, no one thought we were going to war anytime soon. Arguing that I was getting college money, he finally said it was ok. I should have been the one worried about losing him.

I walked past the paint scene again and went back outside to check his shop. It consisted of two rusted shipping containers with an open tent set up between them. I saw, sitting under the tent, the old work table he had when I was four. The same vice and grinder were still mounted on it. I remembered playing in the sparks from the grinder, back when the table had been taller than me.

The left container was just storage, so I looked in the right one, it had clearly been his main shop. There was a slight draft from an exhaust hole cut in the roof. The lighting was poor, even with sunlight flooding through the hole illuminating the fine dust hanging in the air. It was a working man's shop. Everything was covered in a fine layer of grease, oil, and sawdust. The air was filled with the scent of these; it was the smell of my dad.

His old punching bag was mounted on the back of one door. He had made me practice on it thirty minutes a day when I was eleven. I took a lazy swing at it as I walked by. Greasy cardboard boxes filled with saw parts, bar chains, oil, and tools filled the shelves and floor. It was so cramped I could barely walk down the aisle. There were chainsaws in various states of repair lying everywhere. In the back lay an enormous heap of tree climbing gear and ropes.

Walking back outside; I saw pile of random items rusting to death on the ground near the workbench. Something green caught my eye in there and I bent down to discover an antique green Coleman camp stove. It was hardly more than green painted rust, but I knew it was the same stove he had used during my childhood camping trips with him.

I gingerly set the stove down and noticed something else green, half buried under the long grass. Grasping the free end, I pulled out a rotting piece of 30-year-old memory. Barely more than a pile of mold and tent poles, it was the green canvas tent from those childhood camping trips on Mt. Rainier. Still holding the tent, I wondered why he had kept them. I doubted they had been usable in a decade or two, but he had kept them even after moving several times. I wondered if they brought back the same fond memories for him. Maybe they were also the best days of his life? I set the tent down and continued on.

In a daze, I walked around the left shipping container, and saw a log with thirty or so saw cuts in one end. That's how he tested saws after he fixed them. When I was seven, I would break off the slices of wood and try to throw them like Frisbees. I kicked one off and held it, remembering throwing them, but it didn't feel the same. My dad ran Husky Hanks Tree Service for over twenty years. Tree work had been his life. I probably would have joined him, but I hadn't seen him much after the divorce. He hadn't been there much before it anyway.

Everywhere I looked I saw my father. He was standing in front of the work bench grinding saw chains for the next work day. Then he was holding his hand in the sparks. "See, John, they don't hurt," I had been so scared of them.

Suddenly the roar of a chainsaw slicing through a log filled the dusty air. Standing in front of the log holding a chainsaw, wearing scuffed cork boots, faded jeans, a flannel shirt, and torn work gloves he was covered head to toe in saw-dust. Pausing for a moment, he wiped the saw-dust from his face and looked up at me. Then he smiled through his shaggy beard and said, "Hello, son."

It suddenly became too much for me to bear. Everything I saw had become mine, but I didn't want it. Suicide had finally grasped my heart with its icy hand. I sat down among the dusty remains of his life, and I wept.

About the Author

John Hebard was born in 1982 in Forks, Washington. His parents soon moved to Seattle's northern suburbs where he lived until 2001. While in high school, John wrote a short fiction story and made his first attempt at writing a fiction novel. In May 2001, at the age of 19, he joined the Army with an Airborne Infantry contract.

During his nine years enlisted he deployed three times. While overseas, John wrote several poems. He spent three years deployed between Afghanistan and Iraq and another year attempting to pass the rigorous Green Beret training program. He was medically retired during his third enlistment.

A year after retiring, he met his wife Laura and they were married two years later. He's earned an A.A. in Administration of Justice and a B.A. in Criminal Justice and Administration. During his first semester John won an essay competition while also writing his second fiction short story and he attempted to write his second fiction novel.

Shortly before completing his B.A., John and Laura sold everything and bought an RV. After his final class they quit their jobs and hit the road to try their hand at full-time RVing and nomadism. A year after their RV adventure began, John and Laura found themselves cast in the movie RV Nomads, with John also landing a job on the film crew as Supporting Cinematographer and Grip.

While living on the road, John rediscovered his passion for writing. He has begun several more fiction stories but has now completed an autobiography titled #RVLife.

Today, John lives in a fifth wheel with Laura, their dogs Bullet and Kimber, and cat Sox. They travel the country full-time and run a YouTube channel and blog about RV living and traveling called Hebard's Travels.

Made in the USA
San Bernardino, CA
08 March 2019